Liberal democracy into the twenty-first century

Good section in chap 1 (or intro) of the complexity
of the modern critique — could be updated for 2e.
o GG.

Political Analyses

This major new series, a flagship for Manchester University Press, will include some of the best new writing across the range of political science subdisciplines. All of them will present exciting new research or provocative syntheses in an accessible style, and will be available in paperback.

Series editors: Bill Jones, Michael Clarke and Michael Moran

Brendan Evans and Andrew Taylor
From Salisbury to Major: continuity and change in Conservative politics

Michael Foley and John E. Owens
Congress and the Presidency: institutional politics in a separated system

E. Franklin Dukes
Resolving public conflict: transforming community and governance

Stuart Croft
Strategies of arms control: a history and typology

Roland Axtmann
Liberal democracy into the twenty-first century: globalization, integration and the nation-state

Liberal democracy into the twenty-first century

Globalization, integration and the nation-state

Roland Axtmann

Manchester University Press

Manchester and New York

distributed exclusively in the USA by St. Martin's Press

Published by Manchester University Press
Oxford Road, Manchester M13 9NR, UK
and Room 400, 175 Fifth Avenue, New York, NY 10010, USA

Distributed exclusively in the USA
by St. Martin's Press, Inc., 175 Fifth Avenue, New York, NY 10010, USA

British Library Cataloguing-in-Publication Data
A catalogue record for this book is available from the British Library

Library of Congress Cataloging-in-Publication Data applied for

ISBN 0 7190 4304 2 *hardback*
      0 7190 4305 0 *paperback*

First published 1996

00 99 98 97 96   10 9 8 7 6 5 4 3 2 1

Typeset in Great Britain
by Northern Phototypesetting Co. Ltd, Bolton
Printed in Great Britain
by Redwood Books, Trowbridge

Contents

Series editor's Foreword

The Politics Today series has been running successfully since the late 1970s, aimed mainly at an undergraduate audience. After over a decade in which a dozen or more titles have been produced, some of which have run to multiple editions, MUP thought it time to launch a new politics series, aimed at a different audience and a different need.

The Political Analyses series is prompted by the relative dearth of research-based political science series which persists despite the fecund source of publication ideas provided by current political developments.

In the UK we observe, for example: the rapid evolution of Labour politics as the party seeks to find a reliable electoral base; the continuing development of the post-Thatcher Conservative party; the growth of pressure group activity and lobbying in modern British politics; and the irresistible moves towards constitutional reform of an arguably outdated state.

Abroad, there are even more themes upon which to draw, for example: the ending of the Thatcher–Reagan axis; the parallel collapse of communism in Europe and Russia; and the gradual retreat of socialism from the former heartlands in Western Europe.

This series will seek to explore some of these new ideas to a depth beyond the scope of the Politics Today series – whilst maintaining a similar direct and accessible style – and to serve an audience of academics, practitioners and the well-informed reader as well as undergraduates. The series has three editors: Bill Jones and Michael Moran, who will concentrate on domestic topics and Michael Clarke, who will attend to international issues.

Acknowledgements

This book owes much to the kindness of friends and colleagues. It took shape during a workshop on 'Indices of democratization' at the Joint Sessions of the European Consortium for Political Science in Leiden in 1993. Special thanks are due to David Beetham and Bhikhu Parekh whose contributions and interventions inspired me to sit down and write the volume. I am grateful to the Austrian Political Science Association for inviting me to its conference in Prague in November 1994, and in particular to Professor Heinrich Neisser for providing a congenial forum for stimulating intellectual discussion. Colleagues at universities in Nova Scotia, at the University of Ljubljana, the University of Göteborg and the University of Graz were kind enough to comment on my thoughts on 'globalization' as did the participants in the workshop on 'Prospects of democratization in a global perspective' at the conference of the International Political Science Association in Berlin in 1994. I benefited in particular from listening to Philip Resnick's contributions.

I owe a very special debt to the students who took my courses in political theory at the University of Aberdeen in the past. They helped me immeasurably to clarify my thoughts. I was privileged to be invited as a visiting professor by the Department of Sociology at the University of Graz and special thanks are due to the students who allowed me to learn from them. It is a pleasure to record my gratitude to Professor Helmut Kuzmics and his colleagues in the Department of Sociology for making my stay in Austria so rewarding. Over the last few years, as this book has taken shape, I have enjoyed the support of Professor Derek Urwin, Head of the Department of Politics and International Relations at the University of Aberdeen. I am particularly grateful for his granting me sabbatical leave in 1994.

My research for this book has been generously supported by a number of organizations. The Nuffield Foundation and the British Academy awarded me grants to research questions on multiethnicity, cultural diversity and Europe. First results of this research have been incorporated in chapters 3, 4 and 5. The British Council in Canada and in Austria has subsidized my trips abroad. To all of them my sincere thanks.

Finally, my most heartfealt thanks go to Gerti, Lauren and Timmy who always seemed to know when I needed cheering up.

The chapter on globalization develops ideas which have been published in the German journal *Leviathan* in 1995. Some passages of a short review essay, published in *Theory, Culture and Society* in 1995, have been incorporated in the section on 'deliberative politics' in chapter 2.

Introduction

As we move closer to the twenty-first century, the future of politics in Europe has become uncertain. Momentous political changes have occurred in Europe since 1989. They are dominating the continent's political agenda for the 1990s and beyond. The end of the Cold War has changed the political map of Europe. In Eastern Europe, we have witnessed the decomposition of supranational structures with the collapse and dismemberment of the Soviet Union and Yugoslavia. We have witnessed how the renaissance of nationalism and the national striving for political independence and statehood have sometimes resulted in military confrontations, civil war and 'ethnic cleansing'. But we have also witnessed how newly independent states and those only recently formed have embarked upon a policy that amounts to the voluntary political integration into a new supranational structure. Such is the attraction of the European Union that the Baltic states, Hungary, the Czech Republic, Slovakia, Poland, Slovenia and many other Eastern and Central European states aim to gain membership as a matter of urgency.

At the same time in Western Europe, the progress towards supranational integration has begun to slow down. The formation of a European political union has always been justified in both economic and political terms. Economically, it was meant to create the political institutional framework in which closer economic integration could be propelled forward. In political terms, an 'ever closer' political union was seen early on as a necessity in order to lock post-war Germany into the Western system of democratic nation-states, but also to create a politically integrated bloc during the time of East–West confrontation. With the end of the Cold War, the European security architecture has changed and with it the positions and interests of individual states. As the overall objectives of the North Atlantic Treaty Organization (NATO), the West European Union (WEU), the Organization for Security and Co-operation in Europe (OSCE) and the European Union (EU) are being reassessed, the need for an ever closer political union of the

(Western) European nation-states becomes opened up for question as well. As the debates on the Maastricht Treaty and its ratification in the member states in the early 1990s showed, public opinion, too, has become ever more divided about the desirability of political union.

Not only has the process of supranational integration been subjected to searching debate, but questions of national integration have also moved to the centre of the political agenda of many states. In Spain, Italy, Belgium and the United Kingdom, for example, 'regional' and 'ethno-national' movements have been formed or been revived which are mobilizing for regional autonomy and sometimes even for secession. These subnational forces challenge the efficacy and legitimacy of the nation-state, and thus add to the threat to its inviolability as the dominant regulatory political organization that issues out of the transferral of decision-making powers to the supranational arena in Brussels. Yet, while the policy of supranational integration and subnational 'regionalism' have problematized the nature and the future of the nation-state, the revival of xenophobic nationalism, directed mainly against 'ethnic minorities' and resident 'aliens', has aimed at restoring the power and the myth of the strong nation-state.

Nationalism, subnationalism and supranationalism have led to a re-evaluation of the role of the nation-state in Europe in the closing decade of the twentieth century. In a way, this re-evaluation centres on the question whether the nation-state is still capable of guaranteeing the economic well-being, the physical security and the cultural identity of citizens. This question gains even greater urgency once it has been realized that we are now living in a truly 'global' world of dense and ever-increasing inter- and transnational economic, political and cultural interdependence. In this era of 'globalization', how do global forces such as global capitalism, the global media and the global proliferation of nuclear weapons challenge the effectiveness, efficacy and legitimacy of the nation-state? Subnational regionalism, nationalism, supranationalism and global interdependency have created a complex, almost impenetrable mixture of conflicting tendencies and constellations. Decay, disintegration and fragmentation of political and social structures that spur local and regional conflicts are counter-balanced by moves towards unification, integration and co-operation. The empirical analysis of these processes and the emergent local, regional and global structures will become the main challenge to the social sciences in the years to come.

This book, however, sets itself a different, and more modest, task. Cognizant of the problematization of the nation-state at the end of the twentieth century, it offers theoretical reflections on liberal democracy, understood as both a set of institutions and a set of ideas, and discusses the meaning of democracy as we enter the twenty-first century. This analysis takes the close connection between nation-state and democracy as its starting-point.

In the first half of the nineteenth century the idea of the nation-state was a key element in an emancipatory ideology that was directed against the arbitrary rule of princes and small aristocratic elites. It was assumed that:

> the variegated and colorful multitude of traditional monarchies, principalities and in particular the older empires, like the Habsburg or the Ottoman empires, were a source of constant strife and conflict, whereas in modern nation states governed in accordance with constitutional principles and public opinion the peaceful pursuit of the welfare of all would be dominant. (Mommsen 1990: 211)

During the first few decades after the French Revolution the notion of the nation-state came to stand for the idea that legitimate government could only be based upon the principle of national self-determination and that, at least ideally, state and nation ought to be identical with one another. Internally, this meant a high degree of social and cultural cohesion and constitutional government; externally, it meant national independence *vis-à-vis* other rival nations. Yet, as Mommsen argues, in the course of the nineteenth century the idea of the nation-state lost its emancipatory character and became concerned primarily about the exertion of political power and the imposition of its will, if needs be, upon neighbouring peoples: '[I]t came to be associated with the power-status of the established national culture, and the imposition of its values on ethnic or cultural minorities both within and beyond the body politic was now considered essential' (Mommsen 1990: 215). The reasons behind this policy of homogenization and assimilation are manifold, but two would appear to stand out. First, the formation and development of an efficient modern industrial society was seen to require some degree of cultural homogeneity which would allow the functional division of labour and tasks across a wide geographical territory (Gellner 1983). Yet, secondly, not just for reasons of industrial–capitalist 'modernity', but also for reasons of state did homogenization become imperative: '[T]he ethnic and cultural homogeneity of the nation was increasingly considered an essential precondition of the external strength of the nation state in its perennial struggle against rival states' (Mommsen 1990: 215). Imperialism as much as industrialism put a premium on cultural homogeneity and the assimilation or integration of 'minority' groups into the values, cultural traditions and political principles of the dominant, or 'hegemonic', national group.

The notion of the nation-state thus incorporated from the very beginning both the ideas of constitutional government and of cultural homogeneity. And 'democracy' became entangled in this tension as well. During the political and social struggles of the nineteenth century, the notion of constitutionality became broadened into the idea of popular and democratic government, while the concern with cultural homogeneity retained its importance as a mechanism for drawing cultural boundaries between 'us' and 'them', and thereby defining membership in the democratic political community. The conceptualization of popular sovereignty may serve as the most prominent instance of the linkage between democracy and nation-state. In liberal democracies, individuals must be members of the state, must be its 'nationals', in order to possess citizenship rights. 'Nationality' is a necessary, though not sufficient condition for citizenship. As we shall see in the first chapter, in the past even 'nationals' were excluded from political citizenship on the grounds of restrictions regarding gender, property or taxable income, or education, and, in the present, are still excluded on the grounds of age, for example. The principle 'citizenship for nationals' radicalizes the question as to how nationality is acquired. There are three distinct routes to gaining 'nationality' and thus to meeting the prerequisite for acquiring citzenship rights in a state: by descent, that is, having parents who are already nationals (*jus sanguinis*); by virtue of having been born in the country (*jus soli*); or by petitioning for, and being granted, nationality. In contrast to this conceptualization of popular sovereignty as the self-rule of nationals in their capacity as citizens, the radical democratic principle would stipulate that everyone who is permanently subjected to rule and domination in a legal order must have a part in the exercise of that sovereignty that ultimately legitimates that rule. Citizenship status would therefore be distinct from nationality and would adhere to all permanent residents, who would be subject to the same qualifications as the 'nationals'. Such a disjuncture of citizenship and nationality is, however, alien to the political reality of liberal democracy. It therefore demonstrates the systemic linkage between democracy and nation-state.

Democracy became thus linked to the nation-state through the institution of citizenship for members of the national community. Democratic rule by the sovereign people is exercised in the sovereign, territorially consolidated nation-state. Offering *Considerations on Representative Government*, one of the leading liberal philosophers of the nineteenth century, John Stuart Mill, made these connections quite explicit. 'Free institutions', Mill (1861/1991: 428) argued, 'are next to impossible in a country made up of different nationalities. Among a people without fellow-feeling, especially if they read and speak different languages, the united opinion, necessary to the working of representative government, cannot exist'. He maintained that 'it is in general a necessary condition of free institutions, that the boundaries of governments should coincide in the main with those of nationalities' (Mill 1861/1991: 430). His reference to the Habsburg Empire in the explication of this thesis makes it plain that Mill is in favour of the political independence and self-determination of nationalities which are ruled and dominated by an imperial centre. But this 'liberal' endorsement of national emancipation is accompanied by an equally 'liberal' proposition that free institutions and representative government within a state are premised upon the 'blending of nationalities' (Mill 1861/1991: 434).

That we should refer to a liberal thinker in the context of our discussion on the relationship between nation-state, citizenship and democracy is not fortuitous. It was liberalism as a political movement and as a political philosophy which, in the nineteenth century, set the terms for a discussion on these matters. The debate that liberalism initiated, and that raged also within liberal discourse itself, centred upon the relationship between the individual and the state. What are the limits to state power? Which rights, and obligations, does the individual have *vis-à-vis* the state? What are the institutional ramifications of the idea that legitimate government must be based on the consent by the governed? Of course, conflicting answers have been given to these questions, and we shall encounter some of the relevant arguments in the following chapters. Yet there is no denying the fact that the institutions of contemporary Western representative democracies as well as their normative idea(l)s can be traced back to the liberal political tradition. It will be one of the tasks of this book to demonstrate why the contemporary Western democratic systems can justifiably be defined as 'liberal' democracies.

Without wishing to pre-empt the more detailed discussion to follow, a few observations on liberalism as a political theory may be offered at this point. For this purpose, I draw on the concise summary by Michael McDonald (1991: 221–2, where he has recourse to Buchanan 1989). According to McDonald, the basic liberal thesis holds that the state has the duty to enforce the fundamental individual civil and political rights. These rights include rights to freedom of religion, thought, expression and association, the right of political participation, and the right of legal due process. McDonald labels this the 'individual rights thesis' and points out that it contains two assertions fundamental to liberalism: 'The first is that this is a thesis about rights: rights which set limits to the actions of others including the majority or other de jure or de facto holder of political power and authority. The second is that such rights are seen as vested in individuals' (McDonald 1991: 221). The individual as a bearer of rights is a key figure in liberal political theory. And it is asserted in liberalism that it is the task and proper role of the state to protect basic individual liberties. The state has to provide that protective space within which the individual may exercise her or his rights. It is certainly not the task of the state to make citizens 'virtuous'; it has to remain 'neutral' and not aim to promote virtue and punish vice. McDonald calls this tenet of political liberalism the 'neutral or non-virtuous state theses'. Finally, drawing on both the individual rights and the neutral state theses, the 'individual self-determination thesis' maintains that 'there should be official respect for and protection of a realm of individual choice ... [L]iberalism recognizes a domain within which the individual is to be sovereign' (McDonald 1991: 222). Liberalism thus accepts that there is a distinction between a 'private' and a 'public' sphere. It also accepts that individuals are not only bearers of rights, but also, potentially and ideally, the authors of their own lives. As such, interference with their rights and autonomy for it to be legitimate needs the consent of the individual.

These theses are premised on the assertion in liberalism of the equal moral worth of all persons. In political liberalism, this assertion translates into the claim that all people, as citizens, must be treated equally, and laws and rules must be blind to differences of, for example, race, ethnicity, class, sex and gender or religion: as citizens, individuals participate equally in universal rights and entitlements. This idea(l) of universal citizenship is complemented by the liberal model of the public sphere that stipulates 'discursive equality by disqualifying discourse about the differences among actors. These differences are treated as matters of private, but not public interest' (Calhoun 1995: 244). Again, recourse to John Stuart Mill's arguments in his *Considerations on Representative Government* may help clarify this point. Participation of individuals in public affairs, so Mill argues, is valuable for their moral development. Through the engagement in 'public functions', the 'private citizen', Mill suggests, is called upon:

> to weigh interests not his own; to be guided, in case of conflicting claims, by another rule than his private partialities; to apply, at every turn, principles and maxims which have for their reason of existence the common good: and he usually finds associated to him in the same work minds more familiarized than his own with these ideas and operations, whose study it will be to supply reasons to his understanding, and stimulation to his feeling for the general interest. He is made to feel himself one of the public, and whatever is for their benefit to be for his benefit. (Mill 1861/1991: 255)

The individual as citizen/citoyen leaves behind her or his 'private' particularities when entering the 'public' sphere in which public opinion is formed and arguments are decided on their intrinsic merits rather than the merits and identities of the arguer (Calhoun 1995: 244).

These themes and arguments will be developed and assessed in greater detail in the first two chapters. That discussion will show that there have been divergent conceptualizations of 'citizenship', 'civil society' and 'rights' in the liberal tradition. This divergence has not only resulted in conflicting understandings of 'liberal' democracy; it has also meant distinctively different normative evaluations of the legitimacy of political authority and the modern state. In chapter 1, I sketch the model of liberal democracy by emphasizing both its core institutions and core normative ideas. The argument is organized around discussions of the ideas and concepts of 'sovereignty', 'constitutionalism', 'representation' and 'rule by deliberation'. In examining the meaning of these concepts, I shall draw upon the writings of, for example, Thomas Hobbes, John Locke, Jean-Jacques Rousseau and Immanuel Kant as well as upon key arguments advanced in the political debates during the American and French Revolutions. Chapter 2 continues the endeavour to tease out the intrinsic normative and philosophical assumptions of 'liberal democracy'. It discusses the concept of 'citizenship' and 'civil society' in liberalism. It shows that there are two different liberal conceptualizations of the individual as a bearer of rights as a result of the distinction between 'negative' and 'positive' rights and liberties. As we shall see, these divergent conceptualizations lead to fundamentally different assessments of the democratic and liberal credentials of the modern 'welfare' state. In order to bring out more clearly the specificities of the liberal conceptualization of democracy and citizenship, I present a brief account of the alternative tradition of 'republicanism' with its emphasis on 'active' citizenship as a duty and burden proudly assumed rather than a right passively enjoyed, as in liberalism. The chapter then analyses the centrality of the notion of 'civil society' for either tradition, in effect tracing its conceptual history from Aristotle, Hobbes, Locke, Hegel and de Tocqueville to the intellectual debates in Eastern Europe in the 1980s. At issue in these debates is the foundation of legitimate political authority, the rights and obligations of the individual *vis-à-vis* the state, and the limits of state power on the basis of a distinction between the 'public' and the 'private'. These discussions on citizenship, rights and civil society then provide the background for the presentation and critical analysis of the model of 'deliberative politics' that in recent years has been developed by Jürgen Habermas and that, in many ways, combines features of both liberalism and republicanism.

By introducing 'republicanism' and 'deliberative politics' into our discussion, chapter 2 goes beyond a mere explication of 'liberal democracy'. It opens up a line of theoretical reflections on alternative understandings of democracy and citizenship. Chapter 3 continues the problematization of 'liberal democracy'. It takes as its starting-point the idea(l) of universal citizenship that is 'essential' to liberal democracy: citizenship in the liberal, democratic nation-state is founded on the principle of non-discrimination insofar as all citizens participate equally in universal rights and entitlements. In the public sphere, differences are 'bracketed'. Yet it has been argued that this idea(l) amounts to the definition of the individual as a 'disembodied' and culturally 'disembedded' citizen. Both feminism and multiculturalism have challenged the liberal ideal of political universalism. Advocating a 'politics of identity', both demand that concrete differences of women and cultural communities must be accommodated in modern democratic states. In order to allow for the representation of difference without upholding or entrenching inequality and oppression, they further demand that individual rights have to be complemented by group rights. Both, therefore, problematize the institutional and normative structure of liberal democracy. And I shall also show that 'multiculturalism' affects our thinking about nation and the nation-state.

In the final part of chapter 3, I put the 'politics of identity' into a wider context and discuss the 'remoralization of politics' as yet another manifestation of the politics of diversity. The use of nuclear power; genetic engineering; the ecological effects of the industrial mode of production; health policies (for example, with regard to AIDS and HIV or abortion); and individual life-styles (for example, the use of private transport) – all these and many other issues have become opened up for moral debate in recent decades, thus leading to the 'remoralization of politics'. They thus challenge the liberal assumption of the 'moral neutrality' of the state.

In the first three chapters, then, I discuss the norms and institutions of liberal democracy; its 'embeddedness' in political communities structured as nation-states; and theoretical alternatives to this model of democracy. The last two chapters of the book shift attention pointedly to the territorial dimension of democracy. Chapter 1 will have shown that popular sovereignty is considered to depend upon state sovereignty. This presupposition of liberal democracy has been challenged by processes of global interdependence and supranational integration. I argue that at stake is not the 'demise' of the nation-state, but a reconsideration of the idea of 'sovereignty' and the relation between citizens, governments, and supranational institutions. Chapter 4 analyses the challenges that globalization poses to the democratic nation-state. I contend that globalization underlines the importance of the modern state as the dominant form of political organization by raising the issue of collective identity, and, in particular, ethno-national identity. Yet, as I shall argue, globalization undermines the 'sovereignty' of the state, and to the extent that democracy in the liberal model is structurally related to the notion of a *summa potestas*, it poses a challenge to our understanding of democracy.

Centralization and hierarchization of power within states and through states in the international system are steadily replaced by the pluralization of power among political, economic, cultural and social actors, groups, communities within states, between states and across states. In this complex and fragmented world, where is the place of 'democracy'? This is the question with which chapter 4 concludes. In the final chapter I present European integration as one aspect of globalization. By discussing the challenge of European integration to our understanding of democracy and citizenship as institutionalized in historically unique nation-states, I endeavour to advance a tentative answer to the question about the place of democracy in the age of globalization raised in the previous chapter. The chapter addresses a series of interrelated questions. Should there be (or will there be) a development of a sense of being European, a European identity? How does European identity relate to national or subnational identities? How does

European citizenship relate to citizenship in a constituent nation-state? But at the centre of the chapter stands the claim that the 'democratic deficit' of the European Union cannot be overcome by extending the powers of the European Parliament. I discuss the tension between two forms of legitimacy which has severe consequences for democracy in Europe: legitimacy that is mediated through the democratic procedures and institutions of the respective member states, on the one hand, and legitimacy that derives from the political deliberations of the European Parliament on the basis of citizenship rights of individuals and participatory rights of non-state groups, on the other hand. I claim that these two principles of legitimacy are irreconcilable. It follows that there are clear structural limits to the democratization of the European Union. Against widespread claims that the nation-state has lost its significance as the site of democracy to either supranational institutional arrangements or to subnational regions, I argue for the continued importance of the nation-state for citizenship, democracy and freedom.

As we enter the twenty-first century, 'liberal democracy' has survived the ideological challenges of fascism and state socialism. This book looks again at the normative and philosophical suppositions that inform the merged theories of liberalism and democracy. Yet it does not accept that the success of liberal democracy amounts to 'the end of history' (Fukuyama 1992). It cannot be ruled out, for example, that concern with ecological devastations and sustainable growth or with a just and more peaceful world order, will result in the formation of radical theories and political ideologies that go beyond liberalism, Marxism or social democracy (Schecter 1994). Yet, even if we stay within the liberal paradigm and within the institutional framework of liberal democracy, challenges to this type of political rule and its normative and philosophical assumptions and justifications can be seen to gather pace. They demand a response that is likely to lead to fundamental changes to the model of liberal democracy in the twenty-first century. This is a claim put forward in the present book.

1

The model of
liberal democracy

not a necessary linkage

In a liberal democracy, it is the people who have the 'undisputed right to determine the framework of rules, regulations and policies within a given territory and to govern accordingly' (Held 1991: 150). Liberal democracy is premised on the acceptance of the notion of popular sovereignty and its institutionalization in citizenship rights. Sovereignty has been transferred from the (monarchical) ruler to the people, and the people have been defined as the sum of the legally equal citizens. Democratic rule is exercised in the sovereign, territorially consolidated nation-state. In a bounded territory, people's sovereignty is the basis upon which democratic decision-making takes place; and 'the people' are the addressees, or the constituents, of the political decisions. The territorially consolidated democratic polity, which is clearly demarcated from other political communities, is seen as rightly governing itself and determining its own future through the interplay between forces operating within its boundaries. Only in a sovereign state can the people's will command without being commanded by others.

Hence, 'sovereignty' has a spatial dimension in that it is premised on the occupation and possession of territory. This spatial dimension manifests itself most clearly in the drawing of territorial boundaries that separate the 'inside' from the 'outside'. This territorial exclusion is, in turn, the prerequisite for identifying the source of sovereignty within the bounded territory and for defining 'us' in contradistinction to 'them'. Historically, this state sovereignty was achieved through agreements between states in the Treaty of Westphalia in 1648 at the end of the Thirty Years War. Then, governments recognized each others' autonomy from external interference in the most important matter of the time, religious belief. No longer, so governments pledged, would they support foreign co-religionists in conflict with their states. This agreement changed the balance of power between territorial authority and confessional groups in favour of the state. It created the precondition for the build-up of an effective system of control and supervision by the state over the population. It was this 'sovereignty' of the state

10

over its population that has been appropriated and transformed by the people into 'popular' sovereignty in the process of democratization since the eighteenth century (Hirst/Thompson 1995: 410–13).

Popular control over political decision-makers is established through a variety of institutions. Civil liberties, which, for example, guarantee freedom of movement, expression and association, enable citizens to organize independently of government and exert influence on government and governmental policies in their pursuit of shared interests and concerns. Mechanisms of representation are in place to allow the translation of social interests into political issues. First and foremost, there is the recognition of the necessity for public contestation for all political offices and political support. The most important institutional mechanism here is the electoral system which allows for frequent and fairly conducted elections of political decision-makers and serves thus also as one mechanism of elite recruitment and replacement. Electoral competition, and the system of representation more generally, are, in turn, premised on the existence of organized political groups, such as political parties or interest groups. Finally, popular control and its effectiveness are vastly dependent upon the institutional differentiation of the legislature, the executive and the judiciary and upon the division and distribution of power amongst them.

In this and the following chapter I identify and analyse some of the philosophical and theoretical ideas and suppositions which underlie this model of liberal democracy. Once this task has been accomplished, I shall turn to a discussion of some of the main contemporary challenges to this type of democratic rule.

Popular sovereignty and constitutional rule

In a liberal democracy, so I have said, the people are sovereign. But what precisely does this notion of 'popular sovereignty' entail? Let us go back to the historical juncture at which the idea of 'popular sovereignty' gained wide currency, the late eighteenth century. It was during the struggle of the American colonies for independence from Britain and during the crisis and revolutionary overthrow of the French monarchy in the last third of the eighteenth century that a new principle for the political legitimization of political authority was established: the state is legitimate only insofar as it enacts the people's will and is, thereby, responsive and accountable to 'the public'. Not only had the people abolished, or overthrown, an established political order; they had also established a new political principle in that they replaced the idea of the state's authority to define public right and 'welfare' with their claim to a popular mandate to rule.

In the past, the claim of legitimacy of monarchical domination had been based on the notion that the rulers had received their authority 'from the grace of God' (*dei gratia*). As Christ's deputies they were obliged to perform their duties in a devout and just way. They were not seen as sovereign legislator who created and enacted new law. Rather than being 'founders' of new law, they were 'finders' of old law, recognizing and sanctioning law that already existed. Law was seen as representing and expressing perennial norms contained in tradition, ethical values and religious prescriptions; changes in the law were thought of, not as a purposeful creation, but as a 'reformation' of still binding traditional norms and rules, tacitly accepted in a given society (Axtmann 1992; Passerin d'Entrèves 1967: 85–6). Keeping the peace and providing justice under the rule of God as well as under the rule of law were the main responsibilities and justifications of royal authority well into the fifteenth century. The provision of peace and justice (*pax et justitia*) was to result in order (*tranquillitas*). But as the developments in the Holy Roman Empire of German Nations, France, the Netherlands and elsewhere in Europe showed during the sixteenth and seventeenth century, it was the attempt to enforce religious conformity after the Reformation that in effect undermined the establishment of *tranquillitas* in the course of the religious wars that swept across Europe in those centuries. As a result of these wars, political necessities and the concern with the maintenance of the political and geographical integrity of the territory came to inform the policies of the secular authorities in the course of the sixteenth century (Oestreich 1982). The notion of *raison d'état* reflected and legitimized this change and brought about the detheologization and deconfessionalization of political theory: religious issues became subordinated to the secular concerns with the stability and order of the political commonwealth. For the French philosopher Jean Bodin and the group of political thinkers known as *les politiques* in the late sixteenth century, for example, maintaining political order through the consolidation of the power of the state had precedence over the enforcement of religious uniformity and conformity (King 1974; Franklin 1973). The notion of *raison d'état* undermined the conceptualization of the political commonwealth as a *respublica christiana* in which the state-objective (and the duty of the ruler) was defined as the protection of the 'true' faith in order to provide for the best possible precondition for the subjects to attain eternal salvation. Instead of this religious–transcendental foundation of the state-objective, the notion of *raison d'état* focused on the endogenous and autonomous determination of politics, and thus explicitly highlighted the tension between religious ethics and secular political prudence.

This shift in the meaning of monarchical authority found its most significant expression in the increase in the legislative activity of the ruler. The ruler now established himself as law-maker. But this very activity generated theoretical endeavours to assess more precisely the nature of that activity, the kind of power which it both presupposed and entailed. The notion of 'sovereignty' became central in the context of these reflections. It issued out of the basic assumption that:

> there is somewhere in the community, whether in the people or in the prince, or in both the prince and the people united in one body, a *summa potestas*, a power which is the very essence of the State. The decisive contribution of the [rediscovered] Roman [law] doctrine was the new conception of law as an expression of this power, as an instrument which could be used and adapted in accordance with the changing needs of society, as a system of rules that were valid and effective as long as there existed behind them the control of a supreme will: a will which, in virtue of its supremacy, was *legibus solutus*, because it was not accountable to any but itself. (Passerin d'Entrèves 1967: 93)

Henceforth it was one of the major concerns of political and juridical thinking to identify the 'will which legally commands and is not commanded by others' (Passerin d'Entrèves 1967: 93). Bodin and Hobbes conceptualized the king as the source of the law, and it was Hobbes who moved most decisively away from the notion of a sacred foundation of the ruler's legitimacy of rule derived from 'divine right' to a secular notion which saw the ruler invested with sovereignty by the people in the 'covenant'. Yet it was by no means inevitable that a contractual theory of rule should be couched in secular terms. During the period of politico-religious conflict in France, the Netherlands and Scotland in the second half of the sixteenth century, Calvinist political theorists had developed theories of contractual rule in which the notion of *princeps legibus solutus* was challenged by the idea that it was not the ruler but the people who were freed from legal constraint, *populus legibus solutus*. The contractual theory of these Calvinist *'monarchomachs'* was dominated by the idea of a reciprocal bond between ruler and people. This idea was founded on the biblical doctrine of the convenant, the Old Testament *foedus duplex* between God and the people on the one hand, and between the king and the people on the other (Oestreich 1982: 168). By distinguishing between these two pacts – as was the case in the core text of the Calvinist monarchomachs, *Vindiciae contra tyrannos* (1574/79) – the secular rulers were now denied that immediate divine right which the Reformation had initially tended to ensure to them. The law and the contract were now seen to intervene between God and the monarch, and the royal acts were considered to be subjected to the test of mere human reason: should the ruler not fulfil his obligation to ensure piety and provide justice, the people could not be held to obey him (Oestreich 1982: 135–54; Allen 1951: 302–32).

These contractual theories were formulated to justify limitations to the powers of monarchs. But it proved also possible to develop a theory of strong monarchical authority on the basis of a political contract of submission. It could be argued that the people had no right to do anything but endure even the rule of a tyrant, if he had been lawfully instituted. Furthermore, it was also possible to subscribe to a theory of contractual rule without, at the same time, subscribing to a concomitant ethic derived from natural law:

> The foundation of the whole idea of natural law had been the conviction that independently of political institutions, or of human passions, there is a real moral difference between good and evil, which all men have a duty to respect, and by which all human institutions, the state included, must be guided ... It was in this atmosphere that the contract theory had developed in the hands of the religious *monarchomachi* and others of their school ... It had led ... to the idea of the state of nature, in which ... the moral obligation of natural law always held good, and in which men had natural rights – a moral claim that other men, and the state itself when it came into existence, should respect the obligations which were binding on all. (Gough 1936: 110)

As is well known, Thomas Hobbes demolished all this in his political theory which he developed during the revolutionary upheavals in seventeenth-century England. For Hobbes, the state was indeed constituted through the political contract. In this state, all men are subjects, except the man on whom all have agreed to confer power, and who thereby becomes sovereign over them. The rights of individuals and the sovereignty of the 'people' were dissolved in the *potestas* of the *Leviathan*, save the right of self-preservation; whatever the sovereign does is by virtue of the powers men have conferred on him.

It was within this theoretical contractarian tradition, which was complementary to the concept of *raison d'état*, that the notion of the common good, the *bonum commune*, was redefined. In continental Europe since the mid-seventeenth century the purpose of the state was seen, both by the rulers themselves and the majority of political theorists, as going beyond the confines of preserving *pax et iustitia*; it comprised now the task of actively promoting the secular and material welfare of the state and its population. The promotion of this-worldly happiness of the population replaced the ruler's traditional duty to assist in its other-worldly salvation. Hence, to an ever greater extent, justification for monarchical rule was based on the claim that it would bring about and enhance the secular and material welfare of the state and its citizens. This 'state-objective' was particularly characteristic of the political regime of 'enlightened' absolutism that was embraced by rulers across continental Europe in the eighteenth century. Looking back on the changes on the justification of monarchical domination, we notice that the magical and religious–sacral elements of the beliefs that legitimated domination as a 'divine right of kings' became replaced by the secular notions of safety, security and welfare which the rulers strove, and were expected, to provide for their subjects.

The idea of 'popular sovereignty', however, challenged this notion of the

legitimacy of rule, grounded as that notion was in the rulers' performing
their tasks and functions well. It stipulated that, henceforth, political
authority was legitimate only if it was bestowed, and willed, by the people,
and not because of the 'state-objectives', however defined, which it strove
to achieve. The people, not the king, were now seen as the source of the
law. The Virginia Bill of Rights of 1776 made this point very succinctly: 'All
power is vested in, and consequently derived from, the people ... [M]agis-
trates are their trustees and servants, and at all times amenable to them'
(Article 2; in: Morison (ed) 1965: 149–51). A related idea was the assertion
in the French Declaration of the Rights and Duties of Man and Citizen of
1789 that 'The source of all sovereignty is essentially in the nation; no
body, no individual can exercise authority that does not proceed from it in
plain terms' ('Le principe de toute souveraineté residé essentiellement dans la
Nation; nul corps, nul individu ne peut exercer d'autorité qui n'en émane
expressément'; in: Anderson (ed) 1904: 59).

In the past, it had been possible to reconcile the notion of the sovereignty
of the people with the idea of the absolute sovereignty of the monarchs,
since in contractual theory, the sovereignty of the people was constructed
as ceasing with the authorization of the sovereign ruler by the people as a
result of the social contract. The radically new idea, that became prevalent
in the late eighteenth century, was that 'the sovereignty of the people' was
inalienable, that it could not be revoked by, or ceded to, some other body
or person. The first and decisive act of exercising this sovereignty is for the
people to give themselves a constitution under which they agree to live
together. In designing a constitution, the people create a government and
give it powers, but they also regulate and restrain the powers so given.
Thomas Paine, the British-born radical pamphleteer of the American Revolution, argued in *The Rights of Man* (1791) that a constitution was 'a thing
antecedent to the government, and always distinct therefrom' (1791/1985:
192); 'formed by the people in their original character', the constitution
served 'not only as an authority, but as a law of control to the government'
(1791/1985: 187). In the revolutionary period, the idea was reinforced that
the rule of law meant that the state, as much as the citizens, had to submit
to the laws of the land; that, in effect, not only had law to be independent
of the state, constituting, as it were, an autonomous realm, but had also to
be superior to it: then, and only then, could it be conceived of as binding,
not only for the subjects or citizens, but for the state itself. This was the core
idea behind revolutionary constitutional politics: political rule was established through a constitution and, once established, also limited by it.

Once sovereignty of the people had been established as the principle of
legitimate political authority, the question had to be confronted whether
there could be any limits to their sovereignty. Could it be argued that certain areas of individual behaviour had to be delimited over which even 'the

people' have no right to exercise control? One answer to this question typically referred to natural rights, rights of man, or, above all in the twentieth century, human rights. These rights have been seen as a barrier against the exertions of even the sovereign people. The Virginia Bill of Rights of 1776 (Article 1) claimed that:

> all men are by nature equally free and independent, and have certain inherent rights, of which, when they enter into a state of society, they cannot by any compact deprive or divest their posterity; namely the enjoyment of life and liberty, with the means of acquiring and possessing property, and pursuing and obtaining happiness and safety.

The Declaration of Independence a few weeks later expressed the same thoughts in the following famous words:

> We hold these truths to be self-evident, that all men are created equal, that they are endowed by their Creator with certain unalienable rights, that among these are life, liberty, and the pursuit of happiness. That to secure these rights, governments are instituted among men, deriving their just powers from the consent of the governed. That whenever any form of government becomes destructive of these ends, it is the right of the people to alter or to abolish it. (Morison (ed) 1965: 157)

The Declaration thus put the defence of the rights and liberties of individuals against government at the very centre of the foundation of a new political commonwealth. Liberty and property as the natural rights of man had already been discussed in the political philosophy of John Locke. He had argued that God's natural law provided that 'no one ought to harm another in his life, health, liberty or possessions' and that, derived from this law, each person had a natural right to his life, liberty, and property as well as the 'executive right of nature' to protect his natural rights by whatever means necessary. The exercise of this 'executive right' was seen by him as a source of conflict in a state of nature and, as a consequence, men would seek peace by handing it over to a common authority. Through this transferral of the 'executive right', men established a political community (Locke 1689/1989).

But these declarations of the revolutionary era also espoused the idea of natural rights which had also been prominent in Locke's political philosophy. By stating that they considered these rights to be 'inalienable', they also followed Locke's argument that men do not give up these rights when they enter into a political community. Rather, the primary function of a political community, or government, was seen to be the maintenance and protection of these rights. If government violated these rights, it forfeited the trust its citizens had put in it and could be legitimately overthrown. This conceptualization of inalienable natural rights was, of course, quite distinct from the political philosophy of Thomas Hobbes. As we shall see in greater detail in the following chapter, for Hobbes the 'state of nature' was a place of violence and devastation in which the life of man was 'solitary, poore, nasty, brutish, and short'; but once they entered into civil and political society, they surrendered their virtually unlimited rights almost totally to the ruler, or government: only through men divesting themselves of their natural rights could political authority be instituted and peace be achieved. For Locke, on the other hand, the 'state of nature', though lacking security, was potentially a place of civilization and progress in which adult, male, property-owning individuals, who are each others' equals, enjoy freedom to dispose of their powers and possessions as they choose (Keane 1988a: 40). It is here that individuals as bearers of 'inalienable' rights, capable of living within the bounds of natural law, realize their freedom.

But while Hobbes and Locke disagreed about the degree of power at the disposal of the state, they shared a conception of 'negative' liberty. For Hobbes, a free man is a person who 'in those things, which by his strength and wit he is able to do, is not hindered to doe what he has a will to' and who performs his actions freely, in that he 'may refuse to do it if he will' (Hobbes *Leviathan*, chap. 21, 146). In his *Essay Concerning Human Understanding* (chap. 21), Locke embraced this view: 'Liberty, 'tis plain, consists in a power to do or not to do; to do or forbear doing as we will. This cannot be denied.' And for both Locke and Hobbes, 'the law preserves our liberty essentially by coercing other people. It prevents them from interfering with my acknowledged rights, helps me to draw around myself a circle within which they may not trespass, and prevents me at the same time from interfering with their freedom in just the same way' (Skinner 1990a: 305).

We should be aware of the import of this particular political philosophy. For what we encounter here is a condensed summary of the position of classical political liberalism. According to Locke, men enjoy equal rights under the law of nature; therefore, no one can exercise authority over another except by that other person's consent. Political authority in a liberal polity therefore rests on the freely given consent of the governed. Furthermore, governments are instituted by popular consent in order to protect life, liberty and property of the individual. Government finds its legitimacy as well as its limits in the performance of this, and only this, function. It is within the context of this political philosophy that liberalism since the late eighteenth century strove to lay down constitutional provisions that protected citizens from the interference by the state and to stipulate the rights that citizens have in the private sphere. There was a recognition of a separation between 'public' and 'private' spheres, between the 'state' and 'civil society'. Individuals were considered to be more than citizens with political interests, rights and duties; they were seen as possessing capacities and interests of a non-political nature which they were at liberty to express and pursue without the state's interference. Out of this thinking issued a conceptualization

of the constitution as that mechanism that established the state as a guarantor of individual liberty and societal autonomy, while, at the same time,
limiting the state to that function.

Immanuel Kant can justifiably be seen as the philosopher who presented
the principles of this type of rule most succinctly. First, Kant endorsed the
idea of the sovereignty of the people that manifests itself in constitution-
making and law-making: 'The legislative power can only belong to the
united will of the people' (Kant, in: Reiss 1991: 139). Citizens as the members of a society uniting for the purpose of legislating are said to have the
lawful freedom to obey only those laws to which they have given their consent; to enjoy equality before the law so that they possess perfectly symmetrical rights of coercion relative to each other; and to be their own
master, dependent on no other will, but only on themselves, and this 'civil
independence' includes the material means to secure their existence and
sustenance.

Second, Kant conceptualized freedom as 'negative' liberty, defining 'every
restriction of freedom through the arbitrary will of another party' as coercion: 'No-one can compel me to be happy in accordance with his conception of the welfare of others, for each may seek his happiness in whatever
way he sees fit, so long as he does not infringe upon the freedom of others
to pursue a similar end which can be reconciled with the freedom of everyone else within a workable general law – i.e. he must accord to others the
same right as he enjoys himself' (Kant, in: Reiss 1991: 74). But this argument goes beyond a mere statement of the principle of 'negative' liberty. By
rejecting the paternalist idea of happiness which a benevolent state might
want to impose on its subjects, Kant, third, rejected the notion of substantive state-objective and declared that the individuals as citizens know for
themselves what they want to will. It is they, and only they, who have the
right and competence to decide what laws are right and just so that 'the
will of one person can be reconciled with the will of another in accordance
with a universal law of freedom' (Kant, in: Reiss 1991: 133). It is their own
will, and only their will, that is the source of the law. Law is not any longer
seen as manifesting a concordance with a transcendent idea or 'natural
law'; the '*summus imperans*' is not bound, or restricted, by *a* law, but bound
to give laws (Maus 1992: 158–9).

But where, or in what, does the legitimacy of this positive law reside?
From where does it receive its justification and coercive validity if not from
an extra-legal source? For Kant, the legitimacy of the law is dependent upon
the legitimacy of the law-maker. Legitimacy of the law issues out of a procedure of deliberation in which free individuals (as citizens) participate on
an equal footing with each other and in which 'each decides the same for
all and all decide the same for each' (Kant, in: Reiss 1991: 139). The authorization of the legislator to obligate others through his mere will is thus

grounded by the conceptualization of a procedural sovereignty of the people that manifests itself in individuals who, as citizens, deliberate in public with the intent to formulate universal laws (Kant 1965: 25–6; Maus 1992: chap. 8; Brunkhorst 1994: 25, 138, 177–83, 202–3).

Finally, in rejecting the state's objective to provide for 'common welfare' and 'happiness', Kant also denied that a state could coerce its citizens to enter an ethical community, or that a legislator could found a constitution directed towards ethical ends through coercion (Taylor 1984: 109). Through politics, human beings cannot become moral beings. Kant's refusal of any moral telos, or purpose, of the political community was complemented by his view that there was also a disjunction between a republican government and the 'virtues' of individuals:

> [T]he *republican* constitution is the only one which does complete justice to the rights of man. But it is also the most difficult to establish, and even more so to preserve, so that many maintain that it would only be possible within a state of *angels*, since men, with their self-seeking inclinations, would be incapable of adhering to a constitution of so sublime a nature. But in fact, nature comes to the aid of the universal and human rational will ... and makes use of precisely those self-seeking inclinations in order to do so. It only remains for men to create a good organisation for the state ... and to arrange it in such a way that their self-seeking energies are opposed to one another, each thereby neutralising or eliminating the destructive efforts of the rest. And as far as reason is concerned, the result is the same as if man's selfish tendencies were non-existent, so that man, even if he is not morally good in himself, is nevertheless compelled to be a good citizen. As hard as it may sound, the problem of setting up a state can be solved even by a nation of devils (as long as they possess understanding). (Kant, in: Reiss 1991: 112)

Kant thus proposed an institutional arrangement that counteracts interest with interest and passion with passion. Even if we presuppose the existence of only self-interested rational individuals, a republican polity could still be established.

In the following chapter, we shall resume our discussion of this tradition of classical liberalism when we analyse the concept of 'citizenship' and 'civil society' that issued out of this political philosophy. In this chapter, we shall continue in our effort to highlight some of the philosophical implications in the model of liberal democracy.

The representation of interests and government by deliberation

'Liberal democracy' accepts the diversity of social interests and the legitimacy of their pursuit in the political arena. 'Different interests necessarily exist in different classes of citizens', argued James Madison, one of the 'Founding Fathers' of the American constitution:

19

A zeal for different opinions concerning religion, concerning government, and many other points, as well of speculation as of practice; an attachment to different leaders ambitiously contending for pre-eminence and power ... have, in turn, divided mankind into parties, inflamed them with mutual animosity, and rendered them much more disposed to vex and oppress each other than to cooperate for their common good ... The most common and durable source of factions has been the various and unequal distribution of property. Those who hold and those who are without property have ever formed distinct interests in society. (Federalist Papers: No. 10)

Madison recognized that society was composed of different alliances, groupings and parties, all of them pursuing a plurality of interests. Factionalism and political conflict were accepted as an inherent aspect of a political community. Much as we take this view for granted in our time, when Madison and the other 'Federalists' espoused this point, they were taking their leave from a long tradition in political thinking that can be traced back to ancient Greece. The question of 'democracy' had been raised for the first time in the Greek polis in the first half of the fifth century BC. It was there that the idea was formulated and institutionalized that a substantial number of free, adult males should be entitled to participate in governing the political community. However, the classical Greek notion of democracy was premised on the assumption that, in order for democratic rule to uphold the common good of the political community, the citizen body had to be highly homogeneous as high levels of economic inequality, of religious, cultural or racial diversity would tend to produce political conflict and disagreements over the common good. A shared sense of the common good was seen to require a citizen body that was harmonious in its interests. Homogeneity and uniformity of interests and opinions was the prerequisite of democracy; democracy was not seen as that institutional arrangement that would create harmony out of diversity, but as the 'rule of the many' sharing a common understanding of the common weal. It was argued that heterogeneity of interests and opinions could only be avoided in a small city-state. Only in the polis could citizens acquire the knowledge of their city and their fellow citizens by direct observation, experience or discussion that would allow them to gain an understanding of the common good. Furthermore, it was only in the polis that citizens could assemble in public, decide directly on the laws and policies, and participate actively in the administration of the city. Hence, the direct and active participation of the citizens in law-making, law-execution and law-adjudication was seen as the core element of democracy. The idea that citizens could be 'represented' by other people was quite alien to classical democratic thinking. Only through this direct and active participation in public matters for the common good, could human beings realize their 'nature' and be good, 'virtuous' citizens (Dahl 1989).

The conviction that this kind of 'democracy' could only be viable in small republics was received wisdom well into the eighteenth century. In *The Spirit of Laws* of 1748, Montesquieu still endorsed that view, much as he also embraced the idea of the active citizen. He was, therefore, sceptical that in the consolidated, large territorial states of his time direct and active 'democracy' could be established. But Madison turned these arguments on their head. For him, in large republics, there is a greater variety of parties and interests which makes it difficult for permanent majorities to emerge; small republics are particularly susceptible to oppression by a majoritarian faction, whereas in a large republic, the factions are more likely to balance each other off (Pitkin 1967: 190–8). The acceptance of the reality, and even legitimacy, of conflicting interests and competing factions went thus hand in hand with an attempt at devicing an institutional structure that would secure the protection of minorities and the containment of factions. This was the rationale behind the proposed federation of the American states. Roper summed up succinctly one strand of Madison's and Hamilton's argument:

> [A] kaleidoscope of different alliances, groupings and interests across the diverse union would constantly form and reform. Minority groups could gain allies to transform themselves into temporary majorities. Majorities would lose friends, and be relegated to a subordinate influence. Such a democracy was energetic, shifting, changing, such that the prospects of a permanent majority, uniting for unworthy or even benign reasons, or of a regional hegemony were unlikely. (Roper 1989: 58)

This idea of countervailing factions and interests was complemented by the conviction that, in line with Montesquieu's political theory, an institutionalized separation and balance of powers within the state had to be created (Held 1987: 55–66). The 'Federalists' argued that political authority had to be dispersed and many power centres had to be created to prevent the wholesale capture of authority by any one particular interest. It became accepted that in republican regimes there was a need for designing institutional mechanisms to prevent the concentration of power within the state. In the past, forms of 'mixed government' had been advocated in which the interests of 'the one', 'the few' and 'the many' (in the Aristotelian sense) could be represented and pursued. The British Constitution with its institutional separation of the monarchy, the aristocratic upper chamber and the lower House of Commons was one of the longest established forms of government and the one most admired across Europe. Underlying its constitution was the idea that the exercise of power by one section had to be checked by the exercise of a countervailing power by other sections. However, the 'Federalists' developed this idea of the need to check power with power into the concept of the institutional separation of powers. Already in 1776, the Constitution of Virginia had stated unequivocally that 'The legislative, executive, and judiciary departments shall be separate and distinct, so that neither exercise the powers properly belonging to the other' (Morison (ed) 1965: 151–7). The Federal Constitution of 1787 entrenched a division of powers between the national government and the state governments, and within the national government between the three main functions of legislature, executive and judiciary. Through the establishment of the House of Representatives and the Senate, there was a further balance within the legislature, allowing for the interests of 'the people' and those of the individual states to be pursued in different, though closely articulated, institutional settings. This separation of powers was, however, not fully institutionalized. Given, for example, the involvement of both the executive (President) and the legislature in the appointment of Supreme Court judges, and given also the judicial politics of the Supreme Court through the institution of judicial review, we may be entitled to see powers not so much clearly separated as closely interconnected and articulated. Still, the idea that legislative, executive and judicial powers should not be exercised by one person or one group of people or one assembly, but should be institutionally disaggregated has become firmly entrenched in the constitutional and political self-understanding of Western liberal democracy.

But Madison identified yet another safeguard of the common good. Madison was adamant that for a large-scale community, direct democracy was impossible as the people could not meet as a legislative body and had therefore to choose, or elect, representatives to do what they, as citizens, could not do themselves. The Constitution of Massachusetts of 1780 had already stated that 'the people of this commonwealth are not controllable by any other laws, than those to which their constitutional representative body have given their consent' (Art. 10, in: Peters 1978: 48). Contained in this conceptualization of representative government is the idea that law is positive, enacted law; it is reasoned law issuing out of the deliberations of an assembly of individuals who act as the representatives of the people. Madison made this notion of representative government central to his political theory by defining a republic as 'a government in which the scheme of representation takes place' (Federalist Papers: No. 10). As he saw it, the delegation of the government to a small number of citizens elected by the rest had the positive effect to:

> refine and enlarge the public views by passing them through the medium of a chosen body of citizens, whose wisdom may but discern the true interest of their country and whose patriotism and love of justice will be least likely to sacrifice it to temporary or partial considerations. Under such a regulation it may well happen that the public voice, pronounced by the representatives of the people, will be more consonant to the public good than if pronounced by the people themselves, convened for the purpose. (Federalist Papers: No. 10)

As 'proper guardians of the public weal', these representatives cannot be mere delegates or servants of their constituents. 'Representation' was thus conceived as that mechanism through which an 'extended republic' could be governed, and proper representational arrangements would ensure that 'temperate and respectable men', standing for 'reason, justice and truth' (Federalist Papers: No. 63), would be elected, men of 'more cool and sedate reflection' (Federalist Papers: No. 71). A 'virtuous' elite, striving for the common good, was to replace the 'virtuous' citizen.

This view of representation did not go unchallenged. The 'anti-federalist' opponents of the draft constitution of the United States took issue with the idea of the 'virtuous representative'. Many of them, standing as they did in the classical tradition, would have preferred to have no representatives at all, but a 'direct democracy'. Liberty, for them, still referred to the direct political participation in public affairs. But if representation was to be institutionalized, then it should be of a different kind from the Federalists' idea. One 'anti-federalist' argued that:

> the idea that naturally suggests itself to our minds, when we speak of representatives, is that they resemble those they represent. They should be a true picture of the people, possess a knowledge of their circumstances and their wants, sympathise in all their distress, and be disposed to seek their true interests. (Melancton Smith, in: Kramnick (ed) 1987: 44)

Smith insisted that a representative system ought not to seek 'brilliant talents', but 'a sameness, as to residence and interests, between the representative and his constituent' (Kramnick (ed) 1987: 44). In advocating short terms of office for representatives, he, and other anti-federalists, aimed also for a much greater control over the political office-holders, making them much more like mandated delegates than independent representatives.

But while there were these differences between 'Federalists' and 'Anti-Federalists' regarding the qualitative character of representation, they were agreed on one thing: if there was to be representation, it had to be 'actual', not 'virtual'. To put it differently, they were united in their opposition to the idea of representation as developed in the British Constitution. The Americans shared the republican premise that 'the many' can judge and express the common good; within the British tradition, it was maintained that only the 'virtuous few' could do so. The Members of Parliament, as an important part of these 'virtuous few', were seen in the British tradition as representing not a particular place, or the idiosyncratic 'interests' of an individual or a group of individuals, but the whole nation. In his famous 'Speech at the Conclusion of the Poll to the Electors in Bristol', the British–Irish politician and political thinker, Edmund Burke said in 1774 that:

> Parliament is not a *congress* of ambassadors from different and hostile interests, which interests each must maintain, as an agent and advocate, against other

agents and advocates; but Parliament is a *deliberative* assembly of *one* nation, with one interest, that of the whole – where not local purposes, not local prejudices, ought to guide, but the general good, resulting from the general reason of the whole. (Hill (ed) 1975: 158)

Hence, according to Burke, it was not, for example, the 'interest' of the 'common people' that would be 'represented' *vis-à-vis* the king; nor the 'interest' of conflicting or antagonistic classes or status groups which would aim for some kind of peaceful accommodation of these 'interests' in a deliberative assembly. Rather, what was being represented was the common interest of the nation as a whole; and it was in the debate of free individuals that this common national interest could be recognized. It is the duty of Members of Parliament to reason and judge about the good of the whole, and 'the selfish wishes of parts of the nation, the wills of individual voters have nothing to do with it' (Pitkin 1967: 170–1). Samuel Beer has summarized Burke's position well, emphasizing the close connection between the idea of 'representation' and 'parliamentary sovereignty':

> If the many had been enfranchised and deference abolished, the rule of the virtuous few would have collapsed into popular government. The great interests of realm and empire and the various ranks and orders of the governing class would have no longer been assured of their proper weight and voice in government. For that reason, sovereign authority could not be vested in the people but only in that complex body, the parliament, which, including king, lords, and commons, brought all virtues and all interests into a common deliberation in their proper ordering. (Beer 1993: 145)

Burke further argued that representation did not have to be 'actual', in the sense that a constituency elects a Member of Parliament. He argued that disenfranchised groups or localities, which did not send a Member to Parliament, may be 'virtually' represented by some member from some other constituency. This was for the simple reason that Members of Parliament were considered by Burke to represent unattached interests – 'interests to which no particular persons were so specially related that they could claim to be privileged to define the interest' (Pitkin 1967: 210). The agricultural interest, the trading interest and the manufacturing interest, for example, were identified by Burke as such objective, 'fixed' interests which could be 'virtually' represented. This means, for example, that:

> [a]lthough the city of Birmingham elects no members to Parliament, it can still be virtually represented there because Bristol sends members; and these are really representatives of the trading interest, of which Birmingham, too, is a part. Although a member may be called the Representative of Bristol since he is elected there, he really represents Bristol's interest, which may also be the interest of many other cities like Bristol. (Pitkin 1967: 174)

This idea of 'virtual representation' was, manifestly, based on the assumption that one (or some) of the constituencies that do elect members shares the interest of the disenfranchised group. Burke acknowledged that such an assumption could not always be made. Both in the case of the Irish Catholics and the American colonists, Burke asserted that no constituency that was 'actually' represented shared the interest of these excluded groups and he concluded that they had therefore to be represented 'actually' (Pitkin 1967: 177–8). The American colonists had, of course, also proclaimed that their interests had not been represented in Parliament when they demanded 'No taxation without representation'. But as the conflict with the imperial centre progressed, 'independence' from Britain, rather than 'actual' representation in the British Parliament, became the political objective of the American colonists.

In France, too, the question of representation caused much controversy. Could the sovereignty of the people be exercised other than through the direct and immediate participation of all citizens in public affairs? After all, the revolutionary rhetoric had put forward the idea that a multiplicity of individuals was made one, not by the absolute and irrevocable submission to the (individual) person of the monarch, but to the single, unitary (collective) person of the body of citizens as a whole (Baker 1990: 253; Singer 1986: 61–7, 71, 89). In Hobbes's political philosophy, unity was brought to the 'many' members of society by their consent in the covenant to the transferral of sovereignty to the 'Leviathan'; it was the sovereign state which 'represented' the people: 'The Soveraign, in every Commonwealth, is the absolute Representative of all Subjects' (Hobbes, *Leviathan*, chap. 22; also: chap. 16; Baumgold 1988: chap. 3; Pitkin 1967: chap. 2). For Jean-Jacques Rousseau, on the other hand, the people themselves were sovereign and could not be 'represented'; legislative power as the expression of their *summa potestas* had to remain with them. For Hobbes, the common good found expression and manifestation through the sovereign state; for Rousseau, the 'general will' manifested itself in the collective person of the body of citizens as a whole. But there was an ambivalence in Rousseau's thinking. In *The Social Contract*, he argued that the 'general will' was indivisible and could therefore not be 'represented' or 'delegated' (Book II, chap. 1). In his *Considérations sur le gouvernement de Pologne*, on the other hand, he accepted that in a large state like Poland, legislative power could only be exercised through representative institutions. However, in order to uphold the idea of direct democracy as best as possible, he defined the representatives as delegates with a binding mandate, instructed to express, not their personal opinions, but the will of the nation (Baker 1990: 236–7). This ambivalence also informed the arguments of the radical Rousseauian politicians in the National Assembly in 1789. They, too, accepted, grudgingly, the idea of representation but still aimed to ensure the direct participation of all citizens by imposing a binding mandate on their representatives. In the early phase of the Revolution, they therefore endorsed the idea of a suspensive veto of the monarch on the legislation of the representative assembly. Since they did not expect the representatives to be always the organ of the 'general will' of the nation, they construed the suspensive veto of the executive authority of the Crown as the means of enabling the reassertion of the 'general will' because the veto had to be followed by an appeal to the people and its direct vote on the disputed piece of legislation. In short, in this theoretical perspective, 'the unity of general will exists prior to representation, and that, as a result, representation is not to produce a unified political will above society, but simply to mirror the larger unity of purpose present within a politicized social totality' (Singer 1986: 158).

But this Rousseauian notion of direct democracy and representation was challenged from a variety of theoretical perspectives. Amongst those who were committed to the revolutionary transferral of sovereignty from the monarchy to the people, the arguments of the Abbé Sieyès were particularly sophisticated (Singer 1986: 93–108, 153–7). He was quite adamant that in a large, populous state like France popular sovereignty could find its manifestation only in the deliberations of a unitary legislative assembly: 'The people can have but one voice, that of the national legislature ... In a country that is not a [direct] democracy – and France cannot be one – the people ... can speak or act only through its representatives' (Sieyès, in: Baker 1990: 249). The deputies were seen as representatives of not just their localities where they had been elected, but of the entire nation, transcending the necessarily 'particular will' of their constituencies. To be a 'mandated delegate' of his constituency would make the deputy a carrier of that particular will and would not allow him to be the representative of the nation. For Sieyès, representatives were sent to the assembly to discover the national will through deliberations. The deputies came to 'propose, listen, take counsel together, modify [their] opinions, and finally to form in common a common will' (Sieyès, in: Baker 1990: 299). Hence, representation was not seen as a mechanism for the aggregation of particular wills; the 'general will' was more than the sum of particular wills (Forsyth 1987: chap. 7).

In his pamphlet *What Is the Third Estate?* (1789), in which he put forward the initial political programme of the Revolution, Abbé Sieyès had already discussed at some length the idea of a *répresentation nationale*. For him, the representative assembly of the nation had to address matters of common concern: common security, common liberty and the common welfare. He did not suggest that there was no diversity of interests among individuals; but he did not consider personal interest, 'whereby everyone stands apart, thinking of himself only' as dangerous 'since it is insulated. To each man his own. In its diversity lies its own cure' (Sieyès 1789/1963: 158, 159). Hence, individual personal interests will balance each other off, cancel each other out. However, he saw the major difficulty springing from the interest 'by which a citizen allies himself with just a few others. This type of interest leads to conspiracy and collusion; through it anti-social schemes are plotted; through it the most formidable enemies of the People mobilise themselves' (Sieyès 1789/1963: 159). It is thus organized interests which Sieyès detested; or rather, he detested the representation of 'interests' through corporate orders as it had been institutionalized in the *ancien régime*. He negated the political legitimacy of all corporate bodies and the Revolution dissolved them all, 'leaving in their place individuals whose rights were protected by their membership in a nation-state' (Kates 1990: 112). Following Singer (1986: 154–5) we can say that for Sieyès, 'representation is always partial ... [T]he political will ... does not represent the particulars but only what is common to them, leaving, as it were, a stratum of particularity unrepresented ... Ultimately what is represented are not the individual wills ... but the national will that the representation is to produce'. But in any case, as far as the assembly of a nation was concerned, he argued that it should be constituted in such a way that each personal interest it contained was insulated; it should ensure 'that the will of its majority is always consistent with the general good' (Sieyès 1789/1963: 158; also: Hont 1994: 192–205).

We know that in the revolutionary upheavals in France, there was no final constitutional settlement of many of the contentious political issues. However, both the American Revolution and the French Revolution embraced the republican idea that 'the many' are capable of self-rule. They came to accept the necessity for this self-rule to be exercised by representatives who were seen as responsible for the common welfare of the people and accountable to the people through elections. They differed on the legitimacy of the representation of particular interests. In France, the idea of a unified or united nation went hand in hand with the belief that any idiosyncratic particular interests of individuals, groups or corporations had to be submitted, if need be by force, to the national will: '[T]he French did not conceive of representation in terms of separate interests; only a unitary national will could be the ultimate political expression of French sovereignty' (Kates 1990: 114). And it was the National Assembly that was considered to embody the will of the nation – just as it was in the British Parliament that, according to Burke, the national interest was recognized. This kind of reasoning was instrumental in entrenching the notion of parliamentary sovereignty. In America, on the other hand, the legitimacy of particular interests was acknowledged. There, politics became conceptualized as that process in which the interests became represented in the deliberative and decision-making political assemblies in which, in turn, negotiations between particular and divergent ideas and interests of individuals, groups and parties would result, if successful, in the tentative, and fragile, definition of the common weal.

There emerged one further commonality in some of the political thinking of the French and American Revolution; and it was a commonality that also included Burke and other defenders of the British Constitution. For all of them, political rule was exercised as government by deliberation. It was through deliberations in parliamentary assemblies that the 'public good' or the 'general will' was defined. It was defined as a result of political contestation and was, thus, permanently open to redefinition – although the respective degree of openness distinguished the American, the French and the British system.

In the course of time, the idea of representation became linked to the notion of a reasoning public which, exercising the rights of assembly, petition and association formed political associations, political clubs and political parties and, with the help of a free press, deliberated on the issues concerning the political community. The link between this 'reasoning public' and the parliamentary assembly was the electoral process through which parliamentarians were chosen to serve as representatives of public opinion(s). Representation was thus premised on rights of political participation. To that extent, the constitutional provisions that aimed to protect the citizen from the interference of the state and gave him rights to be left alone, was complemented by rights to be involved in the political process.

Democratic government could thus be conceptualized as representative government circumscribed by constitutional constraints. Government was seen to be accountable to the people through the mediation of their representatives assembled in parliament. But parliament itself was also held accountable through the institution of periodical elections. This allowed for the control and sanctioning of parliament by the public as well as the adjustment of parliament to changes occurring in the distribution of political preferences within the public. This reconceptualization of representation and democracy resulted in parliament acquiring a set of distinct functions in democratic systems. As Gianfranco Poggi argues, parliament has become central to this system:

> because it does not simply *transmit* political impulses originating elsewhere; it *produces* political impulses by processing the orientations of the electorate it represents. It is central, too, in that by commenting on and criticizing actions of government and ongoing social developments it feeds information back to the electorate and thereby increases the people's awareness of public issues and both the choices those issues open and the burdens and opportunities they involve. Finally, it is central because and insofar as it forms and selects *leaders* – individuals capable of formulating issues, projecting solutions, voicing and forming public opinion, taking responsibility. (Poggi 1978: 113)

In this perspective, parliament, as a deliberative assembly, is part of the reasoning public, in that it both processes and circulates information emanating from society and also produces information for society. Insofar as parliament is premised on the acceptance of a fluid and varied public opinion and, hence, on the acceptance of public contestation and the legitimacy of opposition, it manifests the idea of the essentially open-ended, contingent nature of politics in Western democracies.

Democracy, participation and the nation-state

I have argued that the legitimacy of the political representation of a plurality of social interests within a constitutional setting of disaggregated institutional powers has become a central aspect of liberal political systems. However, the question has to be asked whether some interests are more likely to be represented than others. It is by considering this question that we are moving towards the issue of democracy. So far, we have only discussed the meaning of popular sovereignty and its institutional and conceptual ramifications. But the question of democracy goes beyond identifying the site of sovereign power. It is centrally concerned with defining the membership of 'the people'; it is concerned with bestowing the status of citizen and thus political entitlements and duties upon individuals. Let us approach this issue step by step. If we assume that the link between a reasoning and 'interested' public and the deliberative parliamentary assembly is the electoral process, then we may also suggest that the representation of 'interests' is heavily determined by the right of political participation in this process. In short, those individuals and groups that can articulate their interests in the electoral process are politically privileged over those who remain disenfranchised. A comprehensive representation of the plurality of social interests has, therefore, as its minimum requirement the universalization of the suffrage so that almost all adults in a state are entitled to participate in elections. Furthermore, no individual or group must be advantaged by having more votes than others; and each vote should have equal value. Such a universal and equal adult suffrage is a necessary condition for the political articulation of the whole diversity of social interests.

As is only too well known, neither universality nor equality of suffrage was achieved until well into the twentieth century. This is not the place to give even a short account of electoral reform in Western Europe since the early nineteenth century. However, a few remarks on the extension of the franchise are nevertheless warranted in the context of our discussion. If we use as a very crude measure of universality of suffrage the question of when, for the first time, more than three-quarters of the population of a country over twenty years of age were enfranchised, then we notice immediately the rather slow progress towards universality. Finland in 1907 (76.2 per cent) and Norway in 1915 (77.1 per cent) were the only two European countries which crossed that threshold before or during the First World War (Flora 1983 for facts and figures in this section). Within five years of the end of the war, a few more states had achieved a greater degree of universality: Austria (85.9 per cent) and Germany (97.9 per cent) in 1919; Denmark in 1920 (82 per cent); Sweden in 1921 (87.9 per cent); the Netherlands in 1922 (80.7 per cent); and the United Kingdom in 1923 (75.1 per cent). Other countries, however, moved towards greater universality only after the Second World War: France in 1945 (88.3 per cent); Italy in 1946 (95 per cent); Belgium in 1949 (91.5 per cent); and Switzerland only in 1971 (80.8 per cent).

A number of mechanisms prevented universality of suffrage. The most decisive mechanism was the exclusion of women. Before or during the First World War, women were enfranchised only in Finland (1906), Norway and Denmark (1915) as well as the Netherlands (1917). After the war, women gained the franchise in Germany, Austria and Luxemburg in 1919; in Sweden and Iceland in 1920; in Ireland in 1923 and in Britain in 1929. In France and Italy women were enfranchised in 1945; in Belgium in 1949 and, finally, in Switzerland in 1971. But while discrimination on the basis of sex was enormously important for restrictions on universality, there were other mechanisms in place as well. During the nineteenth century, income and property qualifications, typically linked to a certain minimum amount of direct tax on property and income, kept the size of the electorate small. This system initially favoured rural proprietors across Europe. Not only were they more likely to be enfranchised than other groups, the distribution of parliamentary seats in favour of rural constituencies also penalized the towns. However, industrialization of the economy and the concomitant acquisition of wealth by the industrial middle class as well as the formation of a professional middle class led to an increase in the social and political clout of the bourgeoisie and resulted in its gradual enfranchisement. It now became increasingly important to determine how to deal with both the working class and the peasantry and their demands for rights of political participation. Initially, property and income qualifications together with educational qualifications were meant to keep the 'lower' classes disenfranchised. In Italy in 1861, for example, the franchise was given to those males over twenty-five years of age who paid a certain minimum amount of direct taxes and could read and write. But in the last quarter of the nineteenth century, it became increasingly difficult to keep the working class disenfranchised, not least because in many countries they were seen by sections of the middle class as potential political allies in the fight against the well-established and entrenched old, and often landed, elite. Stipulations in Norway in the first decade of the twentieth century or in Sweden during the second decade that 'paupers' receiving public assistance or poor relief should be disenfranchised – a stipulation that also applied in the United Kingdom

– demonstrate that attempts were then still made to distinguish at least between a respectable working class and those outside the pale of political society.

While universality of suffrage was slow in coming, so was the equality of votes. The principle of 'one person, one vote' was not widely embraced. 'Plural voting', that gave certain groups one or more additional votes, was widespread during the nineteenth century. As late as the last decade of the nineteenth century, Belgium, for example, while introducing universal manhood suffrage, still upheld the system of plural voting: house owners and owners of real estate whose property was above a certain value, had one additional vote to cast; for citizens with a higher education diploma, the electoral law allowed two additional votes: in total, a person could have up to three votes. But an even more pronounced mechanism for restricting the equality of votes was the division of the electorate into 'estates' or 'curia' with disproportionate numbers of representatives. Again, in order to provide an example, by the turn of the century, the electorate in Austria was divided into five 'curia'. The first 'curia', made up of landowners, had an electorate of about 5,000 choosing eighty-five deputies; the second, made up of members of the chambers of commerce and trade, had about 550 electors, choosing twenty-one deputies. Together, these two curia controlled 25 per cent of all seats by the turn of the century. The third curia was made up of male inhabitants of towns and cities who were of a minimum age of twenty-four and paid a certain minimum amount of direct taxes; they elected 118 representatives by 1897; the fourth curia of male inhabitants of rural communities over the age of twenty-four elected, through indirect elections, 129 representatives. Together, the third and fourth curia controlled 58 per cent of all seats at the turn of the century. Finally, all male citizens over the age of twenty-four were enfranchised in 1897, forming a fifth curia and electing a total of seventy-two seats, or 17 per cent of all seats, yet, similar to the fourth curia, in indirect elections. But as the voters of the first four curia had also the vote in the fifth, they were given two votes in effect.

The extension of the franchise since the late nineteenth century ushered in fundamental changes in politics. It created the precondition of 'mass' politics as it is still with us today. The mobilization of the 'masses' which became necessary for electoral success led to the formation of 'mass' political organizations. And even those social forces which could not hope for the mobilization of a 'mass' following, had to develop relatively competent and efficient party apparatuses. With the organized 'mass' party came the political entrepreneur, the politician as the leader of a political organization which he attempted to control as tightly as he possibly could and whose 'identity' to the electorate at large was built on fairly well defined ideologies and political platforms. Given these structures and processes of 'mass' politics, parliaments 'cease[d] to function as autonomous realms within which contingent decisions can be made purely on the basis of their internal processes' (Poggi 1990: 64). They became places where politicians clash with each other on the basis of policies and political decisions already taken by the political organizations of which they are the parliamentary representatives. Political representation of the individual citizens thus becomes mediated and articulated through organizations.

What we witness in the nineteenth century, then, is a struggle over the extension of citizenship rights. The British sociologist, T. H. Marshall (1963: 74) distinguished three types of citizenship rights: civil, political and social citizenship rights. According to Marshall, civil citizenship rights are instrumental in securing 'liberty of the person, freedom of speech, thought and faith, the right to own property and to conclude valid contracts and the right to justice'. These civil rights can be defended through the system of formal law courts. The state in which civil rights prevail is a constitutional state. The struggle over the establishment of civil rights was waged in the late eighteenth and in the first half of the nineteenth century between the privileged aristocracy and the rising bourgeoisie. The axis of this socio-political conflict was freedom vs. privilege. The challengers to the established order were united by a common belief: liberalism, and a common goal: the establishment of the constitutional state. But the liberal–bourgeois movements of the nineteenth century also mobilized against the established order for political citizenship rights: 'the right to participate in the exercise of political power, as a member of a body invested with political authority or as an elector of the members of such a body'. The state in which such political rights can be exercised is a constitutional parliamentary system. To the extent that the winning of rights of political participation was restricted to the bourgeoisie, the working class, too, became involved in this political struggle, but not just against the old privileged class, but against the newly enfranchised middle class as well. In the struggle of the working-class movements, however, the socio-political struggle which had centred around the issue of freedom vs. privilege was complemented, and somewhat marginalized, by another type of conflict: the struggle of the working-class movement for social justice and economic security against private property, economic power and concomitant political power of aristocracy and bourgeoisie alike. The challengers to the established order demanded not only civil and political liberties; the labour movement now also demanded rights to resources. The struggle was over the establishment of social rights: 'the whole range from the right to a modicum of economic welfare and security to the right to share to the full in the social heritage and to live the life of a civilized being according to the standards prevailing in the society'. The constitutional state with its parliamentary system should become a democratic welfare state. This, at least, was the aim of the social democratic labour movement (Offe 1985).

Ideas

Why should the achievement of citizenship rights have exercised the people in the nineteenth century? Of course, we may adduce philosophical ideas such as self-determination or liberty and equality as moving forces behind the agitation for citizenship rights. And we shall indeed return to such ideas in the following chapters. In the context of our current discussion, however, it is worth mentioning that, for the first time in the nineteenth century, the state had become relevant to the lives of the people. In the past, the state had mainly been an organization geared towards military confrontations with other states in the interstate system. As a geopolitical actor the state had intruded into the lives of its subjects in the person of the tax assessor, tax collector and recruiting officer. Political struggles had been structured by fiscal crises induced by war making:

> As state extraction increased and became more regressive, social tensions were forced to the 'national' political level. Discontent focused on state costs (taxes and military service) and benefits (profitable office holding, economic monopolies, bondholding, and tax and conscription exemptions). These, not the production and market relations of capitalism, constituted the most contentious political economy [before the nineteenth century]. (Mann 1993: 221–2)

The nineteenth century brought dramatic changes. One indicator of these changes is the increase in civilian expenses by the state – from about 25 per cent in the 1760s to about 75 per cent in the 1900s (Mann 1993: 362–78). Another indicator is the expansion of the civilian scope within the state. For the first time, states undertook major civilian functions. They massively extended infrastructures of material and symbolic communication, building, developing or sponsoring roads, canals, postal services, railways, telegraph systems and, most significantly, mass education. They became involved directly in the economy either through the provision of a regulatory and institutional framework for industrialization or as the direct owners of productive industries. And in the last decades of the nineteenth century, most states also set upon developing and implementing welfare programmes (Mann 1993: chap. 14). State interventions into the everyday life of subjects became universal and routinized during the nineteenth century: the postman, the policeman or gendarme, the schoolteacher and the men employed on the railways now became the agents of the state through which individuals came in contact with the state. The state imposed itself in other ways as well:

> Increasingly the state kept records of each of its subjects and citizens through the device of regular periodic censuses ... through theoretically compulsory attendance at primary school, and, where applicable, military conscriptions. In bureaucratic and well-policed states a system of personal documentation and registration brought the inhabitant into even more direct contact with the machinery of rule and administration, especially if he or she moved from one

place to another ... they would be recorded by the machinery for registering births, marriages, and deaths ... Government and subject or citizen were inevitably linked by daily bonds, as never before. And the nineteenth-century revolutions in transport and communications typified by the railway and the telegraph tightened and routinized the links between central authority and its remotest parts. (Hobsbawm 1990: 81)

The state in the nineteenth century thus endeavoured to shape society: by attempting to address the 'social question', restore order through policing 'deviancy', improve moral life and shape the national economy through state subsidies, the elimination of internal trade barriers such as tariffs and the imposition of import duties, or the expansion of the communication infrastructure and education. It also turned its attention increasingly to collecting and collating information about its subjects and citizens. Through its activities, the state became the obvious focus for political activity. It became the reference point for most social groups as they had to strive to capture, or influence, the core institutions of the state in order to advance their own objectives. Thus, the state pulled society into its political space, at the same time as it was trying to shape society according to its own objectives:

> [W]ithout many intending it, 'nationally' regulated railways, roads, public utilities, public health, police forces, courts and prisons, and above all, education and discursive literacy in the dominant language of the state provided centralized-territorial infrastructures for the further flowering of the nation-state. (Mann 1993: 498)

In this process, then, state–society relation was tightened and social relations were 'caged' (Michael Mann) over the national rather than the local–regional or transnational terrain (Mann 1993: 61). The state could no longer be evaded; it therefore became imperative to gain rights of participation in order better to control its activities, share in the benefits it could bring and lessen the negative effects of its policies on the life of individuals, families and communities. Social relationships became bounded by the state's territorial reach. It was only logical that democracy should be 'territorialized' within the confines of the nation-state, too.

For the last century or so, the most contentious issues regarding democracy had to do with the questions of who was to be given citizenship rights and to which areas of social life the principle and the procedure of democracy should be applied. In this chapter we have already touched upon the question of citizenship, and we will broaden our theoretical reflections on it in the following chapters. The issue of the limits to the applicability of democratic ideals and institutions will be addressed when we discuss the similarities and differences between classical liberalism and 'new', social (reform) liberalism in the following chapter. One debate within liberalism was about the extent to which the state was entitled to interfere with 'civil society' and, in particular, the economic activities and property rights of individuals. At stake was the question of social citizenship rights and the development of the 'welfare state'. However, these controversies did not result in undermining the supposition, central to liberal democracy, that the 'state' and 'civil society', that politics and economics, are organized around different structural principles and that each follows its specific code. 'Democracy' is still seen as applicable to the sphere of politics and the 'state', but not to economics and 'civil society'; private property rights, even if held not by individuals but by corporate bodies, are considered to be, in general, inviolable, and, hence, capitalism not to be amenable to democratic control.

Who is a citizen? What rights and duties do citizens have? Where are the limits to democracy? These questions have exercised political thinkers since Greek antiquity, but have been particularly relevant in the age of 'mass politics'. And we will encounter some of the arguments put forward in this debate in the next two chapters. Recently, this canon of questions has been extended by problematizing the territorial dimension of democracy. As we saw, one classical argument perceived democracy as viable only within the territorial confines of a city-state, or polis. It took the revolutionary upheavals of the late eighteenth century to extend the idea and the institutions of democracy to the modern, 'national' state. Yet, in a 'global' world, is this confinement of democracy to the territory of the nation-state still acceptable? In an era of ever-increasing global interconnectedness of people, places, capital, goods and services, has democratic self-government to be institutionalized on the global level? Is the nation-state fundamentally undermined by these global processes so that democracy must suffer as well, linked as it is to this state? In chapter 4 I shall address some of the issues raised by the impact of globalization on the democratic nation-state. I shall argue that globalization will not result in the demise of the nation-state, but it will undermine the 'sovereignty' of the state. To the extent that democracy in the liberal model is structurally related to the notion of a *summa potestas*, it poses a challenge to our understanding of democracy. The final chapter continues with the contemporary concern with territorialized democracy. Analysing the connections between liberal democracy, the nation-state and European integration, it addresses the question of what democracy and citizenship could possibly mean, and how they would have to be institutionalized, in the European Union.

2

Citizenship and civil society: liberalism republicanism and deliberative politics

In the previous chapter, we discussed key theoretical assumptions underpinning liberal democracy. This chapter will analyse how these general assumptions inform a liberal conceptualization of citizenship. In the course of our argument, however, we shall shift our attention to alternative theoretical accounts of citizenship. The theory of republican politics and the theory of deliberative politics will be presented as serious challenges to the liberal paradigm. All three normative theories endeavour to establish a boundary between the 'political' and the 'non-political', and I shall discuss the importance of the concept of civil society for each theoretical model in this endeavour.

Liberal citizenship

Classical liberalism assumes that human beings are atomistic, rational agents whose existence, needs, wants and interests are ontologically prior to society. This presupposition has found its classical formulation in Hobbes's methodological injunction in *De Cive* that we should 'consider men as if but even now sprung out of the earth, and suddainly (*like* Mushromes) come to full maturity without all kind of engagement to each other' (Hobbes 1983: 117 [VIII.1]). This injunction places the individual outside the bonds of community, tradition and history. It paints a picture of the individual as an 'unencumbered self'. Michael Sandel summarizes the 'liberal' picture of the person supremely well:

> No role or commitment could define me so completely that I could not understand myself without it. No project could be so essential that turning away from it would call into question the person I am. For the unencumbered self, what matters above all, what is most essential to our personhood, are not the ends we choose but our capacity to choose them ... What is denied to the unencumbered self is the possibility of membership in any community bound by moral ties antecedent to choice ... Freed from the dictates of nature and the

sanction of social roles, the human subject is installed as sovereign, cast as the author of the only meanings there are ... [W]e are free to construct principles of justice unconstrained by an order of value antecedently given. And as actual, individual selves, we are free to choose our purposes and ends unbound by such an order, or by custom or tradition or inherited status. (Sandel 1992: 18–20)

In this tradition, human beings are seen as competitive individuals naturally pursuing their own interests, and in doing so showing themselves to be 'egoistic calculators of pleasures and pains who regard political activity as a necessary evil to be endured for the ultimate ends of safety, peace, and comfort' (Smith 1989: 236). Each person is seen as by nature free and capable of forming, revising and pursuing her or his definition of the 'good'. As an unencumbered chooser of preferences the individual must be free of any interference from others and its liberty must be protected as long as it is consistent with a similar liberty for others. Individuals are not indebted to government or the state for their right to be left alone. They enjoy these 'negative liberties' on the grounds that these rights are natural and inalienable. Government originates in the rational desires of individuals to protect and defend their subjective rights and prepolitical liberties. The state finds the justification for its existence in this protection and defence. Citizenship is conceived as instrumental to the attainment of non-political goals of autonomous individuals making private choices, and political activity is conceptualized as mainly aiming at establishing a legal framework for the social intercourse of private individuals in their pursuit of idiosyncratic interests.

   In the last half-century or so, these suppositions of classical liberalism have found some of its strongest and intellectually sincerest endorsement and defence through Friedrich Hayek. Liberty, for Hayek, 'describes the absence of a particular obstacle – coercion by other men' (Hayek 1960: 19). Defining liberty as a particular kind of relationship among individuals, Hayek moves away from a Hobbesian understanding of freedom as 'the absence of external impediments' and the logical corollary that it is equivalent with effective power to do whatever we want. Whether a person is free or not, he argues:

> does not depend on the range of choice but on whether he can expect to shape his course of action in accordance with his present intentions, or whether somebody else has the power so to manipulate the conditions as to make him act according to that person's will rather than his own. Freedom thus presupposes that the individual has some assured private sphere, that there is some set of circumstances in his environment with which others cannot interfere. (Hayek 1960: 13)

To be in a state of liberty means that it is left to us to decide what use we shall make of the circumstances in which we find ourselves. This freedom is premised on the existence of the rule of law. Taking a Kantian position, Hayek contends that 'when we obey laws, in the sense of general abstract rules laid down irrespective of their application to us, we are not subject to another man's will and are therefore free' (Hayek 1960: 153). More specifically, Hayek lists as the essential conditions of freedom that human beings are subject only to the same laws as all their fellow citizens; that they are immune from arbitrary confinement; that they are free to choose their work; and that they are able to own and acquire property. Once an individual enjoys these conditions, no other individual or group of individuals can coerce him to do their bidding (Hayek 1960: 20).

Hayek accepts that the notion of equality before the law leads to the demand that all individuals should also have the same share in making the law, and he concedes that this is the point where traditional liberalism and the democratic movement meet. Yet he claims that their main concerns were nevertheless different: 'Liberalism ... is concerned mainly with limiting the coercive powers of all government, whether democratic or not, whereas the dogmatic democrat knows only one limit to government – current majority opinion' (Hayek 1960: 103). Hence, for Hayek, the essential political problem is not who governs but what government is entitled to do. To put it differently, Hayek's concern lies primarily with the protection of the right to be left alone ('negative liberty') and the protection of the sphere within which individuals can act unobstructed by others, not with ensuring the right to be involved in defining and deciding public matters ('positive liberty'). In line with this argument, Hayek can suggest that 'a democracy may well wield totalitarian powers, and it is conceivable that an authoritarian government may act on liberal principles' (Hayek 1960: 103). And he cites approvingly Ortega y Gasset as an elegant statement of this position:

> Democracy answers this question – 'Who ought to exercise the public power?' The answer it gives is – the exercise of public power belongs to the citizens as a body. But this question does not touch on what should be the realm of the public power. It is solely concerned with determining to whom such power belongs. Democracy proposes that we all rule; that is, that we are sovereign in all social acts. Liberalism, on the other hand, answers this question, – 'regardless of who exercises the public power, what should its limits be?' The answer it gives – 'Whether the public power is exercised by an autocrat or by the people, it cannot be absolute: the individual has rights which are over and above any interference by the state.' (Ortega y Gasset 1937: 125, in: Hayek 1960: 442–3)

There are, then, a number of concerns which democracy raises for the liberal. There is the perceived danger of a despotism of the majority over the minority, and the related concern with the right of the individual and of minorities. And there is the challenge posed to individual freedom by the

increase in the role of government as a result of social interests being transformed into political issues through democratic politics. But whereas the
concern with the protection of minority rights remained a key concern of
all variants of liberalism, the same cannot be said about the assessment of
the state's role for individual liberty. Classical liberalism had historically
emerged from the struggle for religious freedom and the attack on traditional political and cultural authority. For classical liberalism the individual
is a rational and reasoning human being capable of unmasking power and
authority upheld by custom and tradition and entitled to self-rule. Industrial
capitalism and urbanization, however, led to the increasing urgency of
social problems at the end of the nineteenth century. In England and the
other industrializing countries across continental Europe, liberal thinking
came to perceive social deprivation and suffering:

> as much an obstacle to human improvement as had been the legal restraints
> on religious opinion or free speech. The great divide was now between rich and
> poor, and liberalism had to recognize this, and act to eliminate poverty, igno-
> rance and disease ... If freedom were to be a value for all, this demanded the
> reconstruction of society to the benefit of the oppressed and disadvantaged.
> (Williams 1991: 150)

In an important early statement that contributed to the theoretical turn in
English liberalism, the political philosopher T. H. Green had argued that true
freedom was not merely the absence of restraint or compulsion but the max-
imum of power for all members of society alike to make the best of themselves (Simhony 1993). State interference in the form of legislation with the
freedom of individuals to enter into mutually binding private contracts was
seen as 'justified on the ground that it is the business of the state ... to maintain the conditions without which a free exercise of the human faculties is
impossible' (Green 1881/1986: 202). Without absence of coercion and
compulsion, there could be no freedom. But for true freedom to be achieved,
the lack of compulsion had to be complemented by a positive capacity of
self-determination that would enable individuals to be the author of their
lifeplan. In this context, the state was defined, not as a force potentially
opposed to individual liberty, as in classical liberalism, but as an instrument
of freedom in that it provided each individual with certain conditions of life
in which he or she could realize her or his powers and capabilities, and
could strive towards her or his 'possible self' (Freeden 1978: 53, 58 and
passim; Vincent/Plant 1984: 59; Nicholson 1990: 140–65; Collini 1979).
Self-development of the individual thus remains the aim of liberalism, but it
is now seen to depend upon the creation of enabling opportunities by a 'welfare' state. Vincent and Plant have succinctly summed up the thoughts of
the 'British Idealists', which profoundly influenced this new liberalism. They
assumed that:

all citizens had capacities and powers, not necessarily of equal amounts or types, yet each should be given an equal footing and a means to develop what they possess. The aim was to achieve the fulfilment of the largest number through their citizenship. The state, by providing the basic services, was attempting to equalize opportunities through intervention. The rationale for this was liberty and citizenship based upon a modicum of economic welfare and a share in civilization. (Vincent/Plant 1984: 87)

But this endorsement of equality of opportunity went hand in hand with the acceptance of diversity of reward. As against the Benthamite form of utilitarianism which defined human beings as rational maximizers, the Idealists put forward a conceptualization of human nature that stressed their desire to develop their capacities and powers. The state's task was to assist in this self-development. At the same time, however, this advocacy for an interventionist state was complemented by an endorsement of 'the operation of the market, with the inequalities to which that would lead and the ownership of private property and the right of accumulation. At the most, their welfare proposals were attempts to ensure that those who were disadvantaged would be able to act more effectively in the market' (Vincent/Plant 1984: 175).

Both liberal traditions share the view of human beings as rights-bearers. But they differ in their understanding of what these rights are. Do they contain only those (civil) rights that protect the individual against coercion by other individuals or by the state? Or do these rights also contain rights to resources and means of self-development? Such 'positive' rights would then comprise economic and social rights which provide individuals with legal claims to positive benefits from the state or another collective body. For example, both traditions would agree that there is a right to life; but they would debate whether this means the right not be killed ('negative' right) or the right to the means of life ('positive' right). They would agree that there is a right to property; but they would debate whether this is a right not to have legitimately acquired property interfered with or a right to the ownership of resources.

As we have already seen, Hayek defined freedom as the absence of intentional restraint and coercion. Only intentional action by a person or group of persons can result in the restriction of liberty. Liberty 'does not assure us of any opportunities'; it does not assure us of any possession of resources and powers; liberty is the freedom from coercion (Hayek 1960: 19). According to this view, the distribution of resources as a result of the operation of a free market, for example, cannot be seen as a limitation of liberty by those disadvantageously affected, because 'the outcomes of markets are an unintended and unforeseen result of individual decisions to buy and sell, taken on all sorts of different grounds' (Plant 1992: 115). To counter this argument, 'positive rights' liberals do not have to confront it head-on. They may ask why we should attach (moral) importance to the idea of non-interference in the first place? Why is the liberty from coercion of overriding significance for our understanding of freedom? Because non-interference allows persons to do what they want to do; because it gives them space to be autonomous agents. But does it make sense to speak of protection from interference in an action that one has no means to undertake (Gould 1988: 198)? Should individuals not therefore be given the means that empower them to act on the basis of this (alleged) autonomy? Does this right to free agency not require for its effective realization a set of positive conditions and provisions? Does the notion of agency that is inherent in the idea of 'negative rights' not involve the provision of resources that contribute to, for example, the physical integrity, survival, well-being, education etc. of the agent? As Plant (1992: 117) argues, 'the right to freedom being secured by rights to these sorts of resources is not freedom to do any individual thing but rather a general set of conditions which will enable the individual to go on to the sorts of things s/he wants to do'. Plant states that, for free agency to be conceivable, negative rights to the freedom from coercion and interference have to be complemented by positive rights to resources which are necessary conditions for acting in a purposeful way at all:

> If we respect a person as a person because of this capacity of rational agency then we cannot both respect him in virtue of this capacity and be indifferent to the question of whether he has the means of exercising that capacity. Hence the principle of respect for persons, which lies behind the negative idea of rights, combined with a limited argument in favour of positive liberty, would yield a set of positive rights to those resources which would satisfy his basic needs of agency. (Plant 1992: 129)

Inevitably, such a provision of positive rights involves some interference with the activities of individuals. But the exercise of civil and political rights is premised on interference, too. These rights, insofar as they can be infringed, not only by the state, but by other people as well, need positive protection by the state to forestall their violation. Gould (1988: 196) argues that the right, for example, of property, as a civil right, would justify laws against the restraint of trade by monopolies, and thus would constitute an interference with the property rights of (and their exercise by) certain economic interests to protect the exercise of this right by other interests. And the right of free speech, too, may involve a curb on media monopolies.

'Positive' liberty as manifested in the right to resources, is thus entrenched in the notions of agency and autonomy. These notions, in turn, give moral significance to 'negative liberty' as that right that is meant to assure a sphere of individual autonomy. And 'positive' liberty as manifested in the political right to be involved and participate in public affairs, is entrenched in the concept of freedom under the rule of law. This is for the simple reason that legal norms that can be enforced by political sanctions are seen as legitimate only insofar as they guarantee the autonomy of the individuals living under them. And this guarantee, in turn, is premised on a democratic procedure that installs the individual as law-maker, acting and deliberating in public in accord with her or his fellow-citizens. But the individual can act as deliberating law-maker only if he or she is protected in her or his personal autonomy by 'negative liberties' that guarantee his dignity and inviolability as a person; individual self-determination is a necessary condition of political self-determination.

We can approach this *problematique* from yet another perspective. The (classical) liberal constitutional model was commensurate with a particular conceptualization of society. This conceptualization presupposed the capability for societal self-regulation and defined the state as the guarantor of individual freedom and societal autonomy only. The liberal constitution was charged with the legal limitation of the state to that role, and with creating institutional mechanisms for binding the state in its activities to societal interests. In effect, this meant the institutionalization of 'negative' rights and the establishment of the rule of law that was binding for the state itself. Hence, liberal constitutionalism aimed to combine an endorsement of the coercive role of the state as the enforcer of civil peace and collectively binding decisions (the Hobbesian tradition) with an endorsement of the right of protection of individuals and social groups against the agency of the state (the Lockean tradition). The political, social and economic dislocations caused by industrial capitalism and urbanization in the course of the nineteenth century led to the realization that the supposition regarding societal self-regulation was erroneous and that the state had to be given an active role to achieve the semblance of a stable and just society. The interventionist state complemented the law-and-order state. The state of the late nineteenth century did not only become ever more involved in the economy as both a regulatory agency and an economic actor in its own right, but also as a provider of social welfare provisions. Furthermore, the 'entry of the masses' into politics raised the question for liberalism as to how to square their status of economic dependency with the theoretical assumptions regarding personal autonomy (Ashford 1986: chap. 2). As we have seen, for the 'new' liberals the answer was to redefine freedom in a 'positive' way and to embrace a policy of social reform, ultimately issuing in the development of the welfare state:

> Their [the masses'] private autonomy had to be secured through reliance on the status guarantees of a social-welfare state. This derivative private autonomy, however, could function as an equivalent of the original private autonomy based on control over private property only to the degree to which the citizens, as clients of the social-welfare state, came to enjoy status guarantees that they *themselves* bestowed on themselves in their capacities as citizens of a

democratic state. This in turn appeared to become possible in proportion to the expansion of democratic control to the economic process in its entirety. (Habermas 1993: 434–5)

Within liberal theory, the welfare state could thus only be justified if it was organized as a democracy. Liberal theory was therefore challenged to develop a concept of citizenship that entailed the three basic ways in which citizens were becoming structurally related to the state (Offe 1987). First, in their collectivity as 'the people', the citizens were the ultimate source of state authority and legitimacy. This was the democratic principle of the modern polity. Second, citizens were the 'subjects' of state authority, bound by the democratically formulated collective political will. Yet, even as 'subjects', they were also enjoying civil rights and liberties that constituted an autonomous, 'private' space of social, economic and cultural action and relationship free of the state's interference. Both aspects together constituted the liberal principle of the modern state. Finally, citizens were (now to become also) the 'clients' of the state, depending upon its provision of services and collective goods to secure their welfare and well-being. This was the principle of social welfare that was now being added to those of rule of law and representative democracy.

In this century, the state has become ever more proactively involved in the planning and management of the economy and in structuring society by meeting social needs and providing utilities and services. The dynamics of 'mass' democracy; the social requirements of capitalism – ranging from state provisions for an efficient legal and technological infrastructure and the reproduction of the labour force (for example, unemployment, education and healthcare) to the opening-up and protection of foreign markets (imperialism); the development of the warfare state as a result of interstate competition and conflict (military–industrial complex); and more 'incidental' events, such as the Great Depression, which clearly demonstrated the possibility and the dangers of market failure were some of the forces behind the increase in the size and scope of the state. As a result, '[b]y the 1960s, both right- and left-leaning political parties had endorsed statism, and accepted the idea that public agencies should manage the economy, regulate commercial and industrial activities, subsidize incomes, provide a wide range of services, manage sizeable social security funds and even own and operate large industrial enterprises' (Midgley 1991: 9). In 1985, on social expenditure alone the OECD countries spent on average almost 25 per cent of their Gross Domestic Product (Glennerster 1991: 164, Tab. 9.1). By that time, however, the welfare state consensus had already come under severe attack, particularly from intellectual forces in Britain and the United States.

The state was no longer seen as the solution to society's problems, but as their cause. The critique of the welfare state was comprehensive. It was argued that the welfare state eroded individual responsibility and initiative; created a large, inefficient bureaucratic welfare apparatus that intruded and violated the privacy of the citizen, diminishing choice and individual preferences; and harmed economic productivity and growth by 'confiscating' private resources in the form of taxation for welfare expenditure, thus depriving the private sector of money needed for capitalization:

> Government welfare programmes are faulted for a breakdown in mutual obligations between groups, a lack of attention to efficiencies in the way programmes are operated and benefits awarded, the induced dependency of beneficiaries on programmes, and the growth of the welfare industry and its special interest groups, particularly professional associations ... By fostering 'dependence' on welfare, beneficiaries of the social services need not work hard, save, or act in a responsible manner. Rather than alleviate destitution, welfare state programmes induce dependency and the proliferation of a culture of poverty. (Stoesz/Midgley 1991: 31)

The policies advocated by the New Right drew on two ideological traditions. First, there was the liberal belief in a free market and limited government. Liberty, freedom and progress were seen as premised on unwinding the coils of welfarism and statism that had fastened around the free economy. To bring about this change, New Right policies aimed at cuts in public expenditure, cuts in taxation, the denationalization of public enterprises and utilities and the privatization of social services. Second, there was the conservative concern with the collapse of traditional values and the breakdown of social order, with the threats to a civilized community by the spirit of social, cultural and sexual permissiveness. A liberal endorsement of 'economic individualism' was to be reconciled with a conservative critique of 'hedonistic individualism'. The conservative project of restoring traditional standards of morality and behaviour by fostering the values of family and community life, of patriotism and nationalism was to be made compatible with the individualist ethos of an unfettered capitalist market economy. In both projects, however, the state was not seen as ultimately 'withering away'; on the contrary, the state was to be a strong state. The restoring of a free and efficient economy required a strong state that could free itself from the domination by sectional interests such as trade unions and could uphold or restore law and order in case of resistance. And in order to combat permissiveness, the state, as a moral agency, had to be strong, too.

We should note that this neo-liberal/neo-conservative attack on the welfare state was in some ways taken up by the 'new social movements' that had been forming since the mid-1960s. In many ways, the women's movement, the environmental movement, the gay and lesbian movement as well as (increasingly) the anti-racist movement were developing strategies to bypass the state in their struggles. They perceived the state as a bureaucratic and centralized apparatus that interfered with every individual's life, moulded individual life-chances, and, instead of combatting economic, gender, sexual and racial discrimination, reinforced capitalism, patriarchy, racism and sexual stereotyping through its policies. These movements grew increasingly sensitive to 'the alienating, decapacitating, and depersonalizing effects that the welfare state and its legal–bureaucratic or professional modes of distribution, treatment, and surveillance can have upon communities and individual '"life-worlds"' (Offe 1987: 506). For the New Right the state's interventions had to be limited by returning the allocation of welfare to markets, while stronger moral intervention by the state was seen as warranted to combat permissiveness. For the 'new social movements', however, the state's interventions had to be limited because it inhibited cultural diversity and individual 'permissiveness'. And it was not the market that should take over the state's task of providing for certain forms of welfare; rather, welfare should be returned to 'more localized, non-hierarchical and non-bureaucratized forms of communal self-administration' (Pierson 1991: 217 and chap. 3 *passim*). Whereas the New Right proposes, in effect, the depoliticization of welfare issues through the privatization of welfare concerns in the form of private insurance schemes, the 'new social movements', in effect, opt for the repoliticization of welfare issues by making them a central concern for the institutions and organizations of a self-governing civil society. Communalization, not marketization, should follow the state's extrication from (some) welfare provisions.

We have seen that the 'liberal' welfare state was linked in its origins to the realization that material inequalities limit individual freedom and make a mockery of the principle of formal legal equality. Yet, on the other hand, attempts by the state to compensate individuals for material inequalities through welfare programmes also tend to impact on the freedom of the individual as he or she is being made the 'client' of the benevolent and paternalistic state. Where to draw the line between (some?) discrimination, on the one hand, in the name of 'freedom', and (some?) paternalism, on the other, in the name of substantial 'equality'? What kind of institutional 'mix' of state, market and community provision is appropriate in the light of the (temporary?) answer to the first question? To address these questions requires (permanent) public debate and reflection, and thus the active involvement of those enjoying social rights. Manifestly, marketization, too, raises the question of individual freedom and inequality as the resources necessary to ensure an adequate level of 'welfare' are unequally distributed. And the idea of welfare provision through the networks of a self-governing civil society can also be reconciled with individual freedom only if the individual becomes actively involved in its organization. Social rights, perhaps more than other rights, would therefore appear to be particularly reliant on their bearers' active involvement, or participation, in the 'community' which bestows them and in which they are to be exercised.

This argument in favour of active political participation can perhaps be couched in a more fundamental way. Liberalism of whatever hue puts rights before politics; individual rights are understood as the presupposition of politics. Rights enable individuals to do, or not to do, certain things and oblige the state either not to interfere with, or else actively to promote, certain vital liberties of the individual citizen. In many ways, such rights pre-empt political and democratic debate in advance. A problem arises, of course, when rights come into conflict with each other. In the case of abortion, for example, how could the 'right to life' argument ever be reconciled with the claim that there is the right of the mother to control her own body; or the freedom of speech with the freedom of privacy, so as to increase freedom overall? Richard Bellamy argues that rights must be related to, and rely upon, particular conceptions of human community and human flourishing as they emerge from the self-understanding of particular political communities (Bellamy 1993: 54; 1994: 429). Gray (1993: 101) puts forward a similar argument when he emphasizes that rights are 'shaped by our judgements of the vital interests, or the conditions of well-being, of the persons, under consideration'. And he continues that 'in political and in moral philosophy, the good is always prior to the right: we make judgements about the rights that people have, only on the basis of our judgements of the interests central to their well-being' (Gray 1993: 102). In a differentiated, plural society such judgements about the greatest liberty are necessarily based on controversial evaluations. For Bellamy, this means that, in order to enjoy liberties, we have the duty to participate in politics in order to determine jointly the character of our community. It is from this perspective that the republican theory of politics gains its renewed importance.

Republicanism and active citizenship

I have argued that liberalism developed a conception of politics that was focused on the activities of private individuals in their pursuit of idiosyncratic interests and the protection by the state of their constitutional and legal rights to life, liberty and property. Though this conceptualization of politics, and its related concept of citizenship, have become dominant in contemporary liberal democratic societies and in political thinking about politics and the rights and duties of citizens, there has been another political tradition that reaches back to Aristotle and Machiavelli and has found one of its most eloquent advocates in the twentieth century in Hannah Arendt. In this 'republican' tradition, political activity is seen as essential for self-fulfilment. It makes the assumption that the liberty of the person can only be achieved and fully assured within a self-governing form of republican community and sees citizenship as an office and a responsibility proudly assumed; not, like the liberal tradition, as a status that makes the person the bearer of a right or a set of rights that are passively enjoyed: 'The first makes citizenship the core of our life, the second makes it its outer frame. The first assumes a closely knit body of citizens, its members committed to one another; the second assumes a diverse and loosely connected body, its members (mostly) committed elsewhere' (Walzer 1989: 216).

In the liberal tradition, rights guarantee freedom from external constraints; in the republican tradition, citizenship rights allow its bearers actively to engage with others in the public realm, to participate as citizens among citizens in a common practice in order to form themselves into politically autonomous creators of a community of free and equal persons on the basis of mutual recognition (Habermas 1992b: 325–9). People can enjoy freedom, or be unfree, only within a political community; freedom is political freedom, and it does not make sense to speak of freedom outside of all social and political context, as in the liberal tradition. Indeed, freedom does not belong to human beings as such, but, as political freedom, adheres only to the citizen (Taylor 1984: 110–11).

This republican tradition can be traced back to Aristotle. For Aristotle, the political community is a shared project; it is an association of people committed to a common purpose: it is 'a community of families and aggregations of families in well-being, for the sake of a perfect and self-sufficing life' (Aristotle, *Politics* 1280^{b}30). Its end is the 'good life' and the 'good' in politics is justice, 'in other words, the common interest' (Aristotle, *Politics* 1282^{b}15). It is only in the political community that human beings achieve their complete realization; it is only in the polis that they can live an honourable life realized through virtuous and noble action in the community. Political life is thus the natural condition of humankind. When Aristotle argues that 'man is by nature a political animal' (Aristotle, *Politics* 1253^{a}1), he suggests that it is only through membership of, and participation in, the political community that we can develop our virtues and excellences.

Membership of this political community means the active involvement of the citizens in governance. To be a citizen means to be a self-governing member of a self-governed community. A citizen has the power to take part in the deliberative or judicial administration of the community and, through exercising his right of deliberating and judging, 'shares in governing and being governed' (Aristotle, *Politics* 1283^{b}42; also 1275^a, 1275^b). Government that emerges out of this active involvement must have regard to the common good and aim to achieve the goals of the community. It is the task of the legislators to ensure 'that all citizens continue to have a common interest in the good of all, and do not use political power to further the interests of particular cliques or groups (such as the rich)' (Jordan 1989: 70; Aristotle, *Politics* 1279^{a}15). It is only in political communities constituted in accordance with strict principles of justice that good laws, combining admo-

47

nition and instruction with compulsion and the threat of punishment, educate individuals to lead a noble life and transcend their narrow self-interests (Williams 1991: chap. 3). It is in such a stable and reasonable political order that human beings 'can develop and sustain the habits of mind associated with contextual discernment, the kind of back-and-forth, universal–particular, thoughtful life that for Aristotle is the human way of being, the human good' (Salkever 1990: 185).

Aristotle thus assumes that human nature embodies certain moral purposes, that human beings are moral beings and that they can only develop and realize their true moral selves in sharing their lives with each other in a self-governing political community that aims at the realization of the good life both for the community as a whole and for each human being individually. Hence, Aristotle can be interpreted as arguing that '[w]e can only be said to be fully or genuinely at liberty ... if we actually engage in just those activities which are most conducive to *eudaimonia*, or 'human flourishing', and may therefore be said to embody our deepest human purposes' (Skinner 1990: 296).

Recent scholarship has placed Machiavelli into this republican tradition. However, whereas Aristotle assumes that the political community is a moral community, no such assumption is made by Machiavelli. His endorsement of popular and participative republican rule is functional. Republican rule is considered indispensable if the city-state is to have any prospect of attaining its highest goals: civil glory and greatness, be it of size, of standing or of wealth, because it allows the struggle between citizens in which they may attain glory for themselves: 'Any city which aspires to bask in the reflected glory of citizens must ... ensure that it leaves them as free as possible from unnecessary restrictions or constraints, and thereby leaves them at liberty to develop and exercise their talents and energies to the uttermost' (Skinner 1992a: 66). Hence, glory accrues to the political community from the self-interests of its citizens, if that community is ruled through self-government. But to ensure self-government and liberty, rulers and citizens alike had to be willing to transcend their private interests in favour of the good of the community. How was this to be achieved? Of the various mechanisms Machiavelli enlists, two deserve our special attention. In line with an Aristotelian position, he claims that good laws will preserve liberty by forcing citizens into discharging their civic duties. But even more important, he argues in favour of a mixed constitution, again in line with Aristotle's arguments. Accepting the existence of opposed factions in each republic, he argues that the ensuing social struggle assures liberty '[a]s the rival groups jealously scrutinise each other for any signs of a move to take over supreme power':

> [T]he resolution of the pressures thus engendered will mean that only those 'laws and institutions' which are 'conducive to public liberty' will actually be

passed. Although motivated entirely by their selfish interests, the factions will thus be guided, as if by an invisible hand, to promote the public interest in all their legislative acts. (Skinner 1981/1992: 74)

Such a mixed constitution would thus be the frame within which human beings could find their self-fulfilment. But in order to ensure that such a constitution would not be corrupted by the power of any one particular faction, public vigilance and thus opposition to the aggrandizing of power was the price of liberty. In short, in order to overcome the perpetual tendency of powerful factions and citizens to take over government, citizens had to commit themselves to public service and civic participation to protect liberty. Citizenship was not to be passively enjoyed, but actively exercised as a duty and obligation out of concern with the good of the community as much as out of self-interest (Goldsmith 1987: 226–9; Skinner 1981/1992: 75; Skinner 1984; Skinner 1992b: 217–22). But since threats to liberty and communal rule could arise, not only from within the community, but also from outwith, republicanism had to be predatory and expansionist. Not only would such a policy contain enemies of the republic, but imperialist expansionism would also add to the glory and greatness of the city-state, and Machiavelli contended that these glorious, violent, and aggrandizing deeds could be better performed by republican citizen–soldiers protecting their liberty and self-interests than by monarchical subjects with nothing to win through their involvement (Hulliung 1983: 27, 58–9, 220).

In this reading of Machiavelli, we have followed closely the interpretations of Quentin Skinner who forcefully emphasized Machiavelli's seminal contribution to the republican tradition (cf. also Pocock 1975). As I presented the argument, republicanism emerges as an essential aspect of power politics; Machiavelli's *The Prince* and the *Discourses* are not two distinct lines of thought, but form a coherent whole. Plato and Aristotle had argued that imperialism and power politics were fatal for city-states because they would inevitably lead to imperial over-stretch, political corruption and the decline of civic virtue; for Machiavelli, on the other hand, such a policy of expansionism was almost the *raison d'être* of republicanism. It was a policy that allowed the city-states, as much as the citizen-soldiers, to attain glory 'abroad' and to protect liberty, as the condition for glory, 'at home'. According to Machiavelli, then, republicanism combined the peaceful institutionalization of social and political conflict 'at home' with a violent, aggressive imperialist policy 'abroad'.

Analysing Skinner's interpretation of the republican tradition, Chantal Mouffe points out that it very skilfully weaves together classical and liberal notions of liberty:

He finds in several forms of republican thought, particularly in Machiavelli, a way of conceiving liberty which though negative – and therefore modern –

includes political participation and civic virtue. It is negative because liberty is conceived as the absence of impediments to the realization of our chosen ends. But it also asserts that it is only as citizens of a 'free state', of a community whose members participate actively in the government, that such individual liberty can be guaranteed. To ensure our own liberty and avoid the servitude that would render its exercise impossible, we must cultivate civic virtues and devote ourselves to the common good. The idea of a common good above our private interests is a necessary condition for enjoying individual liberty. (Mouffe 1992b: 228)

As we have seen, Aristotle conceived politics as a 'natural' part of human existence, as that activity and set of institutions that enabled human beings to achieve their 'natural' or innate telos through virtuous living. While Machiavelli upheld the classical ideal of citizens' direct and active participation in the *respublica*, he did not conceive of the political community as a moral community bound together by an objective conceptualization of the common good and particular manifestations of personal morality. His analysis of republicanism was couched predominantly in terms of military prowess and imperial glory. Hannah Arendt, who has been one of the foremost republican thinkers of the twentieth century, differed from either perspective in significant ways. Against Aristotle she claimed that politics was not natural, but artificial, something that results from the action and speech of human beings in their attempt to establish a world of institutions in their midst that allows them to manifest their plurality. What unites the citizens of a republic is not some set of common values, but the world they set up in common, the public spaces they inhabit together, the acknowledgement of its rules and the commitment to the continuance of its institutions (Canovan 1992: 227; Passerin d'Entrèves 1992). In her analysis of republicanism she downplays the importance of military prowess and thus parts company with Machiavelli. Yet in her assessment of the political relevance of personal morality she places herself in the Machiavellian tradition. Embracing the Kantian argument that even devils, provided that they are rational, can establish a just republic, Arendt argues that human beings do not need to be good as individuals to be able to create a common world. And as Margaret Canovan forcefully argues, Arendt's experience of fascist and Stalinist totalitarianism led her to believe that personal morality could possibly prevent individuals from going along with it, but could not prevent it from happening: 'The only adequate answer was, she [Arendt] concluded, a political one: the agreement of citizens to establish and maintain a republic based on equal rights' (Canovan 1992: 197). According to Canovan, Arendt conceived of personal morality as concerned with one's relation to one's self and to one's neighbours, but for her it did not include concern for the establishment and survival of sound political institutions: 'Such political institutions demand commitments of their own, and these may on occasion conflict with the demands of personal morality' (Canovan 1992: 185).

Politics, for Arendt, was the activity of conducting the affairs of a community by means of speech in the public arena. Politics becomes thus the realm of 'no rule', where human beings face each other as equals and where persuasion, rather than force or violence, 'rule' (Arendt 1958: 25–8; Bernstein 1986: 224). Political participation meant for Arendt the public engagement in discussion, debate and deliberation about matters of public interest (Parekh 1981: 139; Canovan 1992: 225). According to Arendt, political action required 'speech, that is, words which will disclose the aims and intentions of the actor while articulating the meaning of the act' (Wolin 1977: 97). Through speech in the public arena citizens become aware of their plurality while, at the same time, creating a public space that brings them together. But this engagement with others in the public arena is premised on the existence and the sharing of a common culture such that everyone can articulate what they think and what their views are. It is in a public arena structured by such a culture that the self-centred perspective of the individual is constantly challenged by the diversity, plurality and multiplicity of perspectives (Benhabib 1992: chaps 3 and 4). Engagement in the public arena offers the opportunity to see the common affairs from different points of view and to perceive and form one's own interests in the light of the others' response in public encounter.

For Arendt, such a deliberative engagement presupposes a willingness to disinterested reflection, or, as she put it, an enlarged mentality. Political thought was defined as 'representative' in that the formation of an opinion was seen as dependent upon 'considering a given issue from different viewpoints, by making present to my mind the standpoints of those who are absent; that is, I represent them' (Arendt, quoted in: Passerin d'Entrèves 1992: 163; cf. Bernstein 1986: chap. 8). Any judgement, not just political judgement, so she argued:

> cannot function in strict isolation or solitude; it needs the presence of others 'in whose place' it must think, whose perspective it must take into consideration, and without whom it never has the opportunity to operate at all. As logic, to be sound, depends on the presence of the self, so judgement, to be valid, depends on the presence of others. (Arendt 1961: 220–1)

Freedom, for Arendt, thus consisted in the liberty to appear in a public space in the company of fellow-citizens and to create and sustain such a common world through deliberation on the basis of 'representative thinking' and other-regarding political judgement.

Arendt argued that political freedom was threatened whenever 'social' concerns intruded into the public realm (Arendt 1958: chap. 2). In her discussion of the French Revolution she claimed that, when the masses appeared on the scene, the problem of poverty and the concern with the necessity of life appeared with them and resulted in the surrendering of free-dom to necessity, to the urgency of the life process itself: '[T]he revolution had changed its direction; it aimed no longer at freedom, the goal of the rev-olution had become the happiness of the people' (Arendt 1973: 61). In con-trast to the American Revolution, which had been a political revolution dedicated to the founding and constitution of political freedom, the French Revolution was transformed from a political revolution, which it initially was, into a social revolution primarily concerned with liberation from bio-logical necessity:

> Since the revolution had opened the gates of the political realm to the poor, this realm had indeed become 'social'. It was overwhelmed by the cares and worries which actually belonged in the sphere of the household and which, even if they were permitted to enter the public realm, could not be solved by political means, since they were matters of administration, to be put into the hands of experts, rather than issues which could be settled by the twofold process of decision and persuasion ... [W]ith the downfall of political and legal authority and the rise of revolution, it was people rather than general eco-nomic and financial problems that were at stake, and they did not merely intrude into but burst upon the political domain. Their need was violent, and, as it were, prepolitical; it seemed that only violence could be strong and swift to help them. (Arendt 1973: 90–1)

Arendt's conceptualization of politics and political freedom was thus premised on the classical Greek distinction between a 'private' sphere of the 'household' as the unit concerned with production and reproduction and the 'necessities of life', and the 'public' sphere of politics concerned with deliberation, institution-building and the survival of the world we share between us. The 'private' realm is the realm of wants, needs and interests, of particularism; the 'public' is the sphere of universalism where the futility of individual life could be overcome. In it, activities related to a common world; in the private sphere, however, they related to the maintenance of life (Arendt 1958: chap. 2; Cohen/Arato 1992: chap. 4).

This banishing of 'the social question' from the political agenda has seri-ous repercussions for Arendt's theory. Arendt maintained that each person must be given the opportunity to concern herself or himself with public affairs (Bernstein 1986: 248–59). But this opportunity surely includes the attainment of a certain level of education and liberation from poverty and the provision with the basic necessity of life, because only then will it be possible for individuals to participate on a permanent basis in rational public debate. In short, active citizenship is founded on social preconditions; hence, the 'social question' is central to a concept of participative democracy. Fur-thermore, it must surely be left to public deliberation of a reasoning citizenry whether they come to define a problem as of common concern. To relegate the question of poverty, or social problems more generally, from the public

arena means in effect curbing the citizenry's power to determine for themselves what concerns them all. One reason for defining 'social' issues as
'political' problems might be to avoid leaving them to experts who apply
their specialist knowledge to these issues and in doing so, turn citizens into
clients. Finally, if there is no concern with 'the social' in the public arena,
what is left of politics? Schwartz makes the point admirably:

> Arendt's romanticism of the *polis* transfixes upon a 'high politics' of 'glory and
> memorable speeches' about the final ends of the political community. These
> speeches, however, appear to have little in common with the lives of ordinary
> people and the substance of conventional politics in liberal democratic societies.
> War and constitution-making appear to be the only kinds of Arendtian 'poli-
> tics', as if founding and perishing and striving for immortality were the only
> true political concerns. (Schwartz 1989/90: 42)

What we get in Arendt is a concern with participation in discourses about
the 'good life' and the building of a world of common political institutions;
the 'mere life' of the citizens, however, as it is shaped by conflict among
competing social classes and factions is given scant attention. Nor are we
told what will happen once consultation and debate, the exchange of views
and the battle of words is over. Political action is speech, but it is also decision: 'And one must know the way decisions are reached, and the place
from which they ultimately – responsibly – issue' (Sternberger 1977: 145).
But on these issues, Arendt remains silent. This argument can be extended
in a more radical way. Habermas (1977: 6) praises Arendt for showing that
'power is built up in communicative action; it is a collective effect of speech
in which reaching agreement is an end in itself for all those involved'. But
he also argues that politics cannot be identified with the praxis of those who
talk together in order to act in common: 'The concept of the political must
extend to the strategic competition for political power and to the employment of power within the political system' (Habermas 1977: 21). The 'realism' of 'power politics', analysed from Machiavelli and Hobbes to Weber and
Schumpeter, has to be accommodated in any analysis of politics. However,
against the single-minded identification in this tradition of power with a
potential for successful strategic action, Arendt rightly argues 'that strategic contests for political power neither call forth nor maintain those institutions in which that power is anchored. Political institutions live not from
force but from recognition' (Habermas 1977: 17–18; Habermas 1992b:
182–7). As we shall see, this criticism of Arendt's theory is developed by
Habermas into a different conceptualization of deliberative politics that aims
to bring together the strategic and communicative aspects of power.

The concept of civil society in political theory

The concept of 'civil society' is central to the theory of deliberative politics. This is one point that this theory shares with both liberalism and republicanism. Yet, arguably, its particular conceptualization of civil society sets it most decisively apart from the other perspectives. To comprehend both similarities and differences, a brief reconstruction of some of the dominant alternative formulations is warranted. Such a brief review will also serve as a summary of some of the points presented so far in this and the previous chapter.

It is uncontroversial to argue that in the history of the concept of 'civil society' we can discern two distinct conceptualizations. In the classical conceptualization, that stretches from Aristotle well into the eighteenth century, 'civil society' was used as a synonym for 'political society': *civitas sive societas civilis sive res publica*, 'the city-state or civil society or common wealth'. But since the mid-eighteenth century, the term 'civil society' has been used to define a realm of social life that is (or ought to be) separate from the 'state'. As we have already observed, for Aristotle the *societas civilis sive politica*, that is, the polis, was a community of citizens who are united in order to live a 'good', 'virtuous' life. In this self-governed community, citizens engage with each other as free and equal persons and rule themselves through law, not through force, coercion and subjection. This political community is contrasted with the *societas domestica*, the sphere of (economic) production and (social) reproduction, the realm of the *oikos*, that serves the satisfaction of the needs and necessities of life. Only he who controls the *oikos* can be a citizen; the equality of citizenship is premised on the inequality of the household; law as the organizing principle of the political community is shadowed by force as the organizing principle of 'domestic society': unequal distribution of power in the *oikos* is the basis for the constitution of the *societas civilis sive politica*.

Aristotle's equation of *societas civilis* with *res publica*, of civil society with political society, remained a main feature of the conceptual history of civil society over the centuries. One of the major deviations from this tradition occurred in the contractual theories of political authority in the seventeenth and eighteenth century. For Hobbes, for example, civil society was not any longer defined by setting it apart from domestic society, but from the 'state of nature'. For Hobbes, *societas naturalis* was populated by (hypothetically) free and equal individuals. In the 'state of nature', 'the weakest has strength enough to kill the strongest, either by secret machination, or by confederacy with others, that are in the same danger with himselfe'; there is always 'warre, as if of every man, against every man':

> [T]here is no place for Industry; because the fruit thereof is uncertain: and consequently no Culture of the Earth; no Navigation, nor use of the commodities

that may be imported by Sea; no commodious Building; no instruments of moving, and removing such things as require much force; no Knowledge of the face of the Earth; no account of Time; no Arts; no Letters; no Society; and which is worst of all, continuall feare, and danger of violent death; And the life of man, solitary, poore, nasty, brutish, and short. (Hobbes, *Leviathan*, chap. 13: 89).

The 'state of nature' is thus a state of lawlessness, a state in which individuals are not bound by the force of any agreed human laws. Hence it is a condition in which there is a 'full and absolute Libertie in every Particular man' (Hobbes, *Leviathan*, chap. 21: 149). To escape from this violent, dangerous and unsociable 'state of nature', men constitute a civil society through mutual agreement. By covenanting to become subjects of a commonwealth, the individuals put themselves under the authority of the civil laws. In a sense, the individuals forfeit liberty in the act of subjection: 'But Civil Law is an Obligation, and takes from us the Liberty which the Law of Nature gave us. Nature gave a Right to every man to secure himselfe by his own strength, and to invade a suspected neighbour, by way of prevention; but the Civil Law takes away that Liberty' (Hobbes, *Leviathan*, chap. 26: 200).

Society is covenanted; it is not 'natural', as for Aristotle, but 'artificial', instituted through the voluntary association of individuals on the basis of a contract with the view of defending individual interests such as life, property or liberty. Again contrary to Aristotle, this thinking does not place the community above the individual, but rather sees the individual prior to community which is then understood as the product of the actions of individuals in pursuit of their interests. And, yet again deviating from the Aristotelian tradition, providing for the Leviathan, as that agency that enforces the social contract and secures the *status civilis* against any internal or external threats, the member of the commonwealth is now not any longer seen as a peer amongst peers, sharing in governing and being governed, but as a subject of a 'sovereign' political power. What we find here then is a theoretical opening for a systematic differentiation of 'civil society' and the 'state'.

But these theoretical developments remain embedded in a language that still uses the Aristotelian formula of 'political or civil society.' Locke, too, uses this language when he argues that civil society occurs 'wherever any number of Men, in a state of Nature, enter into Society to make one People one Body Politic under one Supreme Government':

For hereby he authorises the Society, or which is all one, the Legislative thereof, to make Laws for him as the publick good of the Society shall require; to the Execution whereof, his own assistance (as to his own Decrees) is due. And this *puts Men* out of a state of Nature *into* that of a *Commonwealth*, by setting up a Judge on Earth, with Authority to determine all the Controversies and redress the Injuries that may happen to any Member of the Commonwealth; which Judge is the Legislative, or Magistrates appointed by it. And where-ever there are any number of Men, however associated, that have no such decisive power to appeal to, there they still are *in the state of Nature*. (Locke 1689/1989, *Second Treatise*, chap. 7, § 89)

Locke thus conceptualizes civil society as synonymous with legal authority and the executive apparatus of the law. But by affirming the right of men to withdraw their consent to these arrangements in case of breach of trust, Locke, too, suggests that political community is not 'natural', but 'artificial', instituted to enable men to enjoy private property and goods. And although Locke does not describe the state of nature in Hobbesian terms as anomic, but populated by rational, property-owning individuals with fundamental rights, civil society is given its relief by comparing it to a (hypothetical) *status naturalis*.

There is yet another common dimension to Hobbes's and Locke's analysis of civil society. For both, civil society is pacified society; a society in which the use of force by private individuals is banned (Baumgold 1993). For Hobbes in *De Cive* (chap. 6, § 13), the state was a 'perfect city' in which 'no Citizen hath Right to use his faculties, at his owne discretion, for the preservation of himselfe, or where the *Right of the private Sword* is excluded'. Hobbes did accept that individuals had a right of self-defence against those 'who shall offer to kill, wound, or any other way hurt his Body' (chap. 2, § 18). But while individuals were thus not divested of the right of self-defence in civil society, they had to renounce the right to kill, which was seen as the monopoly of the state – the 'Right of killing cannot be granted to any private person', it is 'with the Supreme' (chap. 2, § 18).

For Locke, too, violence was inimical to civil society. He had argued that, in the state of nature, there were natural limits on the right of the private sword, which may be used legitimately only for the protection and preservation of property and for punishing violations of the law of nature. Yet, given the absence of positive laws and a common authority to contain conflicts among people and to decide their disputes, the state of nature was unlikely to be a peaceful society. It is this insecurity of the state of nature that makes individuals 'willingly give up every one his single power of punishing to be exercised by such alone as shall be appointed to it amongst them; and by such Rules as the Community, or those authorised by them to that purpose, shall agree on' (Locke 1689/1989, *Second Treatise*, chap. 9, § 127). Hobbes had not accepted that the people, as a collectivity, had a right of political resistance to established government; Locke's theory of the government as a fiduciary power, entrusted by the people as the supreme power to protect their life, liberty and property, raised, however, the issue of the enforcement of governmental accountability (Locke 1689/1989, *Second Treatise*, chap. 13, § 149). He argued, contra Hobbes, that the inalienable right of self-preservation did apply, not only to individuals, but also to societies – yet only in the special circumstances of a 'state of war':

> [W]henever the *Legislators endeavour to take away, and destroy the Property of the People*, or to reduce them to Slavery under Arbitrary Power, they put themselves into a state of War with the People, who are thereupon absolved from any farther Obedience, and are left to the common Refuge, which God hath provided for all Men, against Force and Violence. (Locke 1689/1989, *Second Treatise*, chap. 19, § 222).

This argument also alerts us to Locke's proposition that absolute monarchy is inconsistent with civil society, because an absolute prince remains, in effect, in a state of nature 'in respect of those who are under his Dominion': there is no common authority to appeal to for the adjudication of conflicts between them (Locke 1689/1989, *Second Treatise*, chap. 7, § 90).

Hence, whereas for Hobbes civil society as pacified society required the institutionalization of unconditional and unified sovereignty in the form of absolute monarchy, for Locke it was manifest that 'the People ... could never be safe nor at rest, nor *think themselves in Civil Society*, till the Legislature was placed in collective bodies of Men, call them Senate, Parliament, or what you please' (Locke 1689/1989, *Second Treatise*, chap. 7, § 94). Indeed, Locke comes close to endorsing the principle of parliamentary sovereignty and of rule of law:

> [I]n well-order'd Commonwealths ... the *Legislative* Power is put into the hands of divers Persons, who duly Assembled, have by themselves, or jointly with others, a Power to make Laws, which when they have done, being separated again; they are themselves subject to the Laws, they have made; which is a new and near tie upon them, to take care, that they make them for the publick good. (Locke 1689/1989, *Second Treatise*, chap. 12, § 143)

In either discussion, then, we find civil society defined as pacified society in which individuals have divested themselves of the use of force and have transferred it, either permanently (Hobbes) or temporarily (Locke), to a person or a collective body. In that sense, civil society as pacified society is politically organized society. By designating (collective) actors empowered to deploy legitimate force in (civil) society, either of these theoretical positions creates a space for conceptualizing the actors and agencies involved in the enforcement of order as an – analytically – distinct sphere of society, as 'the state'.

If Hobbes can justifiably be seen as one of the main authors who gave western political philosophy a direction quite distinct from the Aristotelian tradition, then Hegel can be interpreted as that philosopher who reconceptualized the notions of the 'state' and 'civil society' in the most systematic way. Hegel stayed within the Aristotelian tradition in defining the state as an ethical institution membership of which was seen as necessary for moral well-being and moral self-development of individuals. But he took leave from this tradition by arguing that 'civil society' was a sphere quite distinct and separate from the state. Indeed, he conceptualized civil society as the 'stage of difference' between family and the state, mediating between these two spheres (Hegel 1821/1942: §182). Civil society contained three 'moments'. First, it contained the economic relations and institutions of society; it is a 'system of needs' where the individual bourgeois pursues his idiosyncratic private interests and makes his subjective choice. Yet despite the variety and diversity of interests pursued in civil society as an expression of individual particularity, the system of needs is one of reciprocal dependence. A complex division of labour is the chief mechanism of satisfying needs in society. It manifests the 'mutual interlocking of particulars', 'the complex interdependence of each on all' (Hegel 1821/1942: §§ 189A and 199). This economic system also produces various classes and estates, each with its own particularistic set of interests, cultures, habits and ways of life. For Hegel, of the three main estates the chief carrier of civil society is the commercial estate, made up of artisans, manufacturers and merchants and businessmen. Of the other two, the agricultural estate, including the aristocracy, is not systematically treated in the *Philosophy of Right*, whereas the universal estate, or civil servants, are central to his discussion of the state.

The second 'moment' of civil society is the administration of justice. It mitigates the turbulence of the economic sphere by protecting property, regulating conflict and punishing law-breakers. The third moment is the 'police' as that system of administrative power that performs supervisory functions with regard to public morality, but also engages in welfare activities to counterbalance the socially disruptive effects of the workings of the economy, such as poverty. The second and third 'moment' of civil society are thus conceptualized as integrative mechanisms of an antagonistic civil society. And it is in this context of identifying integrative mechanisms that Hegel also discusses corporations. For Hegel these professional associations and voluntary organizations served as a kind of 'second family for its members' (Hegel 1821/1942: § 252), helping to overcome the atomization and alienation of individuals that resulted from market mechanisms. But more fundamentally, Hegel maintained that corporations provided opportunities for developing and manifesting 'civic virtues' and thus contributed to the ethical life even in civil society:

> Under modern conditions, the citizens have only a restricted share in the public business of the state, yet it is essential to provide men – ethical entities – with work of a public character over and above their private business. This work of a public character, which the modern state does not always provide, is found in the Corporation. We saw earlier that in fending for himself a member of civil society is also working for others. But this unconscious compulsion is not enough; it is in the Corporation that it first changes into a known and thought-

ful ethical mode of life ... [I]ts purpose is ... to bring an isolated trade into the social order and elevate it to a sphere in which it gains strength and respect. (Hegel 1821/1942: § 255 A)

Hence, corporations provide an ethical connection between the individuals who share a common 'social standing' (*Stand*) (Hegel 1821/1942: § 253). But they also direct them towards ethical ends, 'and provide a mediating link between the individual's particular life as person and subject, and the individual's common life as a member of a universal society' (Wood 1993b: 421). Hegel can therefore argue that 'the sphere of civil society passes over into the state' (Hegel 1821/1942: § 256). For Hegel then, the corporation is not just a mechanism that integrates variegated social interests into a common structure, but also a source of socialization and education, enabling the individual to overcome particularistic interests and allowing him to perceive a common good (Smith 1989: 236–7; Dallmayr 1993: 122–35; Hegel 1821/1942: § 253). This is an important aspect of Hegel's conceptualization of civil society as that arena in which modern man legitimately pursues his self-interest and develops his individuality, but in which he also learns the value of 'combining together' and social solidarity, and thus becomes educated for citizenship.

If we draw out some of the implications of Hegel's discussion of the second and third 'moment' of civil society, we can argue that for Hegel both public authority and corporation pursue 'the goal of restoring the ethical life which civil society lacks, and of transcending the "stage of difference" by carrying it over into the state' (Kortian 1984: 205). Incorporating the (classical and traditional) 'state' functions of administration of justice and 'police' into civil society could be justified on the grounds that they provided the necessary institutional framework for the pursuit of particular interests, whereas the state proper (as an 'idea') was the manifestation of universality. But this incorporation then allows us in turn to analyse civil society as a kind of 'inferior' state that fulfils state functions but lacks the key characteristics of the 'superior' political state: a constitution and constitutional powers (monarchical power, legislative power and governmental power) as well as the monopolistic power to undertake relations with other states (Bobbio 1989: 30–4; Dallmayr 1993: 145–64).

This political state is conceptualized by Hegel as a constitutional state, a state which upholds, and is bound by, the rule of law. An important aspect of this constitutionality is the representation of the estates of civil society in the legislature:

Regarded as a mediating organ, the Estates stand between the government in general on the one hand and the nation broken up into particulars (people and the associations) on the other. Their function requires them to possess a political and administrative sense and temper, no less than a sense of the interests of individuals and particular groups. At the same time the significance of their position is that, in common with the organized executive, they are a middle term preventing both the extreme isolation of the power of the crown, which otherwise might seem a mere arbitrary tyranny, and also the isolation of the particular interests of persons, societies, and Corporations. Further, and more important, they prevent individuals from having the appearance of a mass or an aggregate and so from acquiring an unorganized opinion and volition and from crystallizing into a powerful bloc in opposition to the organized state. (Hegel 1821/1942: § 302).

There are a number of issues raised in this statement. First, it is through the Estates that people begin to participate in the state (Hegel 1821/1942: § 301A). But it is a participation, not as individuals, but as members of communities and associations. Hegel thus argues in favour of a system of corporate representation: 'The circles of association in civil society are already communities. To picture these communities as once more breaking up into a mere conglomeration of individuals as soon as they enter the field of politics ... is *eo ipso* to hold civil and political life apart from one another ... because its basis could then only be the abstract individuality of caprice and opinion, and hence it would be grounded on chance and not on what is absolutely stable and justified' (Hegel 1821/1942: § 303). Hegel explicitly states that in the corporations (as politically represented in the estate assemblies) the executive meets with legitimate interests that it must respect (Hegel 1821/1942: § 290 A). Hence, contrary to the Aristotelian tradition, 'private' interests and concerns – in Arendt's terminology: the 'social' – can legitimately be raised in public. Second, representation means integration from above. This becomes clearer if we look more closely at Hegel's discussion of (public) opinion. The cacophony of public opinions is transcended in the deliberations of the Estate assembly; indeed, it is through the publicity of these debates that public opinion 'first reaches thoughts that are true and attains insight into the situation and concept of the state and its affairs, and so first acquires ability to estimate these more rationally ... [S]uch publicity ... is ... another antidote to the self-conceit of individuals singly and *en masse*, and another means – indeed one of the chief means – of their education' (Hegel 1821/1942: § 315). Public deliberations of Estates assemblies are thus an excellent education for the citizens in that they allow them to learn how best to recognize the true character of their interests. Publicity in the assemblies is therefore not meant to allow the interlinking of parliamentary debate with the political reasoning of the public in order to criticize and control political power more efficiently. This linkage, as we shall see, is of great importance in Jürgen Habermas's theory of deliberative politics. In Hegel it is a means to organize and influence public opinion from above. Indeed, achievement of anything great or rational is premised on being independent of public opinion: 'Public opinion contains all kinds of falsity and truth, but it takes a great man to find the truth in it. The great man of the age is the one who can put into words the will of his age, tell his age what its will is, and accomplish it' (Hegel 1821/1942: § 318A).

Hegel's concept of civil society, then, is in manifold ways interwoven with the classical perspective. With Aristotle, Hegel shares the view that the family is outside civil society. The family is held together by sentiment and ties of romantic love; in it, the individual enjoys the benefits of ethical cohesion that is cultivated by love. The relationship of members of the family take the form of a 'particularistic altruism' (Avineri); one feels duty-bound to place one's own interests below the common interest of the family and to care for the members of one's own family. This 'altruism' is thus limited to a particular set of individuals. This particularism sets the family apart from both the state and civil society. For Hegel the state is the sphere of 'universal altruism', a community of individuals who will to live together on the basis of an all-encompassing solidarity that expresses the sense of shared values and common sacrifice at the expense of individual interests. It is a community of persons who share a conception of the 'good life' and feel duty-bound to discipline their egoistic inclinations in favour of the advancement of a moral culture and the common good. And it is the class of civil servants, the universal estate, that is analysed as the mediation between the particularism of civil society and the universality of the state, charged with taking impartial care of the universal interests of society (Avineri 1972: chap. 7).

Both particular and universal altruism is alien to civil society. This is the sphere of universal egoism where I treat everyone as a means to my own ends (Hegel 1821/1942: § 187). Whereas for Aristotle it was possible to see the household as both a 'family' unit and a 'production' unit, societal development in Hegel's time had made it possible, and necessary, for him to conceptualize the family and the economy as two functionally differentiated spheres. He could distinguish the two spheres by contrasting their mode of social interaction, that is, particular altruism and universal egoism. But there is yet another difference between civil society, on the one hand, and the family as well as the state, on the other. For Hegel, civil society is the sphere in which individuals enter into contractual relationships with each other. These relationships are abstract, optional, and instrumental. They are abstract, because they do not involve individuals as whole or concrete persons. Rather, they abstract from much of what makes up the identity of an individual and consider him only in a particular respect, for example, as an owner of property that he is willing to exchange for the other person's property. Because of this abstraction, these relationships are optional, or arbitrary, since they are not essential to ('my' understanding of) who 'I' am; they do not define 'me' fully. And they are instrumental, since one enters into these contractual relationships to gain a personal advantage (Westphal 1984).

On the other hand, family and political life, according to Hegel involve substantial ties. These are relationships in which whole or concrete persons relate to each other. They are essential in that they significantly affect who 'I' am: 'Who *We* are in the family and state to which I belong is an essential part of who *I* am, not some peripheral episode which takes place on the surface of my selfhood' (Westphal 1984: 79). As Westphal argues with regard to political life, 'I the citizen am who We the people are. Like the family, the state frees self-consciousness from self-centeredness' (Westphal 1984: 89). Evidently, this position amounts to an attack on political con-tractarianism. Hegel incessantly warns not to confuse the state with civil society and to assume that its specific end was laid down as the security and protection of property and personal freedom, since then the interest of the individuals as such becomes the ultimate end of their association, and membership in the state becomes something optional (Hegel 1821/1942: § 258). Rather, 'it is nearer the truth to say that it is absolutely necessary for every individual to be a citizen' (Hegel 1821/1942: § 75A), because only in the state can the individual as citizen actualize his deepest freedom and realize his nature, not simply as a particular but as a universal, communal being (Pelczynski 1984: 76). Allen Wood sums up succinctly Hegel's thinking about the state:

> The state for Hegel is not a mechanism for keeping the peace, or the enforce-ment of rights, or the promotion of any interest beyond its own existence. Instead, it is most fundamentally the locus of the higher collective ends, which, by rationally harmonizing the rights and welfare of individuals, liberate them by providing their lives with meaning. As Hegel conceives the state, its action on individuals is not the external coercion of policemen, but the internal, eth-ical disposition that fulfills their rational nature and so makes them free. (Wood 1993a: 230)

Hegel's analysis of the state is thus quite different from the classical liberal doctrine that envisages the state as a device necessary for the sake of civil peace and the enjoyment of private property. On the contrary, for Hegel the state was the highest form of human community and conceptualized as independent of any particular interest. But the most influential criticism of Hegel's theory did not come from a liberal perspective but from Karl Marx. He accepted Hegel's distinction between 'state' and 'civil society', but defined each sphere differently and reinterpreted their relationship in a fun-damentally different way. In analysing civil society, he concentrated his attention on the 'system of needs', conceptualizing civil society as compris-ing exclusively material and economic relations; and the complex of eco-nomic relations was seen as coterminous with society itself. In his description of civil society as capitalist society, Marx transformed the picture of the (hypothetical) Hobbesian state of nature into the (historical) reality of bourgeois society (Bobbio 1989: 27–9). This society could be characterized as capitalist society to the extent that it is dominated by a mode of production that rests on the private ownership of the means of production. This private ownership creates a dependent class of wage labourers whose only property that they can sell to secure their means of subsistence is their labour power. By buying labour power, the capitalist buys the one commodity that can create new value; it is value generated by workers in the productive process over and above their wages, and appropriated by the capitalists as 'surplus value'. Marx claimed that this system of exploitation was upheld by the state which he saw as acting on behalf of the capitalist class, though not necessarily at its behest. Even if Marx was thus granting a 'relative' autonomy to the state, 'in the last instance' he (and Friedrich Engels) analysed civil society, the realm of economic relations, as the decisive element, and the state, the political order, the subordinate element, as the political superstructure built upon the material economic base that was civil society.

For Marx, civil society was never more than the sum total of the material conditions of life. As Keane (1988b: 58) rightly points out, Marx did not develop a critical theory of civil society that was oriented not just to the system of production, 'but also to the crucially important dynamics of *other* forms of civil life, including households, voluntary associations, professions, communications media and disciplinary institutions such as schools, prisons and hospitals'. We shall return to this charge later in our discussion. Those contemporary analysts of modern society, however, who have aimed to develop such a critical theory have frequently turned to another thinker of the nineteenth century, Alexis de Tocqueville.

Marx's reluctance of a systematic analysis of intermediate institutions, developing and operating 'between' the 'economy' and the 'state' contrasts not only with Hegel's interest in these organizations, but also with Alexis de Tocqueville's theoretical and empirical treatment of them. In de Tocqueville's analysis, the processes of atomization and individualization in modern society, which had also concerned Hegel, demanded the formation of associations for the sake of the liberty of the individual. According to him, in modern society the ties of family, of caste, of class and of craft fraternities have been cut and 'the woof of time is every instant broken and the track of generations effaced' (Tocqueville 1945: v. II, 99). It is a society in which nothing is stable and in which 'each man is haunted by a fear of sinking to a lower social level and by a restless urge to better his condition. And since money has not only become the sole criterion of a man's social status but has also acquired an extreme mobility ... everybody is feverishly intent on making money' (Tocqueville 1966: 29–30).

But modern society is also a democratic society in the sense that it has led to an increasing equalization of social conditions. As a result, ever more people, although neither rich nor powerful enough to dominate their fellow citizens, 'have nevertheless acquired or retained sufficient education and fortune to satisfy their own wants. They owe nothing to any man, they expect nothing from any man; they acquire the habit of always considering themselves as standing alone, and they are apt to imagine that their whole destiny is in their hands' (Tocqueville 1945: v. II, 99). Hence, not only has the collapse of the old regime set individuals free by cutting them lose from the affective and social ties to families, groups and corporation, membership in which had given them their identity and a sense of belonging; but the structure of modern society is such that it also reinforces this process of individualization by privileging self-centred competitive actions by 'possessive individualists'. As a result, 'democratic' citizens 'do not scruple to show that they care for nobody but themselves' (Tocqueville 1945: v. II, 100).

There is yet another aspect of modern 'democratic' society that figures prominently in Tocqueville's analysis. Democracy as that society that aims at the equalization of conditions, and, in particular, at the abolition of inequalities of power and wealth, in the name of the sovereignty of the people, equal treatment and uniform provision, inexorably leads to the gradual concentration of power in the hands of a centralized state: the political demand for the equality of conditions means in reality the institutionalization of public regulation in the form of the social-welfare state in which the state becomes regulator, inspector, adviser, educator and punisher of social life (Keane 1988a: 55, 58). This centralization has two distinct effects. To start with, it imparts without difficulty:

> an admirable regularity to the routine of business; provides skillfully for the details of social police; represses small disorders and petty misdemeanors; maintains society in a *status quo* alike secure from improvement and decline; and perpetuates a drowsy regularity in the conduct of affairs which the heads of the administration are wont to call good order and public tranquillity. (Tocqueville 1945: v. I, 90)

Centralization thus creates a framework for the peaceful pursuit of private interests and can therefore be interpreted as aiding the development of self-centred individualism. But, second, the incessant increase of the prerogative of centralized government will lead insensibly to the surrender of individual independence as the people perpetually fall under the control of the public administration: 'The eye and finger of government are constantly intruding into the minutest detail of human actions' (Tocqueville 1945: v. II, 325, 313). And Tocqueville continues: 'Private persons are at once too weak to protect themselves and too much isolated for them to reckon upon the assistance of their fellows.' Atomization and individualization are intrinsic features of 'democratic' society; and so is the danger of state despotism that feeds on the 'democratic' demand for equality of conditions and thrives on the individualization in modern society (Tocqueville 1945: v. II, 318).

Under these circumstances the questions arises as to how 'equality' can be combined with 'freedom'? Tocqueville argued that only a vibrant public life that was structured through a plurality of associations could secure liberty. On the one hand, these associations would contain the processes of atomization, giving individuals a sense of solidarity and interdependence. On the other hand, they would provide a barrier against the encroachments by the state on the life of individuals. Both of these aspects are involved when Tocqueville states that, '[i]f men are to remain civilized or to become so, the art of associating together must grow and improve in the same ratio in which the equality of conditions is increased' (Tocqueville 1945: v. II, 110). He claimed unequivocally that:

> If each citizen did not learn, in proportion as he individually becomes more feeble and consequently more incapable of preserving his freedom single-handed, to combine with his fellow citizens for the purpose of defending it, it is clear that tyranny would unavoidably increase together with equality. (Tocqueville 1945: v. II, 106)

He distinguished between two types of associations. Civil associations comprised professional and commercial organizations, but also churches, schools, literary and scientific circles as well as organizations for leisure and recreation. Political associations, on the other hand, comprised not only 'interest groups' and 'parties', organizing 'factional' interests, but also, for example, juries and associations that made up local government (Krumar 1993: 381). According to Tocqueville, political associations were large 'free schools' which taught citizens the 'general theory of association' (Tocqueville 1945: v. II, 116). Compared to civil associations, there was no risk of losing money, he argued, and therefore people were more likely to join political associations and learn the benefits of combining together. While it was thus possible to distinguish between types of association, Tocqueville was adamant that any type of association was premised on the rights of citizens to freedom of expression and association and on the freedom of the press.

In the light of the points made so far, it could be argued that Tocqueville's analysis amounts to a conceptualization of modern society as a tripartite structure. He distinguishes a capitalist economic sphere which is organized around the pursuit of private interests and is dominated by a 'cash-nexus'. This sphere is hardly analysed by Tocqueville. The second sphere is made up of the associative life of the citizens. It is famously analysed in the study on 'Democracy in America'. The third sphere of the state, finally, is dominated, on its executive side, by bureaucracies as well as the police, army, courts and, on the legislative side, by parliamentary assemblies as part of a wider system of formal political representation. If we interpreted this schema in the light of Hegel's analysis, it would seem to be possible to define 'civil society' in a Tocquevillean sense as comprising the first sphere of the economy plus the civil associations, keeping in mind that, for Tocqueville, these associations are both a means for individuals to organize and express particular interests that they have in common with others and a means for transcending their own selfish, conflictual, narrowly private goals (Keane 1988b: 51). Political associations are best seen as necessary for an efficient system of representation. Together with the civil associations, they constitute the 'public' in modern society and, at the same time, a barrier against a potentially tyrannical or paternalistic state.

If we review the arguments put forward by Hegel, Marx and Tocqueville, we may notice that, despite all the differences, they are all premised on two preconditions (Wood 1990: 61). First, that there is, 'in reality', a terrain of human association that is distinct from the body politic, a 'society' with moral claims that are independent of, and sometimes opposed to, the state's authority. As Wood points out, this differentiation was intrinsically linked to the development of private property as a distinct and autonomous locus of social power. It was on this basis that an autonomous 'economy', separated from the 'political', could emerge. And the second precondition is the emergence of (the idea and reality of) the state as an entity with its own corporate identity. Only once these two preconditions were in place could civil society be defined as representing, if not exclusively comprising:

> a separate sphere of human relations and activity, differentiated from the state but neither public nor private or perhaps both at once, embodying not only a whole range of social interactions apart from the private sphere of the household and the public sphere of the state, but more specifically a network of distinctively *economic* relations, the sphere of the market-place, the arena of production, distribution and exchange. (Wood 1990: 61)

In recent years the concept of 'civil society' has been rediscovered in political discourse and used, by and large, in a Tocquevillean sense. As has been pointed out, accepting the reality of a capitalist market-economy, Tocqueville focused his analysis on the juxtaposition of 'the state' and 'society' and advocated associational pluralism and diversity as a means to control state power. For him, freedom belonged to civil society, and coercion, be it tyrannical or paternalistic, to the state: the liberty of the individual could only be secured in the associative sphere outside the state. Tocqueville's concern with avoiding state despotism and creating a space for the autonomous life of voluntary associations is unequivocally 'liberal'. It was this Tocquevillean perspective of opposition to state despotism and the advocacy for associative structures that was dominant in the understanding of 'civil society' in the dissident movements in Eastern and Central Europe in the 1970s and 1980s.

In the state socialist societies in Eastern and Central Europe, it was, of course, quite apposite to conceptualize 'civil society' as juxtaposed to a despotic state, indeed, as the main weapon against an oppressive state (Tismaneanu 1992). 'Civil society' was lined up against the state; what had to be defended was the self-management of society, the independent life of society against the despotic encroachments by the state upon its terrain. As a moral 'ideal', 'civil society' expressed the thought that it was only within an autonomous social sphere that individuals could acquire and manifest mental independence, or, as Vaclav Havel put it, could 'live within the truth':

> What is this independent life of society? ... It includes everything from self-edu-cation and thinking about the world, through free creative activity and its com-munication to others, to the most varied free, civic initiatives, including instances of independent self-organization. In short, it is an area in which living within the truth becomes articulate and materializes in a visible way. (Havel 1978/1991: 177)

Within civil society, every person must have the right of free speech and of free association; and through the exercise of these rights discover what they have in common, recognize each other as peers and begin to regain their liberty. 'Civil society' was the expression of a new ethical vision of social order, signalling a clash of different moralities between the state and soci-ety (Michnik 1985: 87). At issue was the restoration of the dignity of autonomous citizens' initiatives and the creation of a space for the inde-pendent formation and activity of grassroots movements. For the Hungar-ian writer György Konrad, civil society and the activities in it were, approvingly, analysed as amounting to a depoliticization of life; they were seen as 'antipolitical', geared towards limiting the state's interference with the individual's private affairs:

> Antipolitics is the political activity of those who don't want to be politicians and who refuse to share in power. Antipolitics is the emergence of independent forums that can be appealed to against political power; it is a counterpower that cannot take power and does not wish to. Power it has already, here and now, by reason of its moral and cultural weight ... Antipolitics neither supports nor opposes government; it is something different. Its people are fine right where they are; they form a network that keeps watch on political power, exerting pressure on the basis of their cultural and moral stature alone, not through electoral legitimacy. That is their right and obligation, but above all it is their self-defense. (Konrad 1984: 230–1)

Politics, he argued, had flooded nearly every nook and cranny of people's lives; these lives ought now to be depoliticized, ought to be freed from poli-tics 'as from some contagious infection'. And he added: 'I would describe the democratic opposition not as a political but an antipolitical opposition, since its essential activity is to work for destatification' (Konrad 1984: 228). For Havel, at least, such antipolitics that aimed at the creation of a 'parallel polis' was not to be understood as an invitation to retreat into a ghetto and as an act of isolation. The antipolitics of independent initiatives, for example, would help to raise the confidence of citizens and shatter the world of appearances and unmask the real nature of power; in short, the associations and activities of civil society would educate citizens for the task of working for destatification (Havel 1978/1991: 192–6). In a way, the notion of 'antipolitics' was similar to Michnik's concept of 'new evolutionism'. Michnik suggested that the experience of the failures of reform in the past, such as the Hungarian Uprising in 1956 and the reform process in Czechoslovakia in 1968, demanded the recognition that any attempt at change had to accept the geopolitical realities of the Cold War and could not challenge the military or international position of the Eastern bloc lest the Soviet Union would intervene. And, second, he argued that neither revolution from below nor reform from above was likely to achieve anything, and that a realistic policy of reform would have to start with creating a 'civil society' (Michnik 1985). This, of course, amounted to the self-limitation of the transformative strategy that did not envisage a wholesale attack on the state and party apparatuses.

When we now turn to a discussion of the concept of deliberative politics as, after liberalism and republicanism, a third form of conceptualizing democratic citizenship, it would serve us well to remain cognizant of three points raised in the previous discussion on civil society: first, the importance attached to the 'state'–'society' dichotomy; second, the emphasis put on autonomous associations; and third, the idea of 'self-limitation'. All three aspects are central to the discussion of citizenship and civil society in the theory of 'deliberative politics'.

Deliberative politics and democratic legitimacy

The theory of 'deliberative politics' has been most prominently developed by Jürgen Habermas within the context of his discourse ethics. It claims to offer an account of democracy and citizenship at once different from both liberalism and republicanism. In this theory of 'deliberative politics', the concept of civil society plays a pivotal role. This has been well demonstrated by Jean Cohen and Andrew Arato in their book *Civil Society and Political Theory* (1992), and by Habermas himself (1992b). For Cohen and Arato, the concept of civil society designates a societal realm different from both the state and the economy. They define civil society as having the following distinct components:

(1) *Plurality*: families, informal groups, and voluntary associations whose plurality and autonomy allow for a variety of forms of life; (2) *Publicity*: institutions of culture and communications; (3) *Privacy*: a domain of individual self-development and moral choice; and (4) *Legality*: structures of general law and basic rights needed to demarcate plurality, privacy, and publicity from at least the state and, tendentially, the economy. (Cohen/Arato 1992: 346)

This conceptualization of civil society reflects Cohen's and Arato's adoption of Habermas's trichotomous model that distinguishes between the political and economic subsystems and the lifeworld (Habermas 1987). Whereas the subsystems are integrated and steered by the media of power and money respectively, and social interactions are based on a strategic–instrumental rationality, the lifeworld is co-ordinated through action oriented towards reaching understanding and mutual, consensual agreement. In the lifeworld actors confront each other with normative validity claims that must be redeemed in a dialogue. It is the sphere of social life that is co-ordinated through communicative action:

> Under the functional aspect of mutual understanding, communicative action serves to transmit and renew cultural knowledge; under the aspect of coordinating action, it serves social integration and the establishment of solidarity; finally, under the aspect of socialization, communicative action serves the formation of personal identities. The symbolic structures of the lifeworld are reproduced by way of the continuation of valid knowledge, stabilization of group solidarity, and socialization of responsible actors. The process of reproduction connects up new situations with the existing conditions of the lifeworld; it does this in the semantic dimension of meanings or contents (of the cultural tradition), as well as in the dimensions of social space (of socially integrated groups), and historical time (of successive generations). Corresponding to these processes of cultural reproduction, social integration and socialization are the structural components of the lifeworld: culture, society, person. (Habermas 1987: 137)

It is as part of this lifeworld that civil society is being theorized. How does the argument proceed?

According to Cohen and Arato (1992: 347–8), the principle of discourse ethics postulates that 'a norm of action has validity only if all those possibly affected by it (and by the side-effects of its application) would, as participants in a practical discourse, arrive at a (rationally motivated) agreement that such a norm should come into or remain in force'. This principle contains a theory of political legitimacy as it proposes to consider as legitimate only those norms and institutions that would be validated by individuals who engage in a practical discourse. But for such a practical dialogue to produce a rational consensus on the validity of a norm and its institutionalization, procedures must be in place that give all those affected an equal chance to partake in the public deliberations and to initiate and continue

69

communication unconstrained by economic or political force on the basis of a mutual and reciprocal recognition of each by all as autonomous, rational subjects whose claims will be acknowledged if supported by valid arguments. As Seyla Benhabib argues, it follows from this principle that:

> [t]here are no *prima facie* rules limiting the agenda of conversation, nor the identity of the participants, as long as each excluded person or group can justifiably show that they are relevantly affected by the proposed norm under question. In certain circumstances this would mean that citizens of a democratic community would have to enter into a practical discourse with non-citizens who may be residing in their countries, at their borders, or in neighboring communities if there are matters which affect them all. Ecology and environmental issues in general are a perfect example of such instances when the boundaries of discourse keep expanding because the consequences of our actions expand and impact increasingly on people. (Benhabib 1994: 31)

From this perspective, discourse ethics is thus a theory of democratic legitimacy, but goes beyond a concern with legitimation by, first, raising the question of the composition of the democratic constituency, or the membership of the dialogic community, and, second, by insisting on problematizing the boundary between 'public' and 'private' since all issues are seen as potentially open to public debate (Habermas 1992b: chaps 7, 8). Only in and through unrestrained public deliberation will we discover what our deepest disagreements are. It is participation in democratic public discourse that enables individuals to realize what they have in common with others, and what distinguishes them from other individuals. Through participation, 'a narrowly selfish individual would probably discover a life entangled with others in ways he or she previously did not understand and an identity dependent on commitments and responsibilities to publics, communities and groups in ways he or she previously did not recognize' (Warren 1992: 12). Only after public deliberation has been radically opened up in such a way that citizens feel free to introduce any and all moral arguments into the conversational field, will we be in a position 'to agree upon a mutually acceptable definition of the problem rather than reaching some compromise consensus' (Benhabib 1992: 98–9).

Deliberative politics is thus the mode of arriving at a common understanding of what are matters of public concern in a society 'in which a homogeneity of background convictions cannot be assumed and in which a presumptively shared class interest has given way to a confused pluralism of competing and equally legitimate forms of life' (Habermas 1993: 445). Such a practical discourse in post-traditional societies has a number of presuppositions. First, it is premised on mutual respect among the participants in the dialogue. The right of all human beings capable of speech and action to be participants in the moral conversation must be recognized. And so must their 'symmetrical rights to various speech acts, to initiate new topics, to ask for reflection about the presuppositions of the conversation, etc.' (Benhabib 1992: 29). As Gutmann and Thompson (1990: 76–86) have shown, this amounts to a veritable 'political virtue'. Amongst other things, citizens must cultivate a disposition towards openness that allows for the possibility of change in their own moral position. In addition, they must also embrace an 'economy of moral disagreement' in that they seek that rationale that minimizes rejection of the position they oppose; they must search for significant points of convergence between their own understandings and those of citizens whose positions they reject (Gutmann and Thompson 1990: 82; Nauta 1992: 28–33). Implicit in this argument is the further assumption that the capacity of individuals for autonomous judgement on the basis of mutual respect will be enhanced through participation in practical discourses. Individual autonomy is thus achieved only in and through participation in public political discourse.

Discourse ethics thus shares with both the republican and the liberal tradition a concern with 'political virtues'. Insofar as republicanism sees 'citizenship' as an office and not just as a legal status, '[i]t implies acting, doing something, bringing something about. Autonomy and judgement are both conditions for and intended outcomes of citizen action. A citizen is he who has those two qualities to such a degree that he is and remains capable of both ruling and being ruled' (van Gunsteren 1988: 732). In order for an individual to be autonomous, he or she has to be capable of sound judgement, that is to say, has to be capable of dialogic performance in the political community. This presupposes, on the one hand, a knowledge of the language, political culture and those institutions that foster the reproduction of citizens (which includes the constitution) (van Gunsteren 1988). But it also requires, on the other hand, citizens capable of subordinating personal interest to the practice of dialogue and thus citizens with some degree of detachment from self so that they are capable of deliberating well about common ends (Burtt 1993: 361). And liberalism, too, makes assumptions about 'public virtues'. Liberalism has 'a vision of individuals who in some manner take responsibility for their own lives' (Galston 1988: 1287). Arguably the most distinctive liberal virtues are the willingness to question authority and to engage in public discourse on the basis of a general tolerance of diverse interests and opinions and the acceptance of the non-violent pursuit of individual interests. Will Kymlicka and Wayne Norman, following Galston (1988; 1991), divide the 'liberal' virtues required for responsible citizenship into four groups:

> (i) general virtues: courage, law-abidingness, loyalty; (ii) social virtues: independence, open-mindedness; (iii) economic virtues: work ethic, capacity to delay self-gratification, adaptability to economic and technological change; and

(iv) political virtues: capacity to discern and respect the rights of others, willingness to demand only what can be paid for, ability to evaluate the performance of those in office, willingness to engage in public discourse. (Kymlicka/Norman 1994: 365)

All three perspectives thus assume a particular set of 'public virtues'. And while the respective virtues differ in some respects, the main difference between these traditions is arguably to be found, on the one hand, in republicanism and deliberative politics maintaining that these virtues are best 'learned' through participation in the public sphere, whereas liberalism, on the other hand, tends to privilege the 'private' sphere of the family and formal education.

Deliberative politics as one manifestation of discourse ethics is premised on a second prerequisite. Practical discourse assumes the institutionalization of a distinct set of rights of the individual interlocutor. It 'presupposes autonomous individuals with the capacity not only to be self-reflective regarding their own values but also to challenge any given norm from a principled standpoint' (Cohen/Arato 1992: 357). Discourse ethics therefore has a conception of the individual as a person whose autonomy, dignity and uniqueness set external limits to any discourse. The protection of the autonomy of the individual moral conscience demands the institutionalization of inviolable personality rights and 'negative liberties'. Whereas these rights and liberties ground discourse ethics, rights of communication such as free speech and expression as well as rights of assembly, association and participation, are constitutive of discourse and thus implied by discourse ethics. Whereas the first set of rights identifies the subjects who have the right to have rights, it is the rights of communication and association that point to the legitimate domain of formulating and defending rights and constitute that public space in which the rights securing personal autonomy and privacy can be reflexively justified.

Conceptualizing civil society as the institutional framework of a modern lifeworld, Cohen and Arato (1992: 441) analyse it as constituted by three complexes of rights: those securing the socialization of the individual (protection of privacy, intimacy and the inviolability of the person); those concerning cultural reproduction (freedoms of thought, press, speech and communication); and those ensuring social integration (freedom of association and assembly). These clusters of rights ensure the possibility of the reproduction of identities, traditions and solidarities respectively, and form the basis of the societal institutions of reproduction, in particular of those institutions that allow for public communication and publicity and collective action (voluntary associations).

Hence, discourse ethics is premised on a conceptualization of human beings as bearers of rights. As such, our relations to each other must be governed by the norms of formal equality and reciprocity: 'If I have a right to X, then you have the duty not to hinder me from enjoying X and conversely ... The moral categories that accompany such interactions are those of right, obligation and entitlement, and the corresponding moral feelings are those of respect, duty, worthiness and dignity' (Benhabib 1992: 159). But as Benhabib shows, this notion of the 'generalized other' as rights-bearer does not mean that we have to conceptualize 'the other' as an 'unencumbered self' (M. Sandel). On the contrary, endorsing a communitarian argument, the significance of constitutive communities for the formation of one's self-identity may be accepted: 'The 'I' becomes an 'I' only among a 'we', in a community of speech and action. Individuation does not preclude association; rather it is the kinds of associations which we inhabit that define the kinds of individuals we will become' (Benhabib 1992: 71). Thus, we enter into public discourse not just as 'generalized others', but as 'concrete others' with a concrete history, identity and affective–emotional constitution. Our relation as 'concrete others' is governed by the norms of equity and complementary reciprocity:

> [E]ach is entitled to expect and to assume from the other forms of behavior through which the other feels recognized and confirmed as a concrete, individual being with specific needs, talents and capacities ... The moral categories that accompany such interactions are those of responsibility, bonding and sharing. The corresponding moral feelings are those of love, care and sympathy and solidarity. (Benhabib 1992: 159)

The individuals who participate in public deliberation are thus best conceptualized as both bearers of rights and thus worthy of universal moral respect and as 'concrete' persons immersed in ethical relations in the 'lifeworld' whose actions are not exclusively guided by the principles of justice, but also by an awareness of what is expected of them in virtue of the kind of social bonds which tie them to each other (Benhabib 1992: 10).

There is yet another, third, presupposition for this type of discourse. The formation and expression of an autonomous individual moral conscience is only possible in a post-traditional and post-conventional socio-cultural lifeworld. Only such a lifeworld allows for a critical reflexivity that can turn even on its own norms. This lifeworld was constituted as a differentiated societal realm in the process of cultural modernization which, in turn, has to be maintained in the lifeworld as an ongoing, open-ended process of reflexivity: 'A modernized, rationalized lifeworld involves a communicative opening-up of the sacred core of traditions, norms and authority to processes of questioning and the replacement of a conventionally based normative consensus by one that is "communicatively" grounded' (Cohen/Arato 1992: 435). On one level, this simply means that individuals have to accept that the 'ought' cannot just be identified with the 'socially

73

valid'. The 'ought' is thus opened up to critical questioning and hypothetical reasoning. On another level, it means the critique of any role-conformist attitudes and the sustained endeavour at reflexive role-distance, because such a critical self-reflexivity is the necessary precondition for embarking on an open-ended process of discursive will formation that involves a willingness to reverse perspectives and to reason from the other's (others') point of view. In short, discourse ethics presupposes 'modernity'.

Cohen and Arato thus emphasize the close interconnection between an autonomous, active civil society and an intact, protected private sphere that makes possible a practical dialogue that renews, develops and limits societal norms and their institutionalization, but that also allows for collective action in the lifeworld and civil society. But this self-definition and self-limitation, rooted as it is in the tension between privacy, publicity and plurality, does not imply a self-referentiality of civil society. Actors in civil society typically aim to influence the political and economic subsystems, if only to forestall any 'colonization' of the lifeworld/civil society by the subsystems and its subsequent subordination to the functional logic of the media of power and money.

The attempts of actors in civil society to influence the political system are mediated by political society whose institutional structure is made up of parties, political organizations, interest groups, and parliamentary bodies. These institutions act, ideally, as 'receptors' of the will-formation of civil society. According to Cohen and Arato (1992: 412–13), 'political society organized in the form of representative democracy and civil society share two key institutions that "mediate" between them: the public sphere and voluntary associations. The frameworks of politically relevant public discussion (the media, political clubs and associations, party caucuses etc.) and parliamentary discussion and debate are continuous'. In addition to this institutional mediation, political and civil society also share their foundation in communication rights without which public discussion in neither civil society nor the parliamentary public sphere would be possible. Civil and political society are thus the two realms in which deliberative politics can be institutionalized and pursued. They differ, however, in that the parliamentary public sphere is informed by a strategic–instrumental rationality, thus marginalizing communicative interaction that is so characteristic of civil society. This means that, first, politics and publicity is oriented more towards the acquisition, control and exercise of power than politics in civil society. Second, there are intrinsic limits to the democratization of political society:

> The separation of powers, the rule of law, and the requirements of efficient bureaucratic functioning guided by the principle of due process preclude the direct participation of everyone in policy making at the state level. At most,

participants can work at this level indirectly through party and parliamentary supervision, control, and publicity – in other words, through the institutions of political society. (Cohen/Arato 1992: 415–16)

The functioning of societal associations, public communication, cultural institutions, and families is thus considered to be open for potentially higher degrees of egalitarian direct participation and decision-making than, for example, political parties. Finally, political society as an intermediary realm between civil society and the polity is not only, ideally, 'receptive' to messages from civil society but, as the institutional level in which the mechanisms of state are anchored, open to the functional logic of power. As a result, democracy, so Cohen and Arato argue, can go much further on the level of civil society than on the level of political society, 'because here the co-ordinating mechanism of communicative interaction has fundamental priority' (Cohen/Arato 1992: 417).

This assessment is grounded in Cohen's and Arato's belief that democratization must not result in the dedifferentiation of society. One result of the process of modernization has been the institutionalization of a differentiated lifeworld that contains a high level of social plurality and allows for the freeing of the rationality potential of communicative interaction. The other consequence has been the formation of the political and economic subsystems which, co-ordinated through the media of power and money, and thus relieved from the time- and resource-consuming need of responding to normative validity claims, has resulted in high levels of efficient societal steering and productivity. Just as the polity and the economy must be contained in their attempts to 'colonize' the lifeworld, so democratization must find its limits in the acceptance of this societal differentiation. In developing this idea of the self-limitation of democratization, Cohen and Arato stay firmly within Habermas's theory. Habermas, too, has been putting forward the argument that 'the goal is no longer to supersede an economic system having a capitalist life of its own and a system of domination having a bureaucratic life of its own but to erect a democratic dam against the colonizing encroachment of systemic imperatives on areas of the lifeworld' (Habermas 1993: 444). The concept of 'civil society' thus implies a two-fold limitation. Politics and the state are limited by the pressures arising out of the 'public sphere'; and 'the public' in civil society limits itself in that it does not aim to gain direct power within the state or over the economy (Habermas 1992b: 447–50).

The merit of Cohen's and Arato's contribution lies in their clear analysis of the complex interdependencies of lifeworld, civil society and political society from the perspective of Habermas's discourse ethics. They demonstrate how the communicative interactions of 'autonomous' individuals in civil society on the basis of a modern lifeworld that allows for post-traditional

75

and post-conventional reflexivity are connected with the strategic–instrumental interactions in political society on the basis of political rights of participation. They show how these interconnections constitute the public sphere in which popular will-formation takes place: civil society and 'formal' democracy presuppose each other. The deliberative and proceduralist model of democracy that is embedded in these arguments does not depend, as Benhabib rightly points out, on the fiction of a general deliberative assembly. The reason is :

> that the procedural specifications of this model privilege a *plurality of modes of association* in which all affected can have the right to articulate their point of view. These can range from political parties, to citizens' initiatives, to social movements, to voluntary associations, to consciousness-raising groups, and the like. It is through the interlocking net of these multiple forms of associations, networks and organizations that an anonymous 'public conversation' results. It is central to the model of deliberative democracy that it privileges such a public sphere of mutually interlocking and overlapping networks and associations of deliberation, contestation and argumentation. The fiction of a general deliberative assembly in which the united people expressed their will belongs to the early history of democratic theory; today our guiding model has to be that of a medium of loosely associated, multiple foci of opinion-formation and dissemination which impact each other in free and spontaneous processes of communication. (Benhabib 1994: 35)

As Habermas argues, from the point of view of discourse ethics the success of deliberative politics does not depend on a collectively acting citizenry. Such an assumption was, as we have seen, central to the classical republican tradition. For Habermas, however, the success of deliberative politics depends on the institutionalization of the corresponding procedures and conditions of communication. In line with this argument, Habermas analyses popular sovereignty as retreating into democratic procedures and the legal implementation of their demanding communicative presuppositions (Habermas 1994: 10). According to Habermas, such a 'proceduralized popular sovereignty and a political system tied in to peripheral networks of the political public sphere go hand-in-hand with the image of a *decentred society*' (Habermas 1994: 7; Habermas 1992b: 361–5).

To repeat, it is through the interactions between legally institutionalized will-formation (in political society) and culturally mobilized publics (in civil society), that communicative power is generated. But to what use can this power be put? Habermas himself argues that '[t]he public opinion that is worked up via democratic procedures into communicative power cannot "rule" itself, but can only point the use of administrative power in specific directions' (Habermas 1994: 9). Actors in civil society are (beholden) to exercise 'influence', but not 'political power'; they 'deliberate' while others 'decide'. This distinction between 'influence' and 'rule' is yet another reflection of the theoretical endeavour to define the boundary between 'political' and 'civil' society, or, to put it differently, to reassert the conceptualization of modern society as a differentiated system. As we have noticed before, one major manifestation of this social theory was the distinction between, on the one hand, a theory of social integration, that emphasizes the consciousness of the actors involved and focuses on values, norms and processes of reaching understanding, and, on the other hand, a theory of system integration, in which the anonymous media of administrative power and money are seen to achieve integration beyond the minds of actors (Habermas 1987). This theory conceives of 'economy' and 'administration' as self-regulated systems that tend to cut themselves off from their environments and obey only their internal imperatives of money and power, while, at the same time, threatening to 'colonize' the lifeworld. It is via the communicative structures of the public sphere, which are said to comprise 'a far-flung network of sensors that in the first place react to the pressure of society-wide problematics and stimulate influential opinions' (Habermas 1994: 9), that resistance to this colonization is to be fostered, without, apparently, attempting to destroy the colonizers themselves. Yet, what is missing in this theory is a detailed argument as to how 'communicative power' can form or determine 'administrative power' as well as control the medium 'money' and contain the colonizing threat of either subsystem.

As far as Cohen and Arato are concerned, their analysis falls short of a comprehensive theory of democracy for mainly two reasons. First, they do not advance a theory of the state at all. This omission means that the 'intermediary' structure of political society cannot be fully analysed – its linkage with civil society is discussed, but not that with 'the state' (or administrative subsystem). This omission also deprives the authors of the possibility to discuss whether the state/political system can still adequately be conceptualized as the mechanism of societal steering. But even if the authors did not consider this to be an important issue, there is one aspect of the state any theory of civil society should address as a matter of theoretical (and empirical) urgency. The state is a coercive apparatus, an 'actor' with, potentially lethal, force at its disposal. How does civil society prevent the state from using this power to smash its independence? How does civil society 'coerce' the state to uphold the law and a system of legality as its *conditio sine qua non*? Unless this question is addressed one must assume that this theory of civil society presupposes a kind of state that is (already?) 'liberal', that is, willing to respect an autonomous sphere of social life.

Second, in their theory of deliberative politics Cohen, Arato and Habermas have excluded the 'economy' from the realm of 'civil society'. After all, civil society has been conceptualized as a sphere of (potential) social autonomy in the face of both the modern state *and* the capitalist economy (Cohen/Arato 1992: 30; Habermas 1992b: 443). This conceptualization allows them to reject the neo-liberal or neo-conservative equation of civil society with economic society in its manifestation of a capitalist market economy, and both with the 'private' sphere as the sphere of individual freedom. However, not to include 'the system of needs' in 'civil society' raises a number of critical questions. Above all, this exclusion requires us to analyse in which ways the 'economy', and not just the state, may impose itself upon civil society and what limits must be put on the 'actions' of capitalism. However, no such analysis has yet been offered from within this theoretical perspective. If we were to assume that some form of 'economic democracy' constituted such a controlling mechanism, then we would also have to accept some societal dedifferentiation as the economy comes under closer control from actors in either political or civil society (if not state actors).

We may take this consideration of the importance of the 'economy' for a theory of 'civil society' one step further and open up our discussion to the current 'civil society' discourse more generally. We have seen above that John Keane had been criticizing Marx for developing a critical theory of civil society only with regard to the system of production, neglecting, to repeat, 'other forms of civil life, including households, voluntary associations, professions, communications media and disciplinary institutions such as schools, prisons and hospitals' (Keane 1988b: 58). This kind of argument invites us to conceptualize the capitalist economy as part of civil society, while at the same time reducing it 'to one of many spheres in the plural and heterogeneous complexity of modern society' (Wood 1990: 63). In order to counterbalance the (alleged) economic reductionism of Marx, it is suggested that there is no basis for distinguishing between these various institutions and the institutions of capitalism on the grounds of size and scope or social power and historical efficacy:

> the danger [of this position] lies in the fact that the totalizing logic and the coercive power of capitalism become invisible, when the whole social system of capitalism is reduced to one set of institutions and relations among many others, on a par with households or voluntary associations. Such a reduction is, indeed, the principle distinctive feature [of the discourse] of 'civil society' in its new incarnation. Its effect is to conceptualize away the problem of capitalism, by disaggregating society into fragments, with no over-arching power structure, no totalizing unity, no systemic coercions – in other words, no capitalist system, with its expansionary drive and its capacity to penetrate every aspect of social life. (Wood 1990: 65)

Even if one is reluctant to theorize capitalism as a totalizing system, it would appear reasonable to make at least two assumptions. First, if we include the economy in civil society, then we have to pay systematic attention to the oppressive forces operating within it. A theory of civil society that does not do so, is seriously deficient. Second, there can be no doubt that hospitals, for example, and other institutions within the healthcare system, operate within a capitalist environment and are 'ultimately' affected by it. But, as Wood (1990: 65) points out, an analogous proposition about the effects of hospitals on capitalism cannot possibly be conceived. And the same applies to the other institutions of civil society. What lies behind this kind of conceptualization of civil society are the old (fictional) assumptions of pluralist political analysis: that all social 'interests' have an equal capacity to organize and that the competition of organized interests tends towards a power equilibrium in that no interest is strong enough permanently to dominate the other interests or all issue areas at the same time. Again, even if this criticism is not accepted, without a theory of social power civil society theorists will not be in a position to analyse the conflicts and tensions within civil society.

To repeat, a conceptualization of civil society that includes the capitalist economy, but treats its institutions and social relationships as of no more importance than households, schools or voluntary associations, is seriously deficient. And a conceptualization that keeps 'the economy' outside of the conceptual reach of 'civil society' is also unsatisfactory if it neglects to analyse the ways in which 'the economy' can be as much a despotic force prone to coerce civil society as the state. This ambiguity towards capitalism betrays the essentially 'liberal' tradition of this thinking about 'civil society' (Schecter 1994). In this tradition, 'civil society' has been conceived as the realm of consensus and unforced communication and co-operation; the realm of liberty. The state, on the other hand, has been analysed as the monopolist of (legitimate) violence, needed, though, to enforce order, but because of its control of the means of coercion, also a threat to individual liberty. Yet, 'deliberative politics' parts company with that strand of liberalism that would wish to define 'civil society' as the 'private', prepolitical sphere. With Hegel or de Tocqueville, the theorists of 'deliberative politics', see civil society as a space for public action; in a sense, the 'good' citizen operates in both civil and political society. Analytically, civil society emerges as the social and cultural dimension of democracy in that it allows for the formation of those identities, values and institutions without which a democratic public life could not exist.

We have noticed above that Habermas, Cohen and Arato analyse civil society as that arena in which old identities could be confirmed and new ones developed. In many ways, civil society has come to be seen as that sphere of social life where heterogeneity, difference and diversity can prosper and can be accommodated. We shall take up this argument in the following chapter, but broaden it to the question of what this proliferation of diversity, that finds one expression in 'identity politics', means for 'liberal democracy'.

3

Diversity and
the politics of identity

Citizenship in the democratic nation-state established the principle of non-discrimination insofar as all citizens participate equally in universal rights and entitlements. This idea(l) of universal citizenship is premised on the assertion of the equal moral worth of all persons, who, according to Kant, are deserving of equal respect as rational agents capable of directing their lives through principles. This idea(l) asserts that all people, as citizens, must be treated equally, and laws and rules must be blind to individual and group differences. Hence, it denies claims that differences of, for example, race, ethnicity, class, sex and gender, or religion make a difference to people's rights, duties and opportunities: as 'human beings', we are all equal. After all, this assumption of equality underlay the political attack on the *ancien régime* with its system of status and group differences before the French Revolution: 'We have inherited from the Enlightenment an ideal of universal citizenship which, however badly practised, claims to deal with us in our essentially "human" concerns. The vision of democracy that is associated with this ideal claims to treat us as abstract individuals or citizens, regardless of our sex, race or class' (Phillips 1992a: 82; Jones 1990: 810).

Higham (1993) argued in the American case, that, as an egalitarian ideology, universalism manifests itself in three ways. As a civil credo, it promises the protection of everyone's basic rights; as a social vision, it promises to overcome all social barriers external to the self by moving against the privileges of entrenched groups; and as an ideal of nationhood, it promises the integration of a diversity of groups and life-styles as an effect of the logic, and political acceptance, of universal human rights. The notion of human rights, in turn, reinforces the importance attached to the individual in the ideal of universal citizenship since it singles out the individual as bearer of (inalienable) human rights with no regard to her or his social and cultural roots or origin. The notion of 'universal' human rights presupposes a 'particularistic' model of the person:

an active, rational, entrepreneurial person equipped with a certain degree of self-expression, self-help and self-defence: a person who has the opportunity to possess and manage property, to communicate views and pursue happiness along individually chosen lines, to share in government and freely go about everyday activities without interference of officials and prohibitions of the state beyond those strictly necessary for the defence of others. (Berting 1995: 151)

Hence, the discourse of human rights, that is of the utmost importance for liberal democracy, is based, on the one hand, upon a 'particular' conceptualization of the person, and, on the other, is premised on the denigration of 'particularity' by conceptualizing the individual as culturally 'disembedded', as a human being *per se*. Liberal democrats do stress particularity and the value of diversity, but they link diversity to notions of human individuality and choice, and thus ultimately confine it within the narrow limits of the individualist model of human excellence. This leads to a particular logic of democracy, as Copjec argued on the basis of the American case:

> If *all* our citizens can be said to be Americans, this is not because we share any positive characteristics, but rather because we have all been given the right to *shed* these characteristics, to present ourselves as disembodied before the law. I divest myself of positive identity, therefore I am a citizen. (Copjec 1991: 30, quoted in: McLaren 1993: 127)

It is this notion of the abstract, 'disembodied' individual, that is so central to liberal political theory, that has become seriously questioned in recent years. In this chapter, I shall focus my attention on such a critique which has come from feminist political theory and from concerns about questions of multiculturalism.

Yet, before embarking on this discussion, it is well worth noticing that in the republican tradition, too, we encounter the idea of the 'disembodied' citizen. This can be shown in the neo-republicanism of Hannah Arendt. Arendt's concept of politics is, as we have seen, closely bound up with the notion of agency. Her admiration for the founders of the American republic was, after all, based on their capacity to create a political community *de novo*, to embark upon a new beginning. For Arendt, politics is to do with the actions of citizens who create a world between them. Since human beings are capable of action, the unexpected can be expected from them, and they are able to perform what is infinitely improbable (Arendt 1958: 178). It is through innovative action and speech that human beings 'show who they are, reveal actively their unique personal identities and thus make their appearance in the human world' (Arendt 1958: 179). Politics is thus an act of performativity through which a 'new story' can be begun by acting human beings, only then to be enacted further, to be augmented and spun out by their posterity (Arendt 1973: 47). Openness, creativity, and incompleteness are the *sine quae non* of Arendt's conceptualization of politics (Honig 1992).

But we do well to remember that this particular notion of politics presupposed that the realm of necessity, the realm of production and reproduction had been left behind in the 'private' sphere of the household. Necessity, for Arendt, meant irresistibility; it meant the foreclosing of creativity and new beginning, and was thus contrary to everything politics stood for. In this perspective, the body became the most pronounced instance of complete closure:

> The most powerful necessity of which we are aware in self-introspection is the life process which permeates our bodies and keeps them in a constant state of a change whose movements are automatic, independent of our own activities, and irresistible – i.e., of an overwhelming urgency. The less we are doing ourselves, the less active we are, the more forcefully will this biological process assert itself, impose inherent necessity upon us, and overawe us with the fateful automatism of sheer happening that underlies all human history. (Arendt 1973: 59)

Action is the escape from the body and the realm of necessity. Indeed, since the body is 'irresistible', it has to be kept outside the realm of politics, together, as we saw, with 'the social'. To that extent, the person as citizen is 'disembodied'.

The 'disembodied' citizen is thus an imagery that is present in both liberalism and Arendt's neo-republicanism. And we also find a downgrading of the importance of collective identities in her writings. That 'not one man, but men, inhabit the earth', and that this plurality of human beings makes the creation of a world which they can share with each other imperative, is the fundamental human condition that politics must address (Arendt 1958: 234). Any attempt to overcome that plurality must result in 'the exchange of the real world for an imaginary one where these others would simply not exist' (Arendt 1958: 234). Plurality is thus set apart from any notion of homogeneity and is firmly linked to the notion of the enactment of singular identities in performative acts in the public sphere. In Honig's (1992: 227) interpretation of Arendt's theory this argument translates into the assertion that 'a political community that constitutes itself on the basis of a prior, shared, and stable identity threatens to close the spaces of politics, to homogenize or repress the plurality and multiplicity that political action postulates'. Honig takes this argument one step further by reminding us that Arendt considered her own identity as a 'private' matter. In her exchange with Gershom Scholem about her controversial book on the Nazi criminal Eichmann, she refused to accept that her own 'Jewishness' was politically relevant. On the contrary, she considered her Jewishness as only one of the indisputable data of her life. For Arendt this meant, first, that her

Jewishness was not wholly constitutive of her identity, that her (and anybody else's) identity was necessarily multivocal, and, second, that because it was a 'fact', something given and not made, it was not actionable, it was 'irresistible' and as such 'private' (Honig 1992: 228–31). In that sense, both collective and private identities have to be left behind, once we enter the public sphere of action and speech.

In liberalism as well as in Arendt's republicanism, then, we encounter the citizen as an 'abstract' individual who is both 'disembodied' and culturally 'disembedded'. As already pointed out, this premise has been challenged in recent years by feminism and feminist political theory and by the debate surrounding the issue of multiculturalism. To both of these debates we shall now turn.

Feminism and universal citizenship

The discussion of different concepts of citizenship and civil society in the previous chapter allows us to place a core issue of feminist political theory within an already familiar context: the issue of the divide between the 'public' and the 'private'.

We have seen that both the republican and the liberal theory have a notion of the 'public' and the 'private'. For Aristotle, there was one division between the public world of the polis (*societas civilis sive politica*) and the private world of the household (*societas domestica*). In the exposed political sphere, citizens engage with each other as equals in the course of self-rule. The domestic sphere of economic production and social reproduction is hidden, as it were, from the public gaze, though political rule of the (male) citizens is premised on their patriarchal domination over the members of their household. It is the sphere of particularity, of particular interests and concerns which men have to transcend when they enter as citizens the public realm of the polis as the sphere of universality. As we have just been discussing, this transcendence of particularity remained a central concern in Arendt's neo-republicanism.

In the contract theories from the seventeenth century onwards, the boundary between the 'public' and the 'private' was drawn in a different way. Civil society, as we have seen, was the social and political world created through contract; it was the common world of the 'public' sphere that lay beyond the conjugal and patriarchal familial sphere. But this 'public' sphere became in turn reconceptualized. Social and economic changes resulted in the institutional differentiation of economic production and social reproduction. In the words of Hannah Arendt, the 'social' emerged 'from the shadowy interior of the household into the light of the public sphere' (Arendt 1958: 38). The rapid growth of agrarian and commercial capitalism and the gradual formation of a market economy in the seventeenth and eighteenth century provided the context for contractarian theories. They opened up an intellectual space for redrawing the public–private divide. While the conjugal and familial domestic sphere remained removed from the public gaze, the realm of 'civil society' became now divided into the public sphere of 'government'/'state' and the private sphere of the 'social'/'economical'. As Pateman (1989: 135) points out, a conceptual shift occurred that resulted in 'the double separation of domestic life from civil society and the separation of the private from public within civil society itself'. With 'civil' life becoming private in opposition to the 'public' state, and civil society as the sphere of voluntary contractual relations being conceptualized in abstraction from ascriptive domestic life, 'the latter remains "forgotten" in theoretical discussion' (Pateman 1989: 122).

Kymlicka (1990: chap. 7) is right when he argues that we must discern between two types of public–private distinctions in liberalism. Classical liberalism 'glorified' society (Sheldon Wolin), or, as Nancy Rosenblum suggests, for classical liberals:

> private life means life in civil society, not some presocial state of nature or anti-social condition of isolation and detachment ... Far from inviting apathy, private liberty is supposed to encourage public discussion and the formation of groups that give individuals access to wider social context and to government. (Rosenblum 1987: 61)

This ethos still pervades de Tocqueville's reflections in *Democracy in America*. It pits the 'social'/'society' as the 'private' against the 'political'/'state' as the 'public'. The second distinction set the 'personal'/'intimate' apart from the 'public' that now included both the state and civil society. This distinction arose out of the recognition that the 'individual', or, 'individuality', could be threatened not only by political coercion, but also by the seemingly omnipresent pressure of social expectations. It was best expressed in the 'Romantic' invocation of the heroic individual and the notions of self-development, self-expression and artistic creation. 'Modern privacy', as Arendt (1958: 38) argued, 'in its most relevant function, to shelter the intimate, was discovered as the opposite not of the political sphere but of the social'. Privacy became viewed in terms of a retreat from all roles of civil society, thus almost completely reversing the original liberal position. Yet, in the course of intellectual transmutations, which are beyond our current concerns, liberalism incorporated both perspectives in such a way that by now it has become concerned:

> not only to protect the private sphere of social life, but also to carve out a realm *within the private sphere* where individuals can have *privacy*. Private life, for liberals, now means both active involvement in the institutions of civil society, as classical liberalism emphasized, and personal retreat from that ordered social life, as Romantics emphasized. (Kymlicka 1990: 258)

But a right to privacy does not mean the realm to beyond moral scrutiny

What we therefore find in liberal theory is a marginalization of domestic life as paradigmatically private and outside political purview, and a concern with drawing a boundary within 'civil society' between the social and the political, the economy and politics, or freedom and coercion as the respective spheres of the 'private' and the 'public'.

Since the 1960s, feminists and feminist political theorists have claimed that 'the personal is political' and questioned the conventional boundaries drawn between the 'public' and the 'private'. They claimed that 'domestic' life had to be acknowledged as being deeply political. There are at least two distinct dimensions to this claim (Phillips 1991: chap. 4). First, it is argued that the sexual division of housework and of tasks, duties and responsibilities in the family affect the 'political' by restricting women in their participation in public life. For example, while there has been an increase in the proportion of women working in paid employment in the last few decades, women have also retained primary responsibility for raising children, providing care for relatives and organizing the household. This double burden translates into pressures of time that 'will keep most women out of any processes of decision-making on offer' (Phillips 1991: 97). Furthermore, as we have noticed in the previous chapter, there is a sustained argument to be found in liberal political theory that the family is important for instilling civic virtue in its members, a point strongly endorsed in most contemporary analyses of political socialization. Yet, with the unequal distribution of power and options in the family, 'the experience of domestic and familial subservience [arguably] undermines women's self-confidence', and hence their perception of the importance and relevance of their participation in public life (Phillips 1991: 98). This argument, that a more fully realized democracy in the state is premised on equality in 'domestic' life, has been complemented by another perspective on the 'public/private' divide. Here it is argued that the sexual division of housework, domestic violence against women or sexual assault on women and children, in short, 'women's impotence and subordination, their submission and dependence' crucially matter in themselves: the personal can be 'as devastatingly destructive of our human development as anything that governments do' (Phillips 1991: 102). To envelop areas such as sexuality and domestic life in the discourse of privacy is seen as a mechanism whereby women's oppression is constituted, maintained, and, at the same time, rendered apolitical (Frazer/Lacey 1993: 73).

Yet by opening up these areas as 'political', rather than merely 'private', matters, feminists do not offer any general prescriptions about remedies, for example, in terms of state regulation and intervention in the 'private' sphere. Feminists do advocate the provision of resources by the state as of importance to the position of women in society (including the domestic arena); but they are also aware of the state's control over women's reproductive work and life through its policies. As pointed out in the previous chapter, the communalization of welfare provisions, and more generally, the idea of, and political support for, a self-governing civil society that would deal with these 'private' matters as truly public and political concerns has been widely advocated from within the women's movement.

It is, of course, important to remind ourselves that there is considerable debate within feminism about the 'primary' location of women's oppression. 'Liberal' feminism emphasizes the cultural patriarchal traditions that perpetuate the notion of an 'essential' difference between men and women and thus socialize women into a limited range of roles and assumptions. 'Socialist' feminists focus their attention on capitalist relations of production and, for example, their manifestation in gender-segregated labour markets, perceiving women's exploitation in the economic and sexual division of labour as beneficial for capitalism. Against this tendency towards privileging the structure and dynamics of productive relations in capitalism, 'radical' feminists would emphasize relations of reproduction, questions of sexuality, or male violence. While it is evidently impossible to neglect any of these issues, it is still valid to ask about their relative importance, as political strategies to overcome oppression are based on the respective answer. Privileging the sphere of work over the sphere of the family; the realm of production over the realm of reproduction; economic structures over culture and cultural traditions; or patriarchy over capitalism – these analytical assessments inevitably have repercussions for political action. These debates remain unresolved. In recent years, however, they have become superimposed by another debate. Notwithstanding the sphere or structure of social relation in which women are oppressed or disadvantaged, is it not imperative to accept the diversity of women's interests over time and across boundaries such as race, ethnicity, class, sexual orientation, age or physical abilities? To paraphrase Arendt, not woman, but women inhabit the earth, and their respective experience of oppression and disadvantage is closely bound up with their particular positioning within other relations, such as race or class. There is no such thing as the 'essential' woman whose experience could then be universalized into the notion of 'womanhood'. If this argument is accepted, then this position, too, has clear political consequences as it impacts on questions of political aims, strategy and alliances.

One important contribution of feminism to political theory has thus been the questioning of allegedly fixed boundaries between what are public and what are private concerns. In following through this argument, feminists have demonstrated convincingly that women have been incorporated into the polity in ways quite different from men. Not only have they been given citizenship status later than men, as shown in the first chapter, but they have also not achieved formal political equality because the gender division of labour in the domestic sphere and the labour market and its cultural rep-

86

resentation prevent women from participating in public life on an equal footing with men.

The dominant way of dealing with gender inequality in liberal polities has been to pass anti-discrimination legislation. To combat the arbitrary exclusion of women from the pursuit of those goals and things society defines as valuable, equal opportunity laws and policies have been promulgated to ensure that women have equal access to education, employment, political office etc. These sex equality laws and policies are premised on the conviction that, in a liberal society, sex, gender, race, religion etc. must not be allowed to enter into the awarding of social, economic or political benefits. They thus remain firmly within a liberal framework in that they accept the idea(l) of universal citizenship. Undoubtedly, these policies have improved the position of women in many areas of social life. Yet it has been argued by feminists that equal opportunity policies have given women access to a social world that has already been gendered through male supremacy. Indeed, access to this social world only allows women to be 'more like men'. Within a liberal framework, the right to be equal and to be treated equally has typically been perceived to mean the extension of the 'Rights of Men and Citizens' to women. To give women rights equal to those granted to men means that the masculine is conceptualized as the 'same' relative to which the feminine is the 'different' which is to be erased through 'equal' treatment (Bock/James (eds) 1992).

If this is the case 'against equality', should the right to be equal be replaced by the right to be different? Instead of aiming for a gender-blind society, should then the goal be to create a world in which special consideration is given to distinctive characteristics and activities of women; a world in which women are not subject to male-defined institutions and values which pretend to be universally valid? Furthermore, if it is true that there is no 'essential' woman, then there arises the necessity for creating a space in which women can form their own subjectivity and can develop a language in which they express and symbolize their experience, their own unity and diversity as well as sexual difference. These considerations have led to the demand that, instead of leaving behind their particular affiliations and experiences when they act as citizens, women should bring their unique perspectives, interests and experience into the public arena. In a particularly influential contribution to this debate, Iris Marion Young (1990: 164) argued that in a society where some groups are privileged while others are oppressed, 'insisting that equality and liberation entail ignoring differences has oppressive consequences'. Arguing against a politics of assimilation, she advocates a politics of difference that centres on the self-organization of oppressed groups, their assertion of a distinctive identity and their right to group representation in the political system as the best strategy for achieving power and participation in dominant institutions.

According to Young's definition, a social group is characterized by a unique 'culture'. Members of such a group share a similar way of life, and this shared experience translates into a specific affinity with one another. For Young (1990: 172), '[m]embership in a social group is a function not of satisfying some objective criteria, but of a subjective affirmation of affinity with that group, the affirmation of that affinity by other members of the group, and the attribution of membership in that group by persons identifying with other groups'. As a result, membership in these groups defines one's very identity; indeed, 'groups ... constitute individuals' (Young 1990: 45, 260). With its emphasis upon group 'culture', shared 'ways of life', social and personal 'affinity', and 'identity', Young's social groups are, in effect, 'status groups' (Young 1990: 57). Yet, very sensibly, Young does not propose that all these groups should be given rights to group representation. This right adheres only to oppressed groups. For the US–American case, Young (1989: 261) lists the following oppressed groups: '[W]omen, blacks, Native Americans, Chicanos, Puerto Ricans and other Spanish-speaking Americans, Asian Americans, gay men, lesbians, working-class people, poor people, old people, and mentally and physically disabled people'. This is not a definitive list. Young herself added 'Arabs' to this list, but dropped 'poor people' in her book (1990). One 'group' would, however, appear to be excluded from the right of group representation: white, male, heterosexual, middle-aged, able-bodied, non-Jewish middle- and upper-class professionals in employment or self-employed.

What all the other groups share is the experience of oppression. This oppression may manifest itself in a number of ways:

> (1) the benefits of their work or energy go to others without those others reciprocally benefiting them (exploitation); (2) they are excluded from participation in major social activities, which in our society means primarily a workplace (marginalization); (3) they live and work under the authority of others, and have little work autonomy and authority over others themselves (powerlessness); (4) as a group they are stereotyped at the same time that their experience and situation is invisible in the society in general, and they have little opportunity and little audience for the expression of their experience and perspective on social events (cultural imperialism); (5) group members suffer random violence and harassment motivated by group hatred or fear. (Young 1989: 261)

To suffer any one of these forms of oppression qualifies to be considered an 'oppressed' group with the right to group representation. Exploitation and marginalization are the forms of oppression most explicitly linked to the economy. Unemployment, casualization of labour or segregated labour markets are manifestations of such economic oppression. Potentially, then, all wage workers, including the white professionals, would experience it. Hence, on the basis of this list of oppressive forces operating in society, almost everyone could be part of an 'oppressed' group and thus entitled to group representation. Young (1990: 42) asserts that 'no single form of oppression can be assigned causal or moral primacy'; yet in her book she systematically marginalizes the importance of capitalism as an oppressive force, thus downgrading the importance of class collectives in any schema of group representation. In the end, it is those groups which suffer from racism, sexism, homophobia, ageism and ableism that are considered to merit the right of group representation.

According to Young (1989: 261–2; 1990: 184ff.), group representation implies institutional mechanisms and public resources supporting three activities. The first activity is the self-organization of group members so that (1) they acquire the power of asserting a positive meaning for their own identity. As a result of this process of reflective critical understanding of their collective experience and interests, difference comes to mean 'not otherness, exclusive opposition, but specificity, variation, heterogeneity' (Young 1990: 171). The second activity is the voicing of policy positions on those matters (2) that affect them and the generating of their own policy proposals which decision-makers will have to take into consideration. Finally, the last activity is the exercise of veto power regarding specific policies that affect a group (3) directly. According to Young, it is only through such formal mechanisms for representing group difference that political equality can be meaningful.

There are a number of problems with this approach. First, it is unclear which groups precisely are deserving of special representation. We have already noticed that the qualifier 'oppressed' left a very large number of groups indeed which could claim special status. Young is aware that this qualifier still results in an unwieldy agglomeration of groups and thus adds a second rider: groups entitled to the right of group representation must be oppressed or disadvantaged, but they must also 'describe the major identities and major status relationships constituting society or particular institutions' (Young 1990: 266). Would these 'major' identities and status relationships actually include, for example, 'disability'? Would it include 'religion'? In her discussion of oppression through marginalization, Young (1990: 53) mentions single mothers and 'people who are not very old but yet laid off from their jobs and cannot find new work' as well as 'other people involuntarily unemployed'. Who decides whether these people should be entitled to group representation? Young does not say. Second, Young's emphasis upon 'identities' raises serious questions. It may be the case that ethnic groups (communities) approximate the ideal of groups centred on strong, comprehensive identities and distinct ways of life that translate into feelings of affinity and belonging. And I shall return to this question in the following section. But can it really be said that the elderly or the disabled are such groups? And what about women? If we accept the argument that there is no 'essential' woman's experience because any woman's identity is articulated with race, ethnicity, class, sexual orientation etc., then we have to reject Young's rather essentialist notion of group, based, as it is, on the idea of comprehensive identities (Mouffe 1992b: 380). The key concern would then be to conceptualize identities as not already constructed, but as always being open to change and alteration; we would be talking about the construction of (temporary) subjectivities which are permanently articulated with a multiplicity of subject positions.

Young attempts to circumvent this whole problem by suggesting that within groups there should be separate caucuses, so that, for example, there would be a black caucus or a lesbian caucus or a disabled caucus within the women's group. But this then creates the problem of group boundaries: what is the difference between the black caucus within the 'women's' group and the women's caucus in the 'black' group? When do women speak as women, and when do they speak as lesbians, workers, or blacks? Furthermore, if we accept the argument that there is no 'essential' female identity, what could it possibly mean to speak of the 'representation' of women? May women when they speak as women justifiably claim to speak for women? As Phillips (1991: 90) asserts: 'The representation of women *as women* potentially founders on both the difficulties of defining the shared interests of women and the difficulties of establishing mechanisms through which these interests can be voiced'. Multiple, fractured, and shifting identities result in groups whose boundaries and notion of group interests are constantly contested from 'within' and 'without'. How could such groups possibly exercise the power of a legitimate veto? And even if we granted such a power, which are the policies that affect one group only? How would we establish which policy is a concern for all and which a concern for only some? None of these questions is addressed by Young.

Mouffe (1992b: 380) claims that Young's model of group representation as the main plank of her politics of difference is not very different from the interest-group pluralism she criticizes: '[T]here are groups with their interests and identities already given, and politics is not about the construction of new identities, but about finding ways to satisfy the demands of the various parts in a way acceptable to all.' One should add, however, that by providing for institutionalized group representation, Young goes firmly beyond traditional pluralism. One of the main dangers of her approach would seem to be that such mechanisms for group representation 'freeze' the differences between groups into particular forms. Once such a system is in place, dramatizing differences that set one group apart from the other and presenting them as 'essential' and not open to change are likely to be attractive strategies for groups concerned with maintaining their special status. The institutionalization of group representation is thus likely to lead to the ossification of 'difference'. One result could then be an intensification of group conflicts, or, alternatively, the separation of groups from each other.

In view of this dilemma, I find, yet again, Anne Phillips's arguments compelling:

> No democracy can claim to be equal while it pretends away what are major and continuing divides; yet democracy is lessened if it treats us *only* in our identities as women or men ... [W]e do want to 'leave our selves behind' when we engage in democratic politics: not in the sense of denying everything that makes us the people we are, but in the sense of seeing ourselves as constituted by an often contradictory complex of experiences and qualities, and then of seeing the gap between ourselves and others as in many ways a product of change. (Phillips 1991: 8–9, 58–9)

These engagements help us gain a critical distance from the relations within which we live; and through them, we discover, and construct, commonalities and create a world which we will share between us (Arendt). To that extent, they do indeed allow us to transcend (some manifestations of) 'particularity' and to move towards (some form of) 'universalism'.

This argument takes us back to Cohen's and Arato's analysis of civil society. They see the women's movement rooted in civil society and highlight its 'dualistic' politics. On the one hand, its politics of identity is oriented towards redefining cultural norms, individual and collective identities, appropriate social roles and modes of interpretation. This is an essentially 'defensive' politics concerned with 'preserving and *developing* the communicative infrastructure of the lifeworld' out of which new identities can be created (Cohen/Arato 1992: 531). This 'defensive' politics is complemented, on the other hand, by an 'offensive' politics aimed at influencing civil as well as political society in order to achieve changes of the universe of political discourse in a 'politics of reform' to accommodate new needs-interpretations, new identities and new norms (Cohen/Arato 1992: 548–63). It is when moving from the 'politics of identity' in civil society to the 'politics of reform' in political society that the particularism of the concrete 'we' (for example, as 'women') has to be complemented by the universal concerns of 'us' (as a community of citizens), along the lines suggested by Benhabib (1992) and Phillips.

Multiculturalism and group representation

In the previous section we have discussed how the idea(l) of universal citizenship has come under attack from feminist political theory. This idea(l) entails the notion that the respect for the equal dignity of each person requires that we are blind to the ways in which they, as citizens, differ in their individuality. Feminism, however, questions the assumption of this idea(l) that justice coincides with treating people equally by abstracting from their concrete differences. On the contrary, it is claimed that these dis-

91

tinctions have to be taken into consideration and, in order to overcome discrimination, have to be made the basis of differential treatment. In this confrontation, a 'politics of universalism' is pitted against a 'politics of difference'. The 'politics of universalism' aims at the equalization of rights, entitlements and immunities for everyone, or, at least, for every citizen. The 'politics of difference', on the other hand, aims at recognizing the unique identity of concrete individuals or groups, their distinctness from everyone else. Charles Taylor has succinctly contrasted these two types of politics:

> These two modes of politics ... both based on the notion of equal respect, come into conflict. For one, the principle of equal respect requires that we treat people in a difference-blind fashion. The fundamental intuition that humans command this respect focuses on what is the same in all. For the other, we have to recognize and even foster particularity. The reproach the first makes to the second is just that it violates the principle of nondiscrimination. The reproach the second makes to the first is that it negates identity by forcing people into a homogeneous mold that is untrue to them ... The claim is that the supposedly neutral set of difference-blind principles of the politics of equal dignity is in fact a reflection of one hegemonic culture. (Taylor 1992b: 43)

Taylor thus argues that by ignoring or glossing over distinctness, the 'politics of universalism' assimilates unique identities to a dominant or majority identity: 'And this assimilation is the cardinal sin against the ideal of authenticity' (Taylor 1992b: 38). What does this ideal of authenticity entail?

Taylor traces the ideal of authenticity back to the late eighteenth century and the German philosopher Johann Gottfried von Herder who put forward the idea that each of us has her or his own way of being 'human'; her or his own 'measure'. This 'powerful moral ideal that has come down to us' proposes that there is a certain way of being human that is my way:

> I am called upon to live my life in this way, and not in imitation of anyone else's. But this gives a new importance to being true to myself. If I am not, I miss the point of my life, I miss what being human is for me ... Being true to myself means being true to my own originality, and that is something only I can articulate and discover. In articulating it, I am also defining myself. (Taylor 1992a: 28–9)

In line with this ideal of authenticity, defining myself means to determine in what my originality consists; I am beholden to ask in which ways I am different from others. But manifestly, not any difference will do; it must be a 'significant' difference. If I live in a society in which hair colour does not have any 'significance' to my rights, entitlements, opportunities or life-chances, then to see my identity firmly related to my hair colour is meaningless. Yet if I live in a society in which skin colour or gender is socially relevant in determining rights and life-chances, then to define myself on the basis of these features can be highly significant. To quote Taylor once more:

> I can define my identity only against the background of things that matter ... Only if I exist in a world in which history, or the demands of nature, or the needs of my fellow human beings, or the duties of citizenship, or the call of God, or something else of this order *matters* crucially, can I define an identity for myself that is not trivial. Authenticity is not the enemy of demands that emanate from beyond the self; it supposes such demands. (Taylor 1992a: 40–1)

The ideal of authenticity thus does not mean that I work my identity out in isolation. On the contrary, I am embedded in a cultural and social context in two ways. First, to arrive at a meaningful identity, I have to place myself within a 'horizon of important questions', questions the answers to which matter in the society of which I am a member. This means, second, that, not only am I putting forward a claim that some feature, some characteristics that adhere to me are the basis for my 'significant' difference, or otherness, but that I have also to redeem this claim discursively: my inwardly derived, personal, original identity does not enjoy recognition by others *a priori*, it has to win this recognition through exchange, it has to be negotiated through dialogue, and there is the very real danger that I may fail to gain this recognition.

These considerations are relevant for our current concern with multiculturalism for at least two reasons. First, one implication is that 'culture' matters for individuals in their endeavour to define their unique identity. And second, the ideal of authenticity may not only be embraced by individuals, but also by peoples: a concern with 'national' identity was, after all, a key aspect of Herder's discussion of cultural uniqueness.

Taylor's argument regarding the importance of cultural embeddedness for individual self-fulfilment and identity can be developed in a number of ways. Kymlicka (1990: chap. 6) suggests that a key idea of liberalism is the self-determination of the individual. For him, individual autonomy means that, first, we must be free to lead our life from the inside, in accordance with our idiosyncratic beliefs about what gives value to life; that is, it must be left to the individual to choose a particular way of life as approximating most closely to what he or she considers the 'good' life. Second, the individual must be free to question those beliefs and reassess whether a chosen social practice or involvement in a social relationship retains its imputed value; that is, I determine in a process of practical reasoning which ends I want to pursue and which values I want to cherish. Yet, this value pluralism, this process of evaluating distinct 'good' ways of life, is supported by a cultural structure. We choose amongst various options that our culture provides, and it is through this cultural mediation that the options are meaningful to us. It is through membership in cultural communities with their shared

93

memories and values and their common institutions and practices that individuals are provided with meaningful ways of life across the full range of human activities:

> Whether or not a course of action has any significance for us depends on whether, and how, our language renders vivid to us the point of that activity. And the way in which language renders vivid these activities is shaped by our history, our 'traditions and conventions'. Understanding these cultural narratives is a precondition of making intelligent judgements about how to lead our lives. (Kymlicka 1995: 83)

Kymlicka suggests, then, that liberalism wants individuals to be free, not to go beyond the language, conventions and history of their community, but to move around within their culture, to distance themselves from particular cultural roles, 'to choose which features of the culture are most worth developing, and which are without value' (Kymlicka 1995: 90–1). It is through this 'moving around' and 'distancing' that the individual gains her or his individuality. In this perspective, cultural communities are instrumental to the formation and the exercise of the autonomy of the individual, and it is for this reason that they deserve to be protected. Yet this theoretical justification of the relevancy of cultural groups is inherently problematic. It may easily lead to a position in which only those cultural groups which meet the liberal paradigm of individual self-determination will find support from autonomy-based liberalism. Many cultural communities, however, claim group rights so that they can defend their cultural integrity and retain their identity which often does not accord individual self-determination any ultimate value at all. In such circumstances, Kymlicka's foundation of cultural rights in the protection of an individual's freedom autonomously to choose her or his ends prepares the ground for interference with the internal structure of communities in the name of the liberal ideal of autonomy (Kukathas 1995: 239–45). Kymlicka's position stays perilously close to the idea that '[i]ndividual autonomy trumps all' (McDonald 1991: 237). 'Individual autonomy' is upheld as a universal human value that transcends particular cultural contexts. But this idea is controversial since 'it is difficult to determine whether the claim is truly universal, namely, part of what it means to be human, or simply is a set of beliefs specific to a particular culture disguised by the rhetoric of universality' (Macklem 1993: 1,340). In the debate between universalists and cultural relativists, who claim that practices and values of a particular culture cannot be judged by relying on universal standards that transcend such cultural specificity, Kymlicka sides with the universalists.

At the same time, however, Kymlicka appears to commit the mistake of many cultural relativists in insisting on a distinct and homogeneous 'cultural structure' within a particular society. Yet, as Kymlicka's own main analytical and political concern, the position of Aboriginal peoples in Canada suggests, we would do well to query this assumption. In the debate over constitutional changes since the early 1980s, a number of the main Aboriginal groups opposed the application of Canada's Charter of Rights of 1982, that had given Canadians a catalogue of justiciable individual rights similar to the American Bill of Rights (but also a series of 'group rights'), to Aboriginal governments. They saw the Charter with its rights protections as an imposition of a foreign, 'white' culture. Some Aboriginal women's groups insisted, however, that the Charter, and in particular its provisions on gender equality, had to be applied to Aboriginal governments lest traditional practices of discrimination against women should be perpetuated. Howse and Knop (1993: 285) are right to ask which of the two is the authentic voice of Aboriginal peoples: 'the voice that says that Charter rights are a form of external domination or the voice that says they are needed to protect a different kind of Otherness?' For them, the example of the Aboriginal peoples demonstrates that there is a 'multiplicity of Othernesses' and that 'difference itself is plural' (Howse/Knop 1993: 285; also Young 1995). Macklem (1993: 1,343) makes the same point when he rejects a totalizing concept of 'culture' that assumes the existence of one single uniform, dominant culture within a particular society and substitutes the idea of intersecting and competing structures of beliefs.

The reality of the heterogeneity of cultural communities and of their internal divisions, however, poses a challenge, not only to autonomy-based liberalism, but also to tolerance-based liberalism. In his contribution to the debate on cultural rights, Kukathas (1995) rejects the idea that cultural minorities as such have any right to self-preservation or perpetuation. He denies the proposition that fundamental moral claims are to be attached to cultural groups and that 'the terms of political association must be established with these particular claims in mind' (Kukathas 1995: 232). This idea is rejected on the basis of the sociological observation that 'groups are not fixed and unchanging entities in the moral and political universe' (Kukathas 1995: 232). Rather, cultural communities have a mutable nature in that group formation is the product of changing environmental influences that may also lead to changes over time in the group composition and thus to shifting group boundaries. These changes, in turn, contribute to the internal heterogeneity which most groups exhibit at any given moment. To grant rights to such groups would freeze boundaries between groups that would otherwise be fluid and constantly changing, and it would also freeze the position of minorities within such minority groups, restricting their opportunity to reshape their cultural community (Kukathas 1995: 230–6). According to Kukathas, this position does not amount to the claim that cultural communities do not matter for individuals and their sense of identity. It does, however, lead to a particular conceptualization of a cultural community. It is seen as an association of individuals with different interests whose perpetuation is premised on its members' acquiescence in the determining impact of its communal practices on their lives. In Kukathas's argument cultural communities deserve recognition because they are the result of an individual exercising her or his fundamental right to associate. But this right of association has as a corollary the right of dissociation, that is, a right to be free to leave a community or association whose communal practices are no longer accepted by the individual. Out of the right of individuals to associate and dissociate freely issues the recognition that no requirement may be imposed on communities to be communities of any particular kind. The wider society has no right to interfere with communal practices: 'If members of a cultural community wish to continue to live by their beliefs, the outside community has no right to intervene to prevent those members acting within their rights' (Kukathas 1995: 238–9). As long as there is freedom of association, and a right to exit, possible injustice within cultural communities, seen from a liberal point of view, has to be accepted. That may mean that in such communities, freedom of worship may not be respected or women may have opportunities closed off to them: 'internal' minorities or dissidents within these cultural communities must either accept these views, attempt to change them in accordance with communal practices or else leave the community (Kukathas 1995: 247–52).

This line of argument does not allow Kukathas to address the question whether, for example, Aboriginal women have a right to fair participation in the political institutions that govern them. For Green (1995) this line of reasoning is deficient for at least two reasons. First, it is wrong to define and analyse cultural communities as if they were voluntary associations: '[T]he minority groups that are most prized as experiments in living are precisely those in which membership is an "organic" relation, where entry is not voluntary, membership is partly ascriptive, and exit, when possible, is costly' (Green 1995: 266–7). It is precisely because, as Kukathas asserts, cultural communities have a formative impact on an individual's identity that to exit from them is not always a viable option:

> It is risky, wrenching, and disorienting to have to tear oneself from one's religion or culture; the fact that it is possible to do so does not suffice to show that those who do not manage to achieve the task have stayed voluntarily, at least not in any sense strong enough to undercut any rights they might otherwise have. (Green 1995: 266)

The second deficiency in Kukathas's position is the reluctance to contemplate that certain social structures may be unjust, and that they cannot become just merely by becoming avoidable through exit. But this recognition is at the centre of the debate regarding the relationship of diverse cultural communities within the larger society and the position of individuals within cultural communities.

Autonomy-based liberalism and tolerance-based liberalism thus encounter difficulties when dealing with cultural heterogeneity, be it the existence of non-liberal communities within liberal society or of dissenting, and even oppressed, sub-groups within cultural 'minorities'. Respect-based liberalism offers yet another version of liberal reflection on multicommunalism. Arguably, the commitment of the liberal to equal respect for persons and to recognition of their dignity does not extend to their beliefs only, but also to their culture which gives those beliefs 'significance' and 'meaning'. Slighting their culture, holding it up for ridicule, denying its value, hurts them, subjects them to contempt and thus offends their dignity (Raz 1994: 72). Bhikhu Parekh has summarized this argument of respect-based liberalism succinctly:

> Since human beings are culturally embedded, respect for them entails respect for their ways of life. One's sense of personal identity is closely bound up with one's language, characteristic modes of thought, customs, collective memories, and so on, in a word with one's culture. To ignore the latter is to denude the individual of what constitutes him or her as a particular kind of person and matters most to him or her, and that is hardly a way of showing respect. (Parekh 1994b: 103)

We owe respect to other cultures, not because they may contribute to individual autonomy, but because we owe respect to our fellow human beings whose creation and sources of meaning those cultures are. And this respect for other cultures extends also to those cultures that do not embrace liberal individualism. Even staying within Kymlicka's argument, one could contend that 'non-liberal' cultures are valuable for liberals. For the liberal individual to make a genuine evaluation of available choices, he or she has to be in a position to move 'outside' her or his culture to compare and assess alternative options. Waldron (1992: 786) gives the example of a traditional culture that 'may define the role of *male elder*, a patriarchal position of tribal power, as a source of authority and the embodiment of tradition'. In order for a young man to decide whether to aspire to this role, he would possibly want to know 'that the politics of patriarchal authority have, in almost all other social contexts, come under fierce challenge, and that people have developed other means of authoritative governance that do not embody male power and fatherhood in the same way' (Waldron 1992: 786–7). This evaluation of available choices thus presupposes the opening-up of cultures to challenge and comparison from the outside. This seems to be Parekh's position as well:

> We need access to other cultures not so much to increase our range of 'options', for cultures are not options, as to appreciate the singularity as well

97

as the strength and limitations of our own. This means that cultural diversity is valuable not so much because it expands our choices of ways of life but because it extends our sympathies, deepens our self-knowledge, and enables us to enrich our way of life by borrowing whatever is attractive in others and can be integrated in ours. (Parekh 1994a: 208)

Such intercultural dialogues are one means through which cultures possibly gain a degree of heterogeneity on the basis of self-reflexivity. Respect-based liberalism is conducive to the kind of 'deliberative politics' that has been adumbrated in the previous chapter. With its minimalist assumptions on unimpeachable rights, 'deliberative politics' is also the most promising avenue for developing a 'theory of justice' for multicommunal societies.

The theoretical positions, which we have discussed in the previous paragraphs, share the view that, for individuals to exercise their freedom and to define their identity, they need either to be embedded in a culture or have access to cultural material that provides a framework for meaningful choices. This link between individual identity, freedom and culture has become problematic in a number of ways. As is only too well known, the majority of European 'nation'-states are political communities comprising more than one cultural community. Most countries today are multicultural states. For Kymlicka (1995: 18) this means that members of such states 'either belong to different nations (a multination state), or have emigrated from different nations (a polyethnic state)'. A multination state is thus composed of more than one historical community which is more or less institutionally complete, occupies a given territory or homeland, and shares a distinct language and culture. Switzerland with its four linguistic and cultural communities, or Belgium with its two, are good examples of multination states. But so is the United Kingdom, where the Scottish, Welsh and English nations coexist within the same state. Or Canada, whose historical development has involved the federation of three distinct national groups, the English, the French, and the Aboriginals – and one could justifiably consider the indigenous peoples themselves as representing distinct nations. And the United States of America, too, is rightly seen as a multination state, composed, as it is, of, for example, Native Hawaiians, Alaskan Inuit, Native Americans, and the 'commonwealth' of Puerto Rico.

In Europe over the last twenty years or so, the ethno-territorial politics of regionalist movements has been one of the main political manifestations of this 'national' diversity. Migration and immigration have more recently added further ethnic and cultural diversity to the already fragmented ethnocultural structure of many European states. Whereas multination states are composed of several 'nations', in a 'polyethnic state' there coexist several ethnic groups as a result of immigration, none of which occupy a 'homeland'. While these distinctions are useful for analytical purposes, it must not be overlooked that, as a matter of fact, most multination states are at the same time polyethnic states as a result of processes of immigration.

In the last few decades we could witness that in ever more countries national and ethnic communities with distinct languages, histories and traditions have demanded the recognition and support for their cultural identity. These demands have led to arguments and clashes between 'minorities' and 'majorities' over such issues as 'language rights, regional autonomy, political representation, education curriculum, land claims, immigration and naturalization policy, even national symbols, such as the choice of national anthem or public holidays' (Kymlicka 1995: 1). At stake in these controversies is the demand by these 'minorities' for group-differentiated rights, powers, status or immunities that go beyond the common rights of citizenship. These claims may encompass demands for territorial autonomy and self-government in certain key matters; for guaranteed representation in the political institutions of the larger society on the basis of quota systems favourable to the group and guaranteed veto powers over legislation and policies that centrally affect the respective minorities; and for group-specific legal exemptions. They are premised upon the belief that only by possessing and exercising these rights, powers and immunities will it be possible for these communities to ensure the full and free development of their culture.

It is central to Kymlicka's argument that 'national' minorities alone can legitimately claim self-government rights. These national minorities already possess a 'societal culture' whose continuance must be ensured for the sake of the freedom and liberty of its members if the community so wishes. Such a societal culture 'provides its members with meaningful ways of life across the full range of human activities, including social, educational, religious, recreational, and economic life, encompassing both public and private spheres' (Kymlicka 1995: 76). As these cultures tend to be territorially concentrated, their protection through self-government rights could possibly take the form of the devolution of power from the centre to smaller political units within a federal or cantonal structure. For example, discussing the Native groupings in Canada, Kymlicka argues that they have, in effect, become 'a third order of government, with a collection of powers that is carved out of both federal and state/provincial jurisdiction' (Kymlicka 1995: 30). It is their increasing control over health, education, family law, policing, criminal justice and resource development that empowers them to protect their societal culture.

While Kymlicka accepts the claim of national minorities to self-government and the protection of their societal culture, similar claims by immigrant communities, or: 'ethnic' groups, are not endorsed (Kymlicka 1995: 95–6). According to Kymlicka, immigrants have uprooted themselves and have thus voluntarily relinquished some of the rights that go along with their original national membership. When they made the free decision to emigrate, they could know that they would settle in a country which was likely to have a different societal culture. In these circumstances, the expectation of the host country that immigrants should integrate into mainstream society is not unjust. It would also be wrong to compare immigrants with colonists such as the English and French nations in Canada or the USA:

> There was a fundamentally different set of expectations accompanying colonization and immigration – the former resulted from a deliberate policy aimed at the systematic re-creation of an entire society in a new land; the latter resulted from individual and familial choices to leave their society and join another existing society. (Kymlicka 1995: 95)

Both arguments would seem to me to be fundamentally flawed. Kymlicka himself accepts the fact that the world order is unjust and that international inequality is a cause behind international migration. What does 'voluntary' migration mean in this context? How do we deal with those immigrants who, for example as 'involuntary' refugees, have settled in foreign countries? Furthermore, the second argument would appear to be blatantly 'imperialist'. It amounts to saying that, if people come as a colonial vanguard that overpowers and dispossesses indigenous peoples with the intention of creating the new country and society in the image of the one left behind, then they are entitled to the re-creation and maintenance of their societal culture. But if they arrive peaceably as immigrants as a result of 'free' individual and familial choices, then they do not have such entitlements.

While they are not entitled to re-create their societal culture, immigrants can rightfully insist on maintaining some of their heritage (Kymlicka 1995: 97). To this end, they may be granted 'polyethnic' rights:

> For example, Jews and Muslims in Britain have sought exemption from Sunday closing and animal slaughtering legislation; Sikh men in Canada have sought exemption from motorcycle helmet laws and from the official dress-codes of police forces, so that they can wear their turban; Orthodox Jews in the United States have sought the right to wear the yarmulka during military service; and Muslim girls in France have sought exemption from school dress-codes so that they can wear the *chador* (Kymlicka 1995: 31).

Such 'polyethnic' rights can be defended by arguing that to treat people justly requires to treat equal cases equally and different cases differently. Equality must not be equated with uniformity. As Parekh (1994b: 103) argues, 'otherwise different individuals are treated *unequally* if subjected to uniform treatment'. If Jews are required by the law to close their shops on Sundays, they are reduced to opening their shops only five days a week. This amounts to unequal treatment because Sunday is a holiday for Christians, but not for Jews; consequently, Christians have one day more to do business. To clarify this argument further, Parekh reports the case of a Turkish woman in Holland whose unemployment benefit was discontinued by the state because she refused a job in which she would have been the only woman in a group of male workers:

> On appeal the Dutch Central Court of Appeal ruled that the discontinuation of benefit was unjust, as the woman's refusal to accept the job under culturally and religiously unacceptable conditions was fully justified. A white woman's appeal in a similar situation would have received a different treatment. The two women are treated differently but equally, the equality consisting in the fact that they are judged *impartially* on the basis of the *same* criterion of what constitutes reasonable or acceptable working conditions for each. (Parekh 1994b: 105)

According to Kymlicka, such 'polyethnic' rights support the demand by ethnic groups for the manifestation and recognition of their identity and the public acceptance of the value of polyethnicity. They are thus conducive to their integration into the dominant society. While the public sphere is affected in some ways by the granting of such rights and their exercise by ethnic groups, they are primarily designed to affirm 'the right of immigrants to maintain their ethnic heritage in the private sphere' (Kymlicka 1995: 78). Yet, there is an unresolved tension in Kymlicka's argument. He has argued that individual freedom and the capacity to form meaningful identities is premised on a strong, comprehensive cultural context. For such a culture to be socially relevant, 'it must be institutionally embodied – in schools, media, economy, government' (Kymlicka 1995: 76). This means, that unless a culture is a 'societal culture', '[it] will be reduced to ever-decreasing marginalization' (Kymlicka 1995: 80). However, as we saw, Kymlicka would not accept that immigrants/ethnic groups have a right to re-creating a societal culture. Inevitably, therefore, with the decline in the vitality of their own culture they will have to assimilate into the dominant 'societal culture' in order to be 'free'. The 'polyethnic' rights which Kymlicka grants ethnic groups would appear not to be strong enough to stall the evaporation of the cultural traditions of these groups.

It is not clear at all why certain self-government rights should not be extended to ethnic groups. If we take the powers granted to Native groupings in Canada as a measure for such self-government rights, why not grant ethnic groups control over health, education or family law? Let us turn once more to Parekh who suggests that cohesive communities which have democratically accountable self-governing institutions and allow their members a right of exit:

> have a vital role in giving their members a sense of rootedness, harnessing their moral energies for common purposes, and sustaining the spirit of cultural plu-

ralism. Rather than seek to dismantle them in the name of abstractly and narrowly defined goals of social cohesion, integration and national unity, the state should acknowledge their cultural and political value and grant them such support as they need and ask for ... Conducting the affairs of a society as complex as ours is too important a task to be left to the state alone. It requires partnership between the two [i.e., the state and society], and encouraging cohesive communities to run their affairs themselves under the overall authority of the state is an important dimension of that partnership. (Parekh 1994b: 107)

Manifestly, contemplating such a 'partnership', as well as the acceptance of group-differentiated rights more generally, raises the question of the very nature, authority and permanence of the multicultural state of which these various cultural communities are part. Our prevailing assumptions of common citizenship, common identity and social and political cohesion will be questioned. The question will also have to be addressed of how these communities can co-ordinate their actions in areas of common concern or common interest, for example, with regard to the environment, the economy or military security. The much more fragmented, decentralized institutional pattern emerging from this diversity would have to allow for, first, democratic communal self-government; second, a public debate on the matters communities have in common; third, protection of legitimate powers to uphold autonomy; and, fourth, the political co-ordination of the communities that keeps them part of one larger community.

I have argued that multiculturalism challenges the liberal idea(l) of non-discrimination by embracing a politics of difference in which the idea of group-differentiated rights is pitted against the liberal emphasis on individual rights. Yet, its challenge goes beyond that to the liberal universalism of individual citizenship rights. In previous chapters, we have spoken of the individual as the bearer of rights, be they civil, political or social. Indeed, in some of the arguments we have encountered, these rights have been grounded in the idea of 'inalienable' human rights. However, while liberalism as a theory may aim to transcend the time- and space-bound nature of individuals, their concrete embeddedness in specific times and localities and treat them as 'plain' human beings, liberal democracy as a specific institutional arrangement and political practice has always been grounded in the concrete temporal and spatial reality of territorially bounded political communities. To put it differently, the idea and reality of liberal democracy has always been linked to the idea and reality of the nation-state.

We have noticed in the introductory chapter how the idea of popular sovereignty has been closely bound up with the idea of national sovereignty. In the context of our current discussion we may now add to that observation by drawing out some of the implications of the revolutionary origins of the idea of the nation-state. In the revolutionary upheavals of the French Revolution, the 'people' replaced the 'princes' as the sovereign subject of history. It was the sovereignty of the people that bestowed legitimacy upon the newly constituted political order after the demolition of the *ancien régime*. The people as a collectivity installed themselves as the bearers of the rights of political rule, couching their demands for political autonomy and self-determination in the rhetoric of the 'nation'. The new state was to be a 'nation'-state which was to derive its power, and exercise it, for (and not simply over) a nation, a people; it was 'to be a nation's state: the state "of" and "for" a particular, distinctive, bounded nation', expressing that nation's will and furthering that nation's interests (Brubaker 1992: 28).

In the imagery of the 'nation', the plurality and antagonisms of 'society' were moulded into a political entity. The nation became the 'unitary' body in which sovereignty resided. Yet, in which ways should the nation be defined and limited? Who or what was to constitute the nation? In the French tradition, the nation was conceived in relation to the institutional and territorial frame of the state, as 'a political–administrative unit, an aggregate of individuals able to participate in a common political life through their use of a common language and their physical propinquity to each other' (Kamenka 1973: 10). The nation was constituted as a unity of individuals who willed to form a voluntary association between themselves and who, as citizens, enjoyed civil equality and equal political citizenship rights as 'of right'. French nationhood is thus state-centred and constituted by political unity. At the same time, the concept of the 'general will' and the notion of *la République une et indivisible* have imparted on this conceptualization of nationhood a strong sense of uniformity and universality that is adverse to all particularisms. As a logical consequence, and in the tradition of the absolutist state, the centralized post-revolutionary Jacobin state embarked on a policy of centralization, assimilation and the eradication of regional and other differences. What we therefore find in the French case is a state-centred and assimilationist understanding of nationhood that is closely linked to the abstract idea of 'universal' citizenship rights as well as to the idea that cultural unity is expressive, though not constitutive, of nationhood: 'Political inclusion has entailed cultural assimilation, for regional cultural minorities and immigrants alike' (Brubaker 1992: 1).

This assimilationist tendency is not unique to the French conceptualization of nation. It can also be found in that tradition that sees a nation, not as a bearer of universal political values, but as a predetermined community bound by blood and heredity. In this tradition, of which Germany is a main representative, the nation is conceptualized as an organic cultural, linguistic or racial community. Ethno-cultural commonalities form the basis for the integration of a collectivity of individuals into a nation. In this conceptualization of nationhood, membership in the nation, defined as a community of descent with common culture and language, is the presupposition of citizenship in the nation's state. As Brubaker (1992: 10) says, ethno-cultural unity is constitutive, political unity expressive, of nationhood. As a result, territorial boundaries are determined by considerations for ethnic homogeneity; citizenship rights are premised upon membership in the ethno-cultural group; the objective of the state is the welfare of the ethno-cultural community; and ethno-cultural conflicts, including those of a religious or linguistic kind, are politically more sensitive and more important than those linked to socio-economic cleavages or gender issues, for example.

Both types of nation-state would thus appear to accommodate the maxime that a nation-state ought to be in every respect homogeneous and that 'minority' groups would have to adjust to the values, cultural traditions and political principles of the nation. But while such an act of integration and assimilation could be rewarded by the granting of citizenship rights in the French political (democratic) model, no such political integration would be the norm in the German ethnic model. Indeed, as far as the ethnic model is concerned, it must be emphasized that it is generally indifferent to the constitutional structure of the state. As the history of the German state shows, this conceptualization of nationhood can accommodate authoritarianism (Bismarck's Reich), fascism (Third Reich) and democracy (Weimar Republic and Federal Republic).

In both models, then, we can detect processes of homogenization within the state aiming at the eradication of internal differences or else the denial of their existence. This creation of 'sameness' within goes hand in hand with the claim to 'uniqueness' *vis-à-vis* other states and therefore with highlighting substantial differences between states. Concerns with homogeneity and commonality within allow for the dramatization of differences without, but provide also a chance for making visible those individuals and groups within who fail to hold given features in common. The nation-state discourse is thus organized around the notion of 'national' authenticity and identity which translates into strategies of inclusion into, and exclusion from, the national community. And very easily, it also translates into political and cultural concerns with keeping the nation 'pure' or 'unpolluted' or with 'cleansing' and 'purifying' it again if it has become polluted.

In the light of the previous remarks, it becomes evident that multiculturalism challenges liberal democracy, not only because it puts demands for group-differentiated rights on the political agenda, but by problematizing the notion of a popular sovereignty embodied in a 'unitary' nation and manifested in the 'unitary' nation-state. It radicalizes the discourse on difference which is always already implied in the conceptualization of the political community as a nation-state.

As we have seen, from within the discourse of multiculturalism the claim is being advanced that individuals are culturally embedded and that these cultural communities should be considered the basic units of society and treated equally, rather than individuals. This claim has led to the resurgence

of the politics of difference. Based on the ideal of authenticity, it demands
the recognition of unique cultures and identities of 'minorities', and thus
establishes the principle of discrimination (Charles Taylor). In most
instances, such a politics is oriented towards the articulation of claims of
authenticity in the form of group-differentiated rights with the demands for
political inclusion in the form of 'universal' individual citizenship rights. At
stake is the claim that both group 'difference' and 'equality', for communities as well as for their members, can be peaceably and justly accommodated
in a democratic polity.

Yet, we should be aware that the politics of difference may also lead to
different political demands. In recent years, the New Right in Europe has
embraced the notion of a politics of difference as the right to otherness. But
they instrumentalize this right in order to stigmatize the mixing of cultures
and to preserve a 'pure' communal identity. In this conceptualization of the
politics of identity and authenticity, group 'difference' goes hand in hand,
not with equality, but separation. It is a politics of exclusion, ranging from
demands for 'foreigners'/'aliens' to be sent 'home' to genocide in the form
of 'ethnic cleansing'. In his analysis of the French New Right, and the
Groupement de Recherche et d'Etudes pour la Civilisation Européenne and
its intellectual leader Alain de Benoist in particular, Taguieff (1993/94) has
described its embrace of the right to difference as 'differentialist' racism. This
racism is not any longer based on biological assumptions about superior
genetic races that translate directly into hierarchical classifications of races
and civilizations and a political and cultural obsession with the loss of rank
and the debasement of superior people. This new racism is premised on the
acceptance of the right to be different and a respect of the differences
between ethnically and culturally heterogeneous collectives. Indeed, Benoist
(1993/94: 180–1) argues that '[r]acism is nothing but the denial of difference', be it in the form of a hateful and brutal xenophobic repelling of the
other or in the form of a liberal, 'humanitarian' assimilation of the other.
Yet the flipside of this position is the claim that these differences have to be
preserved at all cost; that they must be cultivated, developed and defended
against any attempts to abolish them. As a result, this particular version of
the right to difference is organized around a 'mixophobic' core; it is 'haunted
by the threat of the destruction of identities through inter-breeding – physical and cultural cross-breeding' (Taguieff 1993/94: 101). In effect, it
amounts to a politics of cultural apartheid which is informed by an obsession with avoiding contact and a phobia of mixing. As such, this position
remains closely linked to the political logic of the classic discourse on
nationhood.

The political accommodation of multicommunalism in multicultural
states can thus be organized as a strategy that brings together notions of
difference and equality or, alternatively, of difference and discriminatory

separation. Yet, the articulation of politics and culture is not confined to finding institutional mediations for diverse cultural communities with distinct identities. Increasingly, communal identities are becoming ever more open, ever more fluid and ever more complex as a result of the formation of diasporas in European states. We are witnessing the development of diasporic cultures of displacement and transplantation, created by 'displaced' people in their 'voyage' from their place of 'origin' to a 'new' world. These 'travellers' 'bear the traces of particular cultures, traditions, languages, systems of belief, texts and histories which have shaped them. But they are also obliged to come to terms with and make something new of the cultures they inhabit, without simply assimilating to it' (Hall 1993: 362). They cross and transcend cultural boundaries in time and space, and by amalgamating a hotch-potch of experiences develop their 'mongrel selves' (Salman Rushdie). These cultures of hybridity challenge the binary codes on which communal identities tend to rest: pure/impure; white/black; Western/Oriental etc. They break open the exclusionary cultural boundaries between 'us' and 'them' without either advocating assimilation along the model of the 'melting pot' or the celebration of an 'essential' otherness. In a way, they represent the global human condition in our midst. And we shall return to this theme of 'cultural hybridity' in the following chapter on 'globalization.'

The remoralization of politics

The politics of difference, that is organized around the notions of group-differentiated rights and authenticity and that I have discussed with reference to feminism and multiculturalism, poses a far-flung challenge to the basic idea(l)s of liberal democracy. It fastens on to a notion of diversity that embraces more than just a plurality of idiosyncratic interests that individuals, as citizens, pursue in the political arena in normal 'interest politics'. And this is for the simple reason that this diversity is perceived as ontologically significant because it is the manifestation of distinct identities. However, the issues that are given such ontological status cannot be confined to those discussed in the context of multiculturalism and feminism. It is one of the main characteristics of our contemporary situation that questions of morality have re-entered the public domain and have led to the remoralization of politics.

Over the last few decades, 'modernity' and its ideal of 'progress' have become morally questionable. The use of nuclear power; genetic engineering; the ecological effects of the industrial mode of economic production; health policies (for example, with regard to AIDS and HIV or abortion); and individual lifestyles (for example, the use of private transport, the purchase of a piece of furniture made with special wood or sexual orientation) – all of these, and many other, issues have become opened up for moral debate in recent decades. To the extent that these debates concern questions such as the survival of humankind, the dignity of human beings and the responsibilities towards future generations, they must be conducted as public moral debates within political communities. It is through these debates that the political community constitutes itself as an ethical community concerned with questions of the common good. Yet, as we have seen, liberalism in the Kantian tradition relegates these moral issues to the 'private' sphere. Since different individuals and different groups of individuals differ over the conception of the good, a reasonable way to deal with these differences is not to address them in public; we must accept a 'conversational restraint' regarding these issues:

> When you and I learn that we disagree about one or another dimension of the moral truth, we should not search for some common value that will trump this disagreement; nor should we try to translate it into some putatively neutral framework; nor should we seek to transcend our disagreement by talking about how some unearthly creature might resolve it. We should simply say nothing at all about this disagreement and put the moral ideals that divide us off the conversational agenda of the liberal state. In restraining ourselves in this way, we need not lose the chance to talk to one another about our deepest moral disagreements in countless other, more private, contexts ... Having constrained the conversation in this way, we may instead use a dialogue for pragmatically productive purposes: to identify normative premises all political participants find reasonable (or, at least, not unreasonable). (Ackerman 1989: 16–17)

This argument ultimately claims that morality is a matter of individual choice; hence there is and can be no substantial agreement on the moral norms and rules that ought to guide society and its individual members. Given that morality is a matter of choice, individuals are unable to provide each other with conclusive arguments for their own conception of the good, or of the good or worthwhile life, and no rational way of judging who is right can be found. This position suggests that 'matters of ultimate faith concerning the meaning of life, of the highest good, of the most binding principles in accordance with which we should conduct our lives, [should best be] viewed as rationally "irresolvable" and as issues about which individuals themselves should decide according to their own consciences and world-views' (Benhabib 1992: 108). Therefore, a state, or society, must accept that it ought not to seek to promote any particular conceptions of the 'good', but ought to install procedures that enable members (or citizens) to pursue their ends, as long as they are consistent with a similar liberty for all.

We have seen in our discussion on social rights in the previous chapter that within liberalism there is a tradition which is oriented towards a particular notion of public morality and which would not endorse this view of the (morally) neutral state. And it is, of course, true to remark that liberal-

ism itself is thoroughly 'moral' in its appreciative endorsement of the autonomy and self-determination of the individual. Perhaps we would be well
advised to see the demand for a state that is 'neutral' with regard to moral
matters as a response to a historical reality in which the state has always
been implicated in the definition of 'the good life'.

Since the Renaissance, the notion of human freedom as the right and
ability to self-creation and self-legislation went hand in hand with a comprehensive assault of the profane against the sacred, reason against passion,
norms against spontaneity, rational control against emotional drives and
impulses. The self-enlightened and self-civilizing elite of radical Renaissance
humanists and their philosophical successors in the European Enlightenment, who had emancipated themselves from 'the "animal" or not-suffi-
ciently human, ignorant, dependent, "other side" of their selves', took it
upon themselves to relieve the coarse and uncouth 'masses' of their 'ani-
mality' and to reveal the moral potential hidden in human beings to them
(Bauman 1993: 23). They replaced the Revelation of the Church with an
ethics grounded in the 'nature of Man'. But this 'human nature' was an
ideal to be achieved by overcoming the raw, 'unprocessed', often depraved
empirical nature of humans. For them, human nature was an unfulfilled
potential of which the common people had to be made aware and in whose
realization they had to be assisted by those capable of reason and reflection:

> Two things had to be done first for that potential to turn into daily reality of
> life. First ... people had to be enlightened as to the standards they were able to
> meet but unable to discover unaided. And second, they had to be helped in fol-
> lowing such standards by an environment carefully designed to favour and
> reward genuinely moral conduct. (Bauman 1993: 26–7)

It was these two tasks that turned the philosopher into a teacher and a legislator. They entrenched him firmly in a position of supreme authority as
that 'professional' who possessed 'knowledge' and the ability to put into
practice the knowledge of the knowledgeable. As servants of the 'enlightened' state, the philosopher as teacher-cum-legislator embarked upon cultural crusades that were aimed at 'uprooting and destroying the plural,
manifold, communally sustained ways, in the name of the one, uniform, civilized, enlightened, law-sustained pattern of life' (Bauman 1993: 135). This
war against tradition, against the local, against particularity was fought
through education and legislation on the basis of reason and rationality.

In continental Europe it was the 'well-ordered police state' that embarked
upon the project of uniformalization. In the sixteenth and early seventeenth
century legislation in the form of police ordinances aimed to restore the
'good old order' which had been destabilized by urbanization, monetariza-
tion of the economy and religious conflicts. After the Thirty Years War, the
'moral' project of the state was given a different justification. The state's aim

of achieving financial strength through economic growth gained priority over the maintenance of the old order. In order to achieve and retain 'Great Power' status, rulers had to generate economic growth which could then be channelled into the build-up of standing armies and the conduct of military campaigns. In their effort to achieve economic growth, states strove to 'police' their subjects. This involved the monitoring and surveillance of the population. But as Oestreich (1982: 159) pointed out, it also became a major concern of this new type of state to educate its people 'to a discipline of work and frugality and [to change] the spiritual, moral and psychological make-up of political, military and economic man'. This new man (and woman) was ideally conceived as a human agent capable of remaking herself or himself by methodical and disciplined action, endowed, therefore, with the ability 'to take an instrumental stance to one's given properties, desires, inclinations, tendencies, habits of thought and feeling, so that they can be *worked on*, doing away with some and strengthening others, until one meets the desired specification' (Taylor 1989: 159–60).

The state as a geopolitical actor was thus instrumental in transforming society as well as 'producing' disciplined and self-controlled individuals. Indeed, the modern state achieved societal integration only through developing capabilities for the gathering, storing and controlling of information which became systematically applied to administrative ends in pursuit of standardization and through 'moral' education. Both these objectives came together in the nationalism of the nineteenth century. This line of argument has been further developed by Philip Corrigan and Derek Sayer who, for the English state, have analysed a central feature to be found in any state; namely, how through their very activities, routines and rituals states 'define, in great detail, acceptable forms and images of social activity and individual and collective identity':

> The routines of state both materialize and take for granted particular definitions. 'How things are' (allowed to be) is not simply a matter of ideological assertion ... [I]t is concretized in laws, judicial decisions (and their compilation as case law), registers, census returns, licences, charters, tax forms, and all other myriad ways in which the state states and individualities are regulated ... [This is a] massively authoritative organization of what is to count as reality. This system of power is inseparably also a system of knowledge, both in terms of quantity (how much the state knows, its 'intelligence' ...) and quality (the authority claimed for it, other sources of knowledge being less authoritative by the very fact of being unauthorized). (Corrigan/Sayer 1985: 197, also 3–4)

As a moral regulator, the state 'creates' society; it 'regulates' and 'disciplines' social relationships in that territorial space over which it claims sovereignty. In this perspective, the state, of necessity, is a moral(izing) agent.

In the late twentieth century, however, the state as an integrating force through moral regulation has increasingly become less powerful. This is due to a number of reasons. We have been witnessing an increasing disenchantment with the project of the Enlightenment which was informed by the belief that we could become the masters of our own destiny through the advance of human knowledge of, and the intervention in, the social and material reality. This belief in 'progress' through reason and 'instrumental' rationality has been shattered and it has become evident that 'progress' has resulted in an increase in uncertainty and the creation of new risks threatening the survival of humankind (Giddens 1994; Beck 1994).

In the past, the (welfare) state could provide some kind of protection from socially and industrially produced hazards and damages through voluntary or compulsory insurance schemes. Welfare state programmes covered the hazards and risks of industrial accident, illness (health), old age (pensions), unemployment and poverty (for example, family allowances). And if the state did not provide protection from these hazards through 'national insurance contributions', then, at least in principle, private insurance could be purchased. As Ulrich Beck has pointed out, the insurance principle understands hazards to be 'systematically caused and statistically describable'. It is the foundation of a kind of 'security pact' which, through 'making the incalculable calculable', 'creates present security in the face of an open uncertain future' (Beck, quoted in: Lash/Urry 1994: 34). However, at the end of the twentieth century, while protection from these 'old' risks is still part of the tasks wide sections of the population expect the state to take on, the state is also confronted with a completely new set of tasks. The development of nuclear, chemical, genetic and military technologies has resulted in unprecedented ecological hazards and risks to the well-being and even survival of humankind.

These new risks differ in many ways from the 'old' risks. First, they are limited neither in space nor in time. A nuclear catastrophe in Russia, for example, affects hill-farmers in the Scottish Highlands, possibly for years to come. And mutations of the genetic code as a result of such a catastrophe may only become manifest in future generations. Second, they tend to be unaccountable. The destruction of the ozone layer cannot be traced to any one particular cause and any one particular (group of) person(s) that could be held legally accountable for it. There is thus no liability for damages. Third, they tend to be incalculable. In many cases, such as the building of nuclear reactors or genetic engineering, risks can only be tested and assessed after production; hence, society becomes the laboratory because of the 'anticipatory application of a scientific problem before it has been fully explored' (Lash/Urry 1994: 35). Finally, they tend to be uncompensatable. Causing potentially irreparable global damage, no insurance scheme is available which could provide compensation.

These developments result in the increase in risks and a decrease in protection from them because of their specific quality. At the same time, however, the state is expected to pursue a policy of risk limitation, *vide* the increased importance of environmental policies. But the state can perform this task only under severe restrictions. As a welfare state, the state remains dependent on success in international economic competition as it provides the material resources needed for social policies. This success, however, is premised on the application of scientific innovations and new technologies. A policy that aimed at radically curtailing innovative but risk-producing research would therefore be unlikely to gain wide consensus. The second constraint results from the difficulty in knowing with any great degree of certainty what kind of risks a particular innovation will produce and therefore what the result of a particular policy will be. Genetic engineering, for example, may result in producing plants resistant to bacteriological decease, and thus help to solve hunger; but it may also result in the creation of a 'super-race' through the selection of particular genes. These cognitive problems are compounded by the fact that there is no consensus among the population regarding the moral validity of 'progress' in general and concrete developments, as those just mentioned, in particular. 'Cognitive' uncertainty is thus complemented by 'moral' uncertainty and, increasingly, controversy.

This 'cognitive' and 'moral' uncertainty has opened the space for the public deliberation of moral matters. Yet, notwithstanding the controversies issuing out of these uncertainties, the state has become seriously challenged by these developments. Not only has it become impossible for the state to legislate conclusively in these moral matters and find widespread support for it, but it has also lost the capacity to do so. First, the new risks are not open to a mechanism of 'command and obedience'. Though in some areas, such as the behaviour of individuals regarding the environment, monetary inducements or penalties (fines/taxes) can be used to influence behaviour, with regard to many risks monetary penalties are useless (for example, AIDS). In these instances, the state has to rely on education and persuasion. An authoritative solution to these questions imposed from the 'centre' has become illusionary; instead, the state must attempt to 'convince' the people through dialogue. Second, these new risks are the result, not just of a particular combination of knowledge, practice and social interest that came together in the technocratic manifestation of rationality and reason. Rather, they are deeply implicated in the process of structural differentiation that became the hallmark of modernity.

That modern society is characterized by functional differentiation is, of course, a widely shared view; as a matter of fact, concern with the modern differentiated society has been the hallmark of the modern social sciences since their inception in the nineteenth century. Politics, economics, science, education and religion, for example, have become differentiated in separate

111

'subsystems', or 'structures of social action' (Max Weber), and are each characterized by a distinct criterion of rationality to which all action within that structure/subsystem tends to be subjected. For Weber, it was this specificity of the criterion of rationality that made each structure follow its own independent developmental logic (*Eigengesetzlichkeit*). For Weber this investigation into the internal dynamic of the different structural forms of social action had to be complemented by inquiring into the possible existence of an 'elective affinity' between structures. It had to be analysed whether there existed a relation of structural adequacy which would determine the degree to which structures further or impede or exclude each other. Structures of action were thus seen as constituting each others' environment, forming constraints and opening up opportunities for each other (Weber 1978: 341). In this perspective, then, the differentiated structures remain ultimately interconnected through their enabling as well as their constraining properties by which they affect each other.

We must, of course, take cognizance of the fact that the institutionalization of the separation, for example, of church and state, of politics and economics, or of religion and science was not the inevitable result of evolutionary processes, but rather the consequence of social and political struggles. From a political perspective, the institutionalization of separate spheres of action with considerable (and constitutionally protected) autonomy meant also a diffusion of social power and, by the same token, a limitation to any attempts at centralizing power. Differentiation also allowed for a more 'efficient' realization of the respective goals of the 'subsystems': knowledge could be more efficiently produced once science and religion had become differentiated, or the production of commodities and the satisfaction of needs could be more efficiently organized once politics and economics had become institutionalized as distinct structures of social action.

Restrictions on the exercise of any centralized power as well as the dynamic of the 'subsystems' as a result of the increase in 'efficiency' (in the sense of acting according to the system-specific criterion of rationality) lie behind the incessant drive to ever greater specialization, professionalization and organizational structuration of each 'subsystem'. Yet it must not be overlooked that the functionally differentiated subsystems tend to be interconnected. And this for the simple reason that all subsystems aim to externalize negative effects or costs of their mode of action. For example, the economic subsystem in its capitalist form has always externalized the cost of securing the existence of the worker and let other forms of association, such as family, state or charitable organizations, deal with it. What we are currently witnessing is the radicalization of this method of externalization and the increased dangers for society 'as a whole' issuing out of it. Again, the economic subsystem may serve as an example. Capitalism may be the best system in efficiently allocating scarce resources and satisfying material needs. But in the process of doing so, it depletes the natural resources of the earth and wreaks environmental disaster. A similar argument could be made with regard to the scientific subsystem which is efficient in creating knowledge but, at the same time, produces all kinds of technological risks as an externalized 'cost'.

To put the argument very crudely: functional differentiation meant the diffusion of social power and limitations to the centralization of power – after all, this lies behind the differentiation of 'state' and 'civil society'. It also resulted in 'efficiency' gains and a historically unprecedented degree of societal dynamic. Even if we do not want to hold on to the 'goods' of efficiency, because of the 'bads' of the resultant risks, surely we wish to retain subsystem autonomy because of the 'benefit' of power diffusion? If we therefore do not opt for a strategy of dedifferentiation, bringing the economy under political control, for example (assuming such a policy would be possible in a global world), the question is: how can functionally autonomous subsystems be co-ordinated in such a way that negative costs cannot be externalized (Beck 1993: 78)?

Thus, functional differentiation has not only provided the structural context for the production of 'goods' and 'bads'. It has also resulted in the development of subsystem autonomy that the state cannot undo authoritatively or by coercive means. It has been argued that this has led to a situation in which the centrifugal dynamic of functional specialization threatens the integrity of society; in which functional specialization has created so many independent, and self-referential, centres that social order becomes unattainable in this 'polycentric' society (Willke 1992). This would appear to be too pessimistic a view. After all, some sort of co-ordination is still in place. Over the last couple of decades, policy networks, be they of a more pluralist or corporatist ilk, have been established in Western societies, bringing together state actors and other subsystem actors in formal and informal systems of negotiation (Scharpf 1991). From the point of view of democratic theory, there do, of course, arise important questions regarding this mode of co-ordination. First, who or which collective actors are incorporated into these networks? Second, can the externalization of costs to those not incorporated be prevented? Third, who controls these networks? Are they open to democratic scrutiny? Thus, these neo-corporatist mechanisms raise questions of democratic accountability and the desirability of the rule of experts. It is, of course, a key characteristic of the 'new' risks that they are perceived as not to be amenable to technocratic solutions. On the contrary, they are often seen as caused by 'the rule of the experts', as in the case of nuclear power, and there is therefore widespread popular resistance to the idea that neocorporatist mechanisms of expert rule could provide legitimate and comprehensive solutions to these new risks. It has been around the rejection of expertocracy that many new social movements have formed in the last two or three decades. This is true for the 'classical' new social movements such as the environmental movement and the women's movement as well as for the more recent movements such as New Age or the animal rights movement.

We live in a world of radical uncertainty. A radical plurality and diversity of opinions, norms, values and expectations underpins a politics which cannot any longer be grounded in a recourse to tradition or transcendence and which has to accommodate wide-ranging moral reflection on 'progress' and the ambivalences of 'modernity' without the possibility of appealing to a set of universal principles. The opinions and decisions of the experts are as unlikely as majoritarian decision-making conclusively to settle and solve these 'existential' moral and ethical matters. With the incapability of the state authoritatively to impose decisions; with the delegitimization and demonopolization of experts and their expertise; and with the formation of radical diversity amongst the population at large, new ways have to be found to uphold societal integration. The only sensible way of dealing with this diversity of opinions and moral positions would appear to be the creation of fora of public deliberation about risks and risk prevention which would be populated, not just by experts and the government, claiming to represent the 'demos', but also by the 'demos' itself. What has to be devised are forms and fora of consensus-building co-operation among industry, politics, science and the populace. It is likely that:

> [t]he authoritarian decision and action state gives way to the negotiation state, which arranges stages and conversations and directs the show. The ability of the modern state to negotiate is presumably even more important than its one-sided hierarchical ability to act, which is becoming more and more problematic. (Beck 1994: 39)

In the past, the separation and functional differentiation of powers in the constitutional state was a device to prevent the concentration of authority and power in one centre. It also provided a mechanism for the perception and 'management' of societal problems through specialized institutions and agencies. It would appear that only by developing the modern constitutional and interventionist state in the direction of the 'negotiation state', or, as Willke (1992) calls this new type of state, the 'supervision state', will it be possible to retain the problem-perceiving capacity of the political system and generate its capacity to enable societal communication and deliberation over possible solutions.

4

Globalization and
the democratic nation-state

In the previous chapter I have discussed how feminism and multiculturalism have mounted a challenge to liberal democracy by problematizing its
idea(l) of universal citizenship. Citizenship in the liberal, democratic nation-
state is founded, so I have argued, on the principle of nondiscrimination
insofar as all citizens participate equally in universal rights and entitlements. This idea(l) results in the concept of the 'disembodied' and 'disembedded' citizen. This conceptualization is challenged by 'feminism' and
'multiculturalism'. Both demand that concrete differences of women and
cultural communities must be accommodated in modern democratic states,
and that individual rights have to be complemented by group rights. Both
advocate a 'politics of identity' that challenges the liberal ideal of political
universalism, and 'multiculturalism' also questions our thinking about
nation and the nation-state. Both, therefore, problematize the institutional
and normative structure of liberal democracy. I have also discussed how the
'remoralization of politics' as a result of the 'dialectics of modernity' adds to
this challenge by undermining the liberal idea(l) of 'moral neutrality'.

In the last three chapters, then, I have analysed the norms and institutions of liberal democracy; its 'embeddedness' in political communities structured as nation-states; and theoretical alternatives and challenges to this
model of democracy. In this chapter, I wish to continue my considerations
on challenges to the democratic nation-state. But whereas the last chapter
concentrated on challenges from 'within', this chapter focuses on challenges
from 'without'. It sets out to analyse the ongoing processes of globalization
as a challenge to the democratic nation-state. I shall argue that globalization does not result in the demise of the state. On the contrary, by raising
the issue of collective identity, and in particular ethno-national identity,
globalization underlines the importance of the modern state as the dominant form of political organization. Yet, as I shall argue, globalization
undermines the 'sovereignty' of the state, and to the extent that democracy
in the liberal model is structurally related to the notion of a *summa potestas*,

it poses a challenge to our understanding of democracy.

An analysis of the relationship between the democratic nation-state and globalization could take different forms.

First, we could analyse the global spread of this particular type of political regime. In this exercise, we would operationalize democracy; for example, we emphasize accountability of government to parliament and universal (adult) suffrage as two key institutional aspects of representative democratic government. We then attempt to identify the exact point in time at which these two institutions have been established in the countries under investigation. This would then possibly lead to the construction of time sequences, or 'waves' of democratization. A first 'wave' of democratizing could be seen as 'coming in' around the time of the First World War in Northern and Western Europe with the parliamentarization of constitutional monarchies, the formation of republics and the extension of the franchise. In Central and Eastern Europe, the newly independent states after the collapse of the multinational empires (Austro-Hungary, Ottoman Empire and Russia) start experimenting with democracy at a somewhat later time. The second 'wave' after 1945 would see the defeated states such as Germany and Japan be given democratic constitutions; others, such as Italy and France, institute new democratic regimes. The third 'wave' affects the countries in Southern Europe and in Latin America in the 1970s; and finally, the fourth 'wave' would bring democracy to Eastern Europe after 1989 and would even reach South Africa. From its European heartland, democracy spreads around the world. To complete this kind of research, we would also engage in examining the requisites and causes of democracy and democratization as well as the conditions under which newly established democratic regimes are consolidated. Samuel Huntington's (1991) analysis of 'waves' of democratization provides a prominent example of such a research programme. Fukuyama's (1992) argument regarding 'The end of history' and the (alleged) global triumph of the liberal-democratic idea constitute a philosophical and ideological reflection (and justification) of these developments.

An alternative to this investigation would commence with a reconceptualization of the 'waves' of democratization. Following Robert Dahl (1989), we could see the formation of democracy in the Greek polis in the first half of the fifth century BC as the first time when the idea that a substantial number of free, adult males should be entitled as citizens to participate directly in governing the polis was formulated and institutionalized. Underlying this notion of democracy was the assumption that, in order for democratic rule to uphold the common good, the citizen body had to be highly homogeneous as high levels of economic inequality, of religious, cultural or racial diversity would tend to produce political conflict and disagreements over the common good.

The second transformation occurred once the notion of democracy and its institutionalization could no longer be contained within the city-state and had to be reconceptualized and redesigned for geographically larger territories. As we have noticed in the first chapter, in this phase, two significant additions to the classical democratic tradition were made. First, out of a recognition of the unavoidable heterogeneity of civil and political society arose the awareness of the fragility of civic virtue and the dangers of political corruption. Institutions had to be designed that would prevent the concentration of power. In order to balance the interests of 'the one', 'the few' and 'the many' (in the Aristotelian sense), forms of mixed government were advocated in which these interests were represented and pursued, respectively, the monarchy, the aristocratic upper chamber, and the lower house of commons. This was the solution entailed in the British Constitution. The American Federal Constitution, however, went beyond this model of a 'mixed constitution'. It acknowledged that society was composed of different alliances and groupings, all of them pursuing a plurality of legitimate interests. But, in order for republican virtue to survive the struggle of political factions and social forces, authority was to be dispersed and many power centres were to be created to prevent the wholesale capture of authority by any one particular interest.

The notion of representation was the second idea added to the classical ideal. For large-scale communities, direct democracy was considered impossible as the people could not meet as a legislative body and had therefore to choose representatives to do what they could not do themselves. Democratic government could thus be conceptualized as representative government circumscribed by constitutional constraint. Political contestation was thus institutionalized through the mechanisms for the representation of 'the people' and special 'interests'. Above all, the struggles over universal franchise, free speech and freedom of assembly during the nineteenth and twentieth century broadened the institution of political participation which came to lose its elitist, aristocratic/patrician limitations.

The first 'wave', then, affected the small-scale city-state. The second 'wave' transformed politics in the large-scale communities which developed in the process of the formation of the modern state since about the Renaissance. The third 'wave', so an argument could be put forward, is now upon us. Democracy has to be freed from the shackles of the modern state and has to become global. In an era of ever-increasing global interconnectedness of people, places, capital, goods and services, democratic self-government of the people has to be institutionalized on the global level. Creating structures for a cosmopolitan democracy is the task we have to face should we wish to uphold the ideal of democratic self-government of the people in the twenty-first century. The topic of 'Globalization and the democratic nation-state' would thus engage us in an analysis of the shortcomings of democratic rule that remains wedded to the nation-state in a global age, and challenge us to design democratic institutions and procedures for such a global democracy.

My own interests, while much influenced by the concern with cosmopolitan democracy, are yet somewhat different. In this chapter, I will analyse the effects of globalization on democratic rule in the modern state. I attempt to determine the likely future of the modern state in the era of globalization and ask whether we will experience the end of the modern state. In the first chapter, we have noticed that in the course of the nineteenth century the state began to 'cage' (Michael Mann) much of social activity. Has globalization now begun to replace the state as the decisive framework for social life? I do not think so. However, I will argue that globalization poses yet another challenge to the institutional arrangements of democracy in the modern nation-state.

Manifestations of economic and cultural globalization

We live in an era of ever-increasing global interconnectedness of people, places, capital, goods and services. Globalization is a multi-faceted process that manifests itself in such forms as global tourism and the global reach of nuclear, environmental and health risks. But it has arguably been the emergence of a global economy and a global information system that have been of particular importance for the creation of a 'global' world.

A global economy has emerged which has become institutionalized through global capital markets and globally integrated financial systems; global trade; and global productions networks. In such a 'global economy', the patterns of production and consumption in the world are increasingly interdependent; income and employment are determined at a global level; and national macro-economic management is becoming increasingly anachronistic and doomed to failure. Official international bodies such as the Group of Seven economic nations (G7), the International Monetary Fund (IMF), the World Bank, the Bank for International Settlements (BIS), the General Agreement on Tariffs and Trade (GATT)/World Trade Organization (WTO), or the Organization for Economic Co-operation and Development (OECD) have not amounted to a system of global political governance of the global economy, although they do advance some kind of global economic co-ordination and co-operation. Arguably, however, it is the cartels and joint ventures amongst transnational and multinational corporations that are the most important element of economic (self-) governance (Grant 1992).

This globalization of the economy is driven forward by the interpenetration of the advanced capitalist countries, and, in particular, by the intensification of transfers among three economic macro-regions: North

America/USA; East Asia/Japan; and Europe/European Union. To the extent that capital is buzzing around the world, most of the time it finds a resting place in advanced capitalist countries. To the extent that international trade is increasing, it is an expression of the growing interdependencies of the advanced capitalist countries (Schott 1991; Dicken 1993). And despite processes of deindustrialization in the advanced capitalist countries, most of value-added manufacturing is still taking place there (Rodwin/Sazanami (eds) 1989 and 1991; Martin/Rowthorn (eds) 1986; Gordon 1988). For these three regions, economic globalization has resulted in a trend towards the convergence of the structures of production, finance and technology; in the increasing synchronization of business cycles; and in 'the growing importance of trade, investment and technology flows, both inwards and outwards, within each domestic economy' (Eden 1991: 213). It has also meant an ever greater dominance of transnational corporations. Yet, it should also be noted that each of these macro-regions remains relatively closed in that cross-national investment and trade within a region is greater than between the regions. To that extent, much of economic activity remains 'localized'.

Economic globalization affects all states and all 'national' economies. Yet it does so in ways that differ according to their position within the international division of labour. The dynamics of this process and its socio-economic effects have led to economic regionalization and attempts to institutionalize regional economic co-operation all around the world. Examples of such economic regionalization abound. The North American Free Trade Agreement (NAFTA) between the United States, Canada and Mexico; the European Union; and the Association of Southeast Asian Nations (ASEAN) between Indonesia, Malaysia, the Philippines, Singapore, Thailand and Brunei are, perhaps, the best known. The Asian–Pacific Economic Co-operation (APEC), which was founded in 1989, is likely to become more widely known in the future. Not only does APEC bring together the NAFTA and ASEAN states, but includes also China, Hong Kong, Japan, South Korea, Taiwan, Australia, New Zealand and Papua New Guinea. Obviously, there is great economic, political, and cultural diversity and disparity in this group which will make it rather unlikely that it will develop a high degree of institutionalization. Yet the very attempt at establishing such a co-operation demonstrates the formation of new economic regions as a result of the dynamics of the global economy. While these institutions and mechanism of economic co-operation bring together states and 'national' economies, the global economy has also caused the rise of 'region states' (Ohmae 1993). Ohmae gives as examples of such cross-border region states Hong Kong and southern China; Singapore and its neighbouring Indonesian islands; or Vancouver and Seattle (the Pacific Northwest region state) and Toronto, Detroit and Cleveland (the 'Great Lakes' region state). For Ohmae, these are examples of economically integrated regional entities whose primary linkages tend to be with the global economy and not with their 'host' nations:

> Region states make such effective points of entry into the global economy because the very characteristics that define them are shaped by the demands of that economy. Region states tend to have between five million and twenty million people ... A region state must be small enough for its citizens to share certain economic and consumer interests but of adequate size to justify the infrastructure – communication and transportation links and quality professional services – necessary to participate economically on a global scale. (Ohmae 1993: 80)

There is thus a clear spatial aspect to economic globalization. This spatial dimension finds a further manifestation in migration flows. In the global economy, those countries are disadvantaged which fail to restructure their production, labour market and economic regulations in order to attract global capital. It is from those marginalized and economically less developed countries that many of the world's migrants originate. But as Pellerin points out, in some instances, foreign investment has, in fact, increased migration flows: 'The progressive replacement of traditional or local forms of economic activity with standardized processes of production or the use of modern technology, as well as the greater use of specific categories of labour (such as women and children), tends to increase the number of workers available while the number of jobs available remains relatively stable or decreases' (Pellerin 1993: 245). This situation may then precipitate mass migration.

The geographical dimension of economic globalization is also underlined by the effect of the global economy on different sectors and regions within each state. 'Deindustrialization', for example, is bound to bring disadvantages to the manufacturing industries and industrial regions of advanced capitalist countries, whereas the internationalization of financial services is likely to benefit other geographical locations and socio-economic groups within these countries. One of the effects of global capitalism on the advanced capitalist countries has been the occurrence of socio-economic and socio-political crises which used to be seen as unique to less-developed countries: for example, rising long-term unemployment, increase in income disparities and in absolute poverty, depopulation of the countryside, decay of urban centres and an increase in organized crime (Bonder *et al.* 1993). These effects of economic globalization have led Camilleri (1990: 36–7) to argue that '[t]he emerging international division of labour is therefore a divisive force in domestic society. Insofar as it encourages and accentuates domestic conflict, international integration may provoke national disintegration'. Hence, neither for the global system as a whole nor for its con-

stituent units does economic globalization result in homogeneity and overall integration; rather, it is likely to accentuate heterogeneity and fragmentation. Global capitalism is best analysed as a system of structured
inequality.

The emergence of such a global economy was premised on the development of a technological infrastructure regarding transportation and the
generation and circulation of information. The internationalization of production and the establishment of global production networks has been
dependent upon faster and more cost-effective rail, sea and air transportation and on more extensive interconnections between them. The global
economy more generally has become infrastructurally dependent upon the
spread of global communications networks and the systematic use of radio,
television, telephone, telex, fax, computer and satellite facilities for the generation and dissemination of information. These technological innovations
and their systematic applications in economic transactions have resulted in
the 'shrinking' of distances with faster and improved connection between
places:

> Distances mean little and direction means even less. Relative location is more
> important than absolute location in a tightly connected and integrated world.
> Absolute location, via, where you are, has much less meaning today. What is
> more important as markets, societies, cultures and governments are becoming
> more connected is whether one is 'connected', how far one is from other places
> in time not in absolute distance, and how much one is connected with other
> places. (Brunn/Leinbach 1991: XVII)

Whether states can avail themselves of the advantages and benefits of these
global communications and information networks depends therefore upon
their respective access to these technologies. As in the global economy, it is
the (technologically) advanced capitalist countries of the West (including
Japan) that dominate the development and deployment of these technologies and that control the access of other countries to them (Smith 1980).
The structure of inequality and dependence of the global economic system
is thus buttressed by the control over the communication media, and in particular the satellite systems on which they rely for speed and global reach,
by the economically powerful states and capitalist institutions. Since many
of these technologies were initially associated with military surveillance and
have become an ever more integral part of the global military order, they
also buttress (as well as manifest) the geopolitical dominance of the West.

By meeting the communications and information requirements of both
global capitalism and modern warfare, these technologies have created the
conditions for a global system of symbolic interaction and exchange (Turner
1994a: 156). These new communication media allow the generation and
dissemination of economically valuable data; but they also make possible

the transfer of mental images, exposing the recipients of these images to similar, 'standardized', ways of thinking and acting. In other words, these media and the images they transport have arguably an impact on the culture and identity of the societies exposed to them. They could be seen as foreign cultural invaders diluting 'indigenous' cultures and being instrumental in creating a 'global' (Western) culture (Janelle 1991; Ferguson 1993).

The technical revolution in telecommunications and information systems allows the world-wide spread of the 'culture-ideology' of consumerism that 'transforms all the public mass media and their contents into opportunities to sell ideas, values, products, in short, a consumerist worldview' (Sklair 1991: 76, also 72–81, 129–66). Arguably, to the extent that global mass media firms and transnational advertising agencies succeed in creating globally shared consumption needs, 'the consumption of the same popular material and media products, be they Schwarzenegger, Cheers, Pepsi, Big Macs, Disney Worlds, clothes, cars or architectural fashions, creates a meta-culture whose collective identity is based on shared patterns of consumption, be these built on choice, emulation or manipulation' (Ferguson 1992: 80). Since this nascent global mass culture must speak across many languages and native cultural traditions, it is dominated 'by television and by film, and by the image, imagery, and styles of mass advertising' (Hall 1991b: 27). It thus operates mainly through the packaging of imageries as articulated by the visual and graphic arts and their diffusion through world-wide telecommunications networks.

The 'culture-ideology' of consumerism and the global diffusion of particular (Western/American) images and imagery spread through world-wide telecommunications networks are not the only manifestations of this 'global' culture. Western culture, in its 'modern' form, finds its stable foundation, above all, in a particular cognitive style. This method of cognition has eliminated the sacred and the magic from the world by postulating that 'there are no privileged or a priori *substantive* truths ... All facts and all observers are equal ... In inquiry, all facts and all features are separable: it is *always* proper to inquire whether combinations could not be other than what had previously been supposed' (Gellner 1992: 80). This modern scientism and its implementation led to the 'disenchantment' of the world (Max Weber) and made it a cold, morally indifferent place. Yet it also enhanced the economic, military and administrative power of those societies that embraced it. The application of this cognitive style to economic activities and political organization led to the development of the bureaucratic state, disciplined, modern technological warfare and capitalism in the West. These institutional innovations allowed the West to impose its dominance throughout the world. The practical success of this style of thought has been, and still is, inducing all of humankind to adopt this style, at least in some measure:

Scientific/industrial civilization clearly is unique ... because it is, without any shadow of doubt, conquering, absorbing all the other cultures of the Earth. It does so because all those outside it are eager to emulate it, and if they are not, which rarely happens, their consequent weakness allows them to be easily overrun. (Gellner 1988: 200)

The 'global culture argument' has thus a variety of facets: 'A global culture would operate at several levels simultaneously: as a cornucopia of standardized commodities of denationalized ethnic or folk motifs, as a series of generalized "human values and interests", as a uniform "scientific" discourse of meaning, and finally as the interdependent system of communications which forms the material base for all the other components and levels' (Smith 1990: 176). Smith is correct to point to the element of timelessness inherent in the idea of global culture as 'for its purposes the past only serves to offer some decontextualized example or element for its cosmopolitan patchwork'. But he is quite wrong to argue that global culture is also context-less, 'a true melange of disparate components drawn from everywhere and nowhere' (Smith 1990: 177). Global culture remains centred in and bound to the 'West' (and Japan) in its reliance and dependence on 'Western technology, the concentration of capital, the concentration of techniques, the concentration of advanced labour in the Western societies, and the stories and the imagery of Western societies: these remain the driving powerhouse of this global mass culture' (Hall 1991b: 28). Drawing together these different elements, cultural globalization could then be defined as the universalization, that is, global spread, of Western 'modernity' and instrumental rationality in its institutionalized forms of scientism, capitalism and the bureaucratic state and the popular representation of its commensurate value system in the images and imageries of 'Western' mass culture (Rieff 1993; Madsen 1993).

Global culture and collective identity

Will cultural globalization result in global cultural homogeneity? Will localisms and traditions of variance be swept away by the forces of Western cultural 'imperialism'? Or will cultural globalization, similar to economic globalization, result in generating and upholding heterogeneity as a feature as much inherent in its 'logic' as homogenization? While it would be highly problematic to argue that national or cultural identities are not open to influence by mass communication media at all, this does not mean that they are necessarily shaped or constituted by them. The argument that media determines culture and cultural experience, systematically denies the contextuality of culture. The social groups and collectives that are the recipients of the 'global message' interpret, or bestow meaning upon, these messages on the basis of their own specific experience and memories as they

123

grew out of their own particular histories and cultures; they creatively modify 'messages' and cultural products in light of their own local needs and requirements. It is exactly the timelessness, but also the context-specific 'Westernness', of the global cultural message that is undermining its capacity to create a global collective identity, 'those feelings and values in respect of a sense of continuity, shared memories and a sense of common destiny of a given unit of population which has had common experiences and cultural attributes' (Smith 1990: 179). Sachs expresses the gist of this argument, and the actual experience to which it relates, extremely well:

> Having a memory, relating to others, participating in a larger story, calls for involvement, require presence. This presence, naturally, is lived out in particular physical settings like piazzas or streets, mountains or seashores. And these locations are in turn imbued with experience past and present. They become places of density and depth. Therefore, certain places have a special 'thickness' for certain people. It is there that the ancestors walked the earth and the relevant memories are at home. It is there that one is tied into a web of social bonds and where one is recognized by others. And it is there that people share a particular vantage point and that language, habits and outlook combine to constitute a particular style of being in the world. (Sachs 1992: 111)

Though Sachs evidently discusses ethno-cultural identity, one should not forget that there are other types of collective identities, such as those formed on the basis of class, caste, gender and religion as well as those connected with colonialism. These identities ensure the heterogeneity of local experiences and refract the past in a variety of ways and become, at least partially, constitutive of ethno-national identity. But they also ensure that cultures do not become static, but remain 'fields of struggle' on which they are constructed, deconstructed and reconstructed. These collective identities thus relate to ethno-national identity in a variety of ways, constituting its context while at the same time preventing its fixity. But to the extent that an ethno-national identity does exist, it is centred on historically and emotionally entrenched shared memories (including those of past struggles) which are sustained through a sense of continuity between generations.

The global diffusion and global acceptance in the twentieth century of the idea of the nation-state as an institutionalized global norm and ultimate symbol with regard to what a viable society should 'look like', has itself been an important feature of globalization. It has meant the extensive global legitimation of the strong centralized state as a primary feature of the world system, thereby constraining societies to participate in the interstate system 'along the "acceptable" lines of possessing relatively homogeneous state apparatuses' (Robertson 1992: 69). Historically, it was in the wake of the American and French Revolutions that nationalism aimed 'to overcome local ethno-cultural diversity and to produce standardized citizens whose

124

loyalties to the nation would be unchallenged by extra-societal allegiances' (Robertson 1990a: 49). In the nineteenth century, this political nationalism was complemented, and increasingly marginalized, by the nationalization of culture in the pursuit of the creation of a national–societal identity. In particular in Central and Eastern Europe, belonging to a nation was being defined as belonging to a particular culture. In some cases, supposedly primordial cultures were 'discovered' or 'invented', but, in any event, elaborated – through philology and the consolidation of national languages; through literature and the discovery, or forging, of national epics; and through history and the construction of narratives of the 'nation' (Buell 1994: 42). In all cases, cultural achievements became routinely claimed for 'nations', that is, culture became 'nationalized' and 'territorialized' (Nederveen Pieterse 1994: 179). Hence, hand in hand with the universalization of the nation-state norm there also went the 'nationalization' of culture that found one expression in 'the expectation of uniqueness of identity' (Roland Robertson), and thus the norm of particularism and localism. While the universalization of the nation-state norm contributed to the global spread of the interstate system, (the idea of) the cultural homogenization within the nation-state reinforced the cultural diversity of that system.

It is a key aspect of the contemporary stage of global interconnectedness that concrete societies situate themselves in the context of a world complex of societies; that they conceptualize themselves as part of a global order. As a result of this global self-reflection, the criteria for societal change and conduct tend to become 'matters of inter-societal, inter-continental, inter-civilizational, and inter-doctrinal interpretation and debate' (Robertson/Chirico 1985: 237; Turner 1994b). Such a situating of societies may engender strains or even discontent within societies. It heightens the significance of the problem of societal order in relation to global order and is thus likely to give rise to a large number of political–ideological and religious movements with conflicting definitions of the location of their society in relationship to the rest of the world and the global circumstance as a whole. In short, it radicalizes and politicizes the search for identity. This identity, however, is the possible result of the confrontation of a particular locality with others in the emerging world of global capitalism, global information and communication networks, global transportation technology and global tourism. Particularistic identity in the age of globalization is thus constructed in full awareness of the rest of the world. It is an identity that does not aim at insulation from the world, but allows local units conscious, if potentially fraught, interactions with it (Robertson 1992: 69–70; Mlinar 1992: 5–12; Walker 1993: 176–9).

Since this process of identity formation in the age of globalization is embedded in this structure of interactivity, it is always precarious and fragile. This interactivity finds expression in the impact of non-Western cultures on the West or the local reception of Western culture in the form of the indigenization of Western elements, but also in the influence that non-Western cultures are exercising on one another (Buell 1994: Part 2). Global tourism is one mediating mechanism in this structure of global interactivity:

> Global tourism increases intercultural exchange and forces cultural elites to come to terms with the heritage industry ... Tourism tends to make cultures into museums, as cultural phenomena which can be viewed as quaint, peculiar and local. Tourism paradoxically is a quest for authentic local cultures, but the tourist industry, by creating an illusion of authenticity, in fact reinforces the experience of social and cultural simulation ... [E]thnic or national cultures become local or folk cultures which are available to the tourist gaze. (Turner 1994b: 185)

Migration is another mediating mechanism that triggers greater cultural reflexivity. As Nederveen Pieterse (1994: 165) points out, 'the migration movements which make up demographic globalisation can engender absentee patriotism and long-distance nationalism, as in the political affinities of Irish, Jewish and Palestinian diasporas and emigré or exiled Sikhs in Toronto, Tamils in London, Kurds in Germany, Tibetans in India'. This is the structural underpinning of many of the questions raised by 'multiculturalism'/'multicommunalism' that we have discussed in the previous chapter. At stake is the formation of 'diasporic' identities and their articulation with a 'national' identity. With regard to the United States of America, Appadurai (1993: 424) argued that such an articulation may lead to the formation of a truly 'postnational imaginary' as people migrate to the USA to seek their fortunes but without being any longer content to leave their homelands behind:

> For every nation-state that has exported significant numbers of its population to the United States as refugees, tourists or students, there is now a delocalized *transnation* which retains a special ideological link to a putative place of origin but is otherwise a thoroughly diasporic collectivity. No existing conception of Americanness can contain this large variety of transnations. In this scenario, the hyphenated American might have to be twice hyphenated (Asian-American-Japanese or Native-American-Seneca or African-American-Jamaican or Hispanic-American-Bolivian) as diasporic identities stay mobile and grow more protean. Or perhaps the sides of the hyphen will have to be reversed, and we can become a federation of diasporas.

The effect of both migration and global tourism is the increase in, and the awareness of, greater cultural diversity, differentiation and heterogeneity. This experience of heterogeneity, multiplicity and hybridity is likely to bring 'all social groups within the globalizing process into a self-awareness of the relativity of their own belief systems' (Turner 1994b: 17). It is for this

126

reason that global interactivity makes identity formation a potentially fraught and conflictual process.

'Particularistic' identity, that issues out of cultural reflexivity, does not of necessity express itself in 'ethno-national' terms. Samuel Huntington (1993) has controversially argued that the question of collective identity in a 'global' world is likely to pose itself in civilizational terms. He contends that, concomitant with the increase in interactions between peoples of different civilizations, there does occur an intensification of civilization consciousness and awareness of differences between civilizations and commonalities within civilizations. These differences will become politically radicalized through the operation of the global system in which the West in effect 'is using international institutions, military power and economic resources to run the world in ways that maintain Western predominance, protect Western interests and promote Western political and economic values' (Huntington 1993: 40). A 'clash of civilizations', as the title of Huntington's article puts it, is therefore by no means inevitable. Even if we took no offence at Huntington's ideological construction of an 'essential' and 'unified' civilizational 'us' and 'them', the 'other', we may argue with Huntington against Huntington that a 'clash' is premised on a global system of inequality and power differentials; that is, without Western dominance, no clash of 'civilizations'. Notwithstanding these qualifications of Huntington's political argument, he is right to argue that it is within this context of global inequality that a de-Westernization and indigenization of elites are currently occurring in many non-Western countries, counterbalancing the impact of Western cultures, styles and habits that have become popular among many groups (Huntington 1993: 27).

Yet, these elites are still concerned with building modern institutions such as bureaucratic states and modern armies as well as technologically advanced economic structures; but by aiming to preserve indigenous values and ideas, they strive to 'modernize but not to Westernize' (Huntington 1993: 41). They attempt to embrace 'modernity' in its institutionalized forms of the centralized bureaucratic state, capitalism and scientism in order to overcome the position of powerlessness that comes with a lack of 'modernity'. The question they have to face is whether those 'modern' institutions are inextricably interlaced with 'Western' values. Is capitalist modernization premised on the acceptance and endorsement of individualism? Is the 'modern' state necessarily a secular state? Is it possible to embrace the 'modern' form of political organization and postulate, at the same time, that it should express and reflect the collective (religious) values of the moral community that constitutes it (Juergensmeyer 1993)? As the example of Japan forcefully shows, the embrace of 'modernity' enabled it to defend and uphold its indigenous traditions. The same appears to be true for the other 'Tiger' economies in South-East Asia (Funabashi 1993). In fact, the Confucian revival in industrial East Asia since the Second World War was not only a response to the previous Westernization of the political and cultural elites, but constituted a forceful critique of modern Western culture in its attempt to understand some of the effects of industrialization, urbanization, bureaucratization and widespread influence of mass communication. At the same time, however, '[t]here is strong evidence to show that the dynamic cultural forms enhancing economic productivity that industrial East Asia assumed have benefited from Confucian ethics' (Wei-ming 1991: 772).

But the various manifestations of 'religious fundamentalism' across the world attest to the socio-political and socio-cultural dislocations that the policy of 'modernization', even without an accompanying conscious endeavour to embrace 'Western' values, causes in many countries. The rise of radical ('fundamentalist') Islamist movements in the Middle East in the 1960s, gathering pace in the 1970s and 1980s, must be seen as a response to the failures of the various policies of modernization. Neither the secular nationalist regimes of a socialist and/or pan-Arabist (rather than pan-Islamist) orientation, nor Kemalism in Turkey or the 'White Revolution' in Iran were perceived as a success: 'Thus, Islamic revival can be regarded at least partly as a function of the eclipse of the Arab radical nationalist movement and of other developmental experiments in the Middle East' (Ayubi 1991: 65; Sivan 1985: chaps 2 and 3). Culturally, the general Islamic resurgence 'represents a rejection to alienation and a quest for authenticity' (Ayubi 1991: 217). But as the institutionalization of 'fundamentalist' Islam in Iran shows, even there this 'cultural nationalism' aims to allow for the existence of a militarily strong, centralized, bureaucratic state and a capitalist market economy. Islam, both in its 'liberal' and 'fundamentalist' manifestation, provided the link between Iranian cultural particularity and modern global universality; in either case, modernity was to be achieved through a revitalization of Islamic cultural difference, not at the cost of it (Beyer 1994: chap. 7).

Religious 'fundamentalism' is, of course, not just a phenomenon of the non-Western world, as the example of the New Christian Right in the United States attests. This religious movement has been analysed with good reasons as a reaction to processes of globalization, in this case, the decline of American hegemony since about the Vietnam war and the ensuing status crisis of the United States as a state in the world system. The repositioning of the United States in the global system created an opening for the New Christian Right as a social movement and gave some *prima facie* credibility to its claim that '[r]eligious revival is the essential prerequisite of moral regeneration which in turn will cause the United States to recover its leadership role in the world' (Beyer 1994: 122). Like Islamic 'fundamentalism', the New Christian Right reasserts a particular (American) group-cultural exclusivity as uniquely morally and ethically valid; and it, too, 'dogmatically' refuses to accept the validity of some 'modern' values (such as science), while, at the same time, holding on to other 'modern' features, such as market-based capitalism.

Religious 'fundamentalism' as a response to the global condition can thus be found in many parts of the world. We should, however, be aware that such a religious response may manifest itself, not just in a particularistic modification of global universality, but possibly also in its wholesale embrace. An exemplar of such a response is the Latin American liberation theology movement. This movement developed in the 1960s, at a time of accelerated incorporation of Latin America into the global system and out of a concern with the spiritual and material effects of the ensuing changes on the people. Rather than respond to these dislocations by reviving or reasserting particular and exclusive religio-cultural traditions, this movement embraced the 'modern' values of progress and equality and based its politics of combating the globalization-induced social and spiritual problems on the application of science and the tools of instrumental rationality (Beyer 1994: chap. 6). As this movement shows, reasserting cultural particularisms as much as embracing global universality are thus possible reactions to processes of globalization and their 'local' manifestations. It would, of course, warrant detailed analysis of each case to determine the factors causing either of these reactions in concrete circumstances; but it would be a sound assumption that in each case, both 'tendencies' are likely to vie with each other for (temporary?) supremacy.

How to be 'modern' without becoming 'Western'? The tension that this dilemma creates can find expression in 'religious fundamentalism' as much as in 'ethno-nationalism', both of them, at the same time, manifestations of a politics of cultural uniqueness that is a societal response to the challenges of globalization. They can be analysed as attempts to reconstruct traditions in permanent civilizational encounters and locally to interpret and apply universal principles. To that extent, ethnic revivalism and nationalism as much as 'religious fundamentalism' can be understood from the point of view of the analyst as a necessary aspect of globalization. From the point of view of the participant, they may appear as an adequate response to what can be seen as the homogenizing threat of globalization, and thus as a reaffirmation or reinvention of a particularistic collective identity.

In many non-Western countries, we are thus witnessing a playing-out of the dialectical tensions between 'modernization' and cultural 'indigenization'; between the 'universal' and the 'particular'; the 'global' and the 'local'; in short, the dialectic of homogeneity and heterogeneity. It is this tension that informs the search for an idiosyncratic collective identity and the politics of cultural uniqueness in the era of globalization. For the 'West', this *problematique* presents itself, too, but in a different way. To the extent that globalization affects the polity and politics of the democratic state, it reinforces concerns with collective identity. It does so by problematizing the identity-bestowing notion of 'citizenship'.

The challenge of globalization to the democratic nation-state

As we have already discussed in chapter 1, in the democratic state, sovereignty has been transferred from the (monarchical or autocratic) ruler to the people, and the people have been defined as the sum of the legally equal citizens. It is the people who possess sovereignty and thus the 'undisputed right to determine the framework of rules, regulations and policies within a given territory and to govern accordingly' (Held 1991: 150). Political democracy is premised on the acceptance of the notion of popular sovereignty and its institutionalization in citizenship rights. The mechanisms for inclusion into, and exclusion from, the 'polity' ('who precisely constitutes the people?') are organized around social criteria (for example, class, age, gender) as well as ethnic criteria (for example, race, place of birth). Citizenship rights are thus typically built around the notion of a universalism of rights and a particularism of identity. The 'demos' component is normally dominant though the debate over the extension of citizenship rights to non-natives, such as guest workers or immigrants/aliens, makes manifest the dormant, and easily awakened, power of the 'ethnos' component. With international migration likely to become ever more pronounced as a consequence of changing world labour markets, ecological devastation and displacements caused by political–military interventions, the discourse of 'ethnicity', and even 'race', will also become more pronounced in debates about citizenship (Brubaker (ed.) 1989).

The relative weighing of the 'demos' and the 'ethnos' component has, of course, always been problematic. The precise mixture of these components, their form and mode of institutionalization and the respective mode of legitimation are an important element of the collective identity of a political system. In the past, one political tradition saw the state as a nation unified by a common culture: the state is both a political and a cultural unity. In the (French) republican version of this tradition, the nation has been defined as a political community, based on a constitution, laws and citizenship. It has allowed for the possibility of admitting newcomers to the community provided they adhere to the political rules and are willing to adapt the national culture. But in this version, the required cultural assimilation of newcomers is not couched in terms of ethnic homogeneity of the state. This 'ideal' of the ethnically homogeneous state is prominent in those states in which membership of the nation is defined in terms of ethnicity, with a strong emphasis upon common descent, language and culture. In such states, a policy of ethno-cultural assimilation can be understood as an attempt to confront the issue of actual ethnic diversity and turn the 'ideal' into reality. But this ideal and the related policies clash with another prominent idea that sees a culture as being a state in embryo. This idea allows cultural minorities to make the claim that they possess a right of resistance to policies of cultural assimilation and even more, a right to secession and independent statehood. While the first conceptualization might possibly lead to internal ethnic conflict resulting (possibly) in secession, the second is likely to lead to international conflict as a result of irredentist nationalism that expresses itself in demands that people who are members of a common 'cultural nation' but who happen to be citizens of another state be allowed to join the (new) state. In either case, the issue at stake is not the disappearance of the state, but how (ethnic, religious, and cultural) diversity can be accommodated within individual states and within the international state-system.

Whatever the precise criteria for inclusion into the community of citizens, citizenship status is the prerequisite for partaking in democratic rule. As we saw, this democratic rule is exercised in the sovereign, territorially consolidated nation-state. Popular sovereignty is premised upon state sovereignty. However, in a world of global interconnectedness both people's sovereignty and state sovereignty have been challenged since '[t]he very process of governance can escape the reach of the nation-state. National communities by no means exclusively make and determine decisions and policies themselves, and government by no means determine what is right or appropriate exclusively for their own citizens' (Held 1992: 21; Connolly 1991: 216). For example, the formation of a global economy outreaches the control of any single state; multi- and transnational corporations, stock brokers and international money and securities dealers make production and investment decisions that affect the economic well-being of states and people without being accountable to them. Global communication and the processes of informationalization make it difficult for governments to control information and its dissemination; and with power adhering increasingly to those actors who have unconstrained access to information flows, 'the nation-state – with its more traditional geopolitical concerns for policing jurisdictively its territories, populations, and markets – often comes up short with nothing near complete closure over events within its boundaries' (Luke 1993: 239). Exterritorial global forces both invade the political space of the nation-state and, because of their exterritoriality, are operating outside the controlling reach of the nation-state. Both as space invaders and as space evaders do they challenge the democratic polity. They affect the life of citizens by imposing constraints and limits on democratically constituted political agency without allowing the citizens substantial control over them. In this context, William Connolly has observed:

This is the double bind of late-modern democracy: its present terms of territo-

rial organization constrict its effective accountability, while any electoral cam-
paign within its territory that acknowledged the import of this limitation would
meet with a predictable rebuff at the polls. Who wants to elect representatives
who concede the inefficacy of the unit they represent ... or who compromise
the principle of sovereignty through which the sense of the self-sufficiency of
established institutions of accountability is secured? (Connolly 1991: 217)

There is no denying the fact that states can no longer afford not to be part
of the global economy; opting out of global capitalism has grave consequences for the developing national economies and the social and political
structure of a country. Of course, opting in has severe consequences for
countries as well. Some of the consequences derive from the fact that global
capitalism is a system of structured inequality. Others follow from the institutional 'logic' of the global economy:

> Competing for world market shares, whether oil or semiconductors or air
> travel, means accepting the established structures and customs of those mar-
> kets. Competing for foreign capital means accepting the terms and conditions
> set by the major financial centres and the major international banks, insurance
> firms, law firms and accountants ... It means accepting the imperative of nego-
> tiating with foreign firms which have more control than national governments
> over access to major world markets, and have ownership of and control over
> advanced technologies; and whose co-operation can also gain access to the for-
> eign human and financial capital necessary for economic growth and a secure
> balance of payments. (Strange 1995: 161)

The closing down of certain policy options as a result of opting into global
capitalism is, without any doubt, an important aspect of the current phase
of economic globalization. Internationally mobile capital and volatile international markets as well as the change to flexible methods of production
and the concomitant re-shaping of the composition of the labour force have
affected the level of economic activity and employment within states and
their capacity for political regulation of the economy. Yet we should ask
whether the democratic state has ever controlled all that obtained within
its territorial space? Has capitalism ever been controllable by the state? Has
the state ever controlled finance capital? And has capitalism never in the
past set any limits to what the state could do? Furthermore, it may be
argued that the actors in the world economy have an interest in a regulated
international business environment: 'Calculable trade rules, settled and
internationally common property rights, and exchange-rate stability are a
level of elementary security that companies need to plan ahead and, therefore, a condition of continued investment and growth ... Companies may
want free trade and common regimes of trade standards, but they can only
have them if states work together to achieve common international regulation' (Hirst/Thompson 1995: 425–6). This international regulatory 'func-

tion' of the states, so Hirst and Thompson propose, gives them considerable leverage over economic actors. Furthermore, they point out that not all economic actors operate globally, but benefit from their embeddedness in national business systems:

> Companies benefit from being enmeshed in networks of relations with central and local governments, with trade associations, with organized labour, with specifically national systems of skill formation and labour motivation. These networks provide information, they are a means to co-operation and co-ordination between firms to secure common objectives, and they help make the business environment less uncertain and stable – a national economic system provides forms of reassurance to firms against shocks and the risks of the international economy. (Hirst/Thompson 1995: 426–7)

This argument alerts us to the fact that economic globalization does not necessarily, or generically, result in a wholesale decline in political opportunities for national economic management. States as social organizations may benefit economic actors in both the national and global environment. As far as the question of democracy is concerned, the problem posed by globalization would therefore appear to be somewhat more complex than the issues raised by Falk or Strange would seem to suggest. Political legitimacy in the sovereign, democratic nation-state has typically been linked to the state's capacity to deal relatively effectively with the demands and expectations of its citizens and with the citizens' democratic rights to exercise control over the ruling elites through elections and other forms of political participation as well as through the use of law. This legitimacy is strained because policy issues increasingly require international agreement and collaboration and are therefore not any longer open to the problem-solving capacity of individual nation-states. But once policy issues are no longer susceptible to comprehensive governmental control, no one can be held democratically accountable for them. As long as it is possible for states to find acceptance amongst their citizens for the claim that the global policy interdependence can be confronted through international and intergovernmental arrangements which leave nation-states with a veto, this challenge to political legitimacy will not result in a crisis of legitimacy: the citizens will still maintain that their governments are democratically accountable to them for their policy decisions (Gamble 1993).

However, when and if it becomes apparent that intergovernmental collaboration is less efficient in addressing and solving global policy issues and that transnational decision-making bodies would have to be created whose decisions became binding on nation-states, the question of legitimacy would be raised again. One response to the realization of the diminished problem-solving capacity of states both as 'sovereign' and 'autonomous' actors and as participants in international and intergovernmental arrangements, is

likely to take the form of demands for, in political terms, a 'splendid isolation' and, in economic terms, protectionism, and thus for a policy of 'exit-
ing' from the world-system. The issue of a distinct identity of a political
collectivity, which Roland Robertson discusses in the context of globalization, will resurface as a manifestation of popular disappointments with the
ability of democratic regimes to meet the expectations of their citizenry and
solve pressing policy issues. As the rise of right-wing extremism in many of
the democratic countries of the West in recent years shows, there is a distinct possibility for 'xenophobic nationalism' to function as the mobilizing
ideology for the establishment of authoritarian regimes in which the
'ethnos' component of citizenship will marginalize the 'demos' component.
It is also an open question whether the countries which have established
democratic regimes in the last two decades or so, will return to more
authoritarian rule once it becomes clear that the rising expectations of the
population, which are part and parcel of the democratic process, cannot be
met in the world of global interdependence and (still increasing) global
inequality.

The argument put forward in the preceding paragraphs may be cast in a
somewhat different way. The success of the nation-state in the last two hun-
dred years or so as well as its universality and legitimacy were premised on
its claim to be able to guarantee the economic well-being, the physical security and the cultural identity of the people who constitute its citizens. But
global forces such as global capitalism, global proliferation of nuclear
weapons and global media and culture are now undermining this claim and
challenge the effectiveness of the political organizational form of the nation-
state (Beetham 1984). They are thus weakening the links between the citizens and the nation-state. The citizens demand political representation,
physical protection, economic security and cultural certainty. But in a
global system that is made up of states, regions, international and supranational organizations and transnational corporations and that does not
have a clear-cut power hierarchy, the nation-state finds it increasingly difficult to accommodate these interests and mediate between its citizens and
the rest of the world (Horsman/Marshall 1994).

It is within this structural configuration that nationalism can become a
strong political force. And this for a variety of reasons. First, nationalism is
structurally embedded in the changes of the interstate system. After the end
of the Cold War, the geostrategic interests of the superpowers can no longer
be defined as necessitating the perpetuation of the freezing of international
borders on the grounds of security. As a result, demands for independence
within states can be voiced more persuasively along nationalist lines.
Second, the formation of regional blocs (such as the European Commu-
nity/Union) makes it feasible for 'small' states, such as the Baltic States, the
Czech Republic, Slovenia or Scotland, to conceive of themselves as viable,

'independent' states in a 'Greater Europe'. It thus allows for nationalist mobilization in pursuit of secession and independence. Third, the restructuring of the global economy adds to chances of 'survival' of (at least, some) smaller states: with the increasing importance of high-tech, high-knowhow economies, scale and space become less important in economic terms, as Hong Kong and Singapore demonstrate. Even 'city-states' have thus a good chance of establishing themselves in the global system. Finally, globalization, and in particular, global capitalism, has brought in its wake regional disparities and economic dislocations. Deindustrialization and unemployment, rising prices and declining living standards have intensified the demands by citizens for protection and security. The citizens 'call on governments to act in the national interests at a time when policy tools at the disposal of the nation-state are no longer up to the task' (Horsman/Marshall 1994: 86). In this situation, extreme nationalism and right-wing extremism can become popular amongst those social classes and groups most affected by the processes of globalization.

Nationalism, of necessity, thrives on the creation of 'otherness' and the distinction between 'us' and 'them'. However, 'otherness' and 'difference' are not only a result of political structures; they are also issuing out of economic structures. Recent changes in economic production and reproduction, which aimed to establish regimes of flexible work organization, flexible technology and flexible labour in an economy geared towards batch production and niche marketing, have radicalized questions of collective identities. In particular, flexibility of labour meant, in effect, the division of the work force into a skilled employed core and an unskilled and only partially employed periphery with a clear boundary divide between these segments. These economic changes caused the '[d]isorganization of broad, relatively stable, and encompassing commonalities of economic interest, associational affiliations, or cultural values and life-styles' (Offe 1987: 527). According to Offe, this disorganization led 'to the virtual evaporation of classes and other self-conscious collectivities of political will, economic interest, and cultural values whose existence [is a] necessary condition for solidarity and collectivist attitudes and ideologies' (Offe 1987: 528).

The differentiation of social structure is complemented by the pluralization of life-styles: '[C]apital has fallen in love with difference ... [A]dvertising thrives on selling us things that will enhance our uniqueness and individuality. It's no longer about keeping up with the Joneses, it's about being different from them ... [C]ultural difference sells' (Rutherford 1990: 11). This has put a premium on privileging life-styles and consumption, rather than life-chances and production, as means of social differentiation and distinction. It tends to privilege 'status' politics over 'class' politics. Together, these changes in economic production and reproduction as well as the commodification of 'otherness' can be analysed as leading not only

135

to the destruction or undermining of the older ('fordist') bases of political and social identity and collective solidarities, but also to the fragmentation of the (modern) 'self' and the formation of multiple personal identities as well as to the fragmentation and differentiation of culture. This process of fragmentation and multiplication can be understood as the creation of that space that enables individuals to develop new loyalties and identities after the fracturing of the old 'narratives'. As Stuart Hall argues, this fragmentation of self has led to an:

> enormous expansion of 'civil society', caused by the diversification of the different social worlds in which men and women can operate ... Of course, 'civil society' is no ideal realm of pure freedom. Its micro-worlds include the multiplication of points of power and conflict. More and more of our everyday lives are caught up with these forms of power, and their lines of intersection. Far from there being no resistance to the system, there has been a proliferation of new points of antagonism, new social movements of resistance organized around them, and consequently, a generalization of 'politics' to spheres which hitherto the left assumed to be apolitical. (Hall 1991a, as cited in: Lipschutz 1992: 415)

Global capitalism can thus be analysed as creating the 'space' for the formation of a plurality of collectivities, such as 'new social movements' that, as we have already seen in a previous chapter, can become the carriers of a 'politics of difference', based, for example, on gender or sexual identities. However, the effect of capitalism on identity formation goes beyond affecting the constitution of new collectivities in a 'postfordist' economic regime. Mitchell (1993) has provided us with a good case study of this *problematique* in the context of global capitalism. In her discussion of Vancouver as a 'global city', she analyses how, since the mid-1980s, the influx of capital from Hong Kong, but particularly the residential settlement of Hong Kong Chinese, have led to perceptions by the long-term white residents of threats to their established ways of life and to fears of exclusion from business activities. These anxieties were expressed as concerns about individual and national identity and about urban change (rather than in an explicit 'racist' language). But these tensions, that had been triggered off by international spatial (economic) integration and that found one expression in the search (or assertion) of a collective identity (be it in local or national terms), have to be controlled if the ongoing expansion of capitalism is to be secured. As a result, multiculturalism has been reworked as 'an ideology of racial harmony and bridge-building' (1993: 288). Multiculturalism appears as that ideological moment that contributes to the removal of local barriers to the spread of capitalism; barriers that could be sustained, *inter alia*, by the racialization of society. The discourse on 'multiculturalism', that presents racial diversity in a positive way, can thus be read as 'an attempt to gain hegemonic control over concepts of race and nation in order to further expedite Vancouver's integration into the international network of global capitalism' (Mitchell 1993: 265). It is the expression of the contradictory nature of capitalism that it generates, on the one hand, attempts to reassert particularistic (ethno-national or racial) identities in response to its global spread and, on the other, that it can only thrive when these sets of particularistic identities are peacefully contained and accommodated in the ideology of multiculturalism.

Yet, as we have already seen in chapter 3, multiculturalism is more than an ideology. Increasingly, in the era of globalization, Western societies become 'multicultural' societies in which distinct and cohesive communities demand the recognition and institutionalization of group rights in order to preserve their culturally and morally distinct way of life. States are increasingly resembling an assemblage of national, ethnic, cultural or religious communities with distinct languages, histories, traditions and more or less complete institutional structures. In order to ensure the full and free development of their culture, these communities demand the right to govern themselves in certain key matters, urging the transfer of power and legislative jurisdictions from central government to their own communities. As we have noticed, this raises a series of controversial questions regarding both the institutional structure of the modern, Western state and its underlying normative philosophy.

So far in this chapter my argument has been that political, economic and cultural aspects of globalization will result in the proliferation of cultural 'particularisms', collective identities and the political creation of 'otherness'. Yet, we can also detect trends towards the formation of a global consciousness. Ever more individuals define their identity by reference to the 'global' world. To start with, global capitalism has created a denationalized global business elite that shares a kind of homogenized global culture of experience, symbols and infrastructure that supports its way of life. But what this global elite lacks is any global civic sense of responsibility – unless one accepts the pursuit of global business as a true manifestation of such civic concerns (Falk 1994). However, during the last two decades or so, the threats to the survival of the human race posed by nuclear, biological and chemical warfare and by dangers of an ecocatastrophe as well as a concern with political and social injustice world-wide, be it with political prisoners or discrimination on the basis of race or gender, have led to the formation of movements that do not limit their activities to any one particular territory. For activists in the environmental and peace movements or in Amnesty International, the 'one world' has become the point of reference for their concerns (Falk 1992: chaps 4, 6; Hegedus 1989; Thränhardt 1992; Meyer/Marullo 1992; Heater 1990: 229–41; Roszak 1979). To a certain extent, this holds also true for the women's movement. Such a global orientation is also becoming prominent within religious organizations. For the World Council of (mostly Protestant and Orthodox) Churches, for example, the spiritual and ethical concern with 'Justice, Peace and the Integrity of Creation' is, of necessity, global (Beyer 1994: chap. 9). The participants in these movements act on the basis of a global consciousness. They have been defined as 'citizen–pilgrims' whose 'commitment is radical and essentially religious in character, not depending on any validation by the prospect of immediate results' (Falk 1992: 74):

> [Their] ethos implies a reorientation of citizenship in order to go beyond loyalty and diligent participation in the collective life of a territorially delimited society that qualifies as a sovereign state. The citizen sensitive to the claims of this emergent ethos needs to extend his or her notions of participation in dimensions of both space (beyond the territory of any particular state) and time (beyond the present, reclaiming past wisdom and safeguarding future generations). (Falk 1992: 153–4)

'Think globally, act locally' as much as 'Think locally, act globally' is the core of this ethos that is 'necessarily deferential to the local and the diverse' (Falk 1992: 153). As Sachs (1992: 112) put it, '[t]he globe is not any longer imagined as a homogeneous space where contrasts ought to be levelled out, but as a discontinuous space where differences flourish in a multiplicity of places'. Arguably, through their global orientation, the 'citizen–pilgrims' are participating in the creation of a global civil society. It is significant for our understanding of these processes that, for example, more than 1,500 non-governmental organizations (NGOs) took part in the UN Conference on Environment and Development (the Earth Summit) held in Rio de Janeiro in 1992. Yet, we must not forget that these social movements and movement organizations are formed mostly within national civil societies and, to a great extent, depend for their success, and even their survival, on other institutions such as political parties, trade unions, churches and the media. A global civil society that is built around the global linkages of these nationally 'embedded' movements is thus inherently fragile and premised upon a 'national' environment congenial to movement politics (Shaw 1994).

Such a democratic global civil society needs a public space for deliberation and the co-ordination of activities. Though such a space has not yet been institutionalized, the new information and communication technologies could possibly provide its infrastructural underpinning once their 'empowering' potential has been released (Keane 1991: 116–62). James Rosenau has suggested that these technologies have already enhanced the competencies of citizens:

> The advent of global television, the widening use of computers in the workplace, the growth of foreign travel and the mushrooming migrations of peoples, the spread of educational institutions at the primary, secondary, and univer-

sity levels, and many other features of the post-industrial era [such as the revolution in information technology] have enhanced the analytic skills of individuals. (Rosenau 1992: 275)

This skill revolution, so he argues, increasingly enables citizens to hold their own against political authority 'by knowing when, where, and how to engage in collective action' (Rosenau 1992: 291). To the extent that these technologies can become sites of resistance, they will also be the sites of political struggle in the future.

We may use arguments put forward by Roland Robertson and Frank Lechner to place these developments into a theoretical perspective. They have argued that in the present global circumstance we see the creation of a world order that is no longer intelligible solely on the basis of a Hobbesian realism that 'focuses on societies as independent self-interested entities ... constrained only by considerations of prudence and expedience'. It has now become a world order which increasingly takes on the form of an international society, 'in which states are the primary actors but are necessarily related to other states on the basis of common rules and institutions [and in which] there are limits to sovereignty' (Lechner 1991: 271–2). This global order becomes therefore intelligible on the basis of a Grotian internationalism.

This 'relativization of societies' thus involves 'the situating of concrete societies in the context of a world complex of societies' and results in the criteria for societal change and conduct becoming 'matters of inter-societal, inter-continental, inter-civilizational, and inter-doctrinal interpretation and debate' (Robertson/Chirico 1985: 237). This 'relativization of societies' is complemented by the 'relativization of the selves' which involves 'the situating of selfhood in the more inclusive and fundamental frame of what it means to be of mankind' (Robertson/Chirico 185: 234). According to this argument, there occurs a relativization of personal identity, with identity becoming detached from reference to the national society/state, towards a conception of selfhood which is based on the realization of the transnational bonds between human beings and common humanity. A Kantian cosmopolitanism and universalism replaces a Lockean individualism as the appropriate conceptual approach for understanding this emergent global condition (Lechner 1991: 271).

In this perspective, the transnational movements discussed above could be seen as manifestations of the 'relativization' of both societies and 'selves.' Another prominent manifestation of these processes of relativization can be detected in international law. A major concern of international law is still the development and maintenance of a legal framework for regulating the relationship between states. The normative core of this framework is expressed in the principles of the sovereign equality of states; the self-determination of peoples; the non-intervention in the internal and external affairs of other states; the prohibition of the threat or use of force; and the peaceful settlement of disputes. But increasingly, attention is also given to establishing an international legal framework for upholding and protecting the right of individuals as human beings, in particular, through the protection of 'human rights', as well as to the conceptualization of humankind through the development of the legal notion of the 'common heritage of mankind' (Cassese 1986: chaps 6, 11, 14).

As is well known, the notion of the 'common heritage of mankind' can be found in article 136 of the Convention on the Law of the Sea in which the sea-bed and ocean floor and subsoil thereof, beyond the limits of national jurisdiction, and its resources are defined as 'the common heritage of mankind'. But it should also be remembered that, first, the United States and United Kingdom, for example, did not sign the Convention, objecting, in particular, to this very article and that, secondly, this very notion was introduced to forestall the ongoing process of *de facto* 'etatization' of the seas, that is, the appropriation of sea resources by individual states. In fact, therefore, the Convention and its 'failure' confirm the importance and power of individual states in the state system and thus the (ultimate) political weakness of the notion and norm of 'mankind' and shared fate. Still, this notion could arguably be held to indicate developments towards some kind of conceptualization of 'cosmopolitanism' in international legal theory.

The point to be made is not that states have given up the use of force in the pursuit of what they see as their interests and are, instead, using international law to settle conflicts. Indeed, it could be argued that international law, as it currently stands, expresses the power political interests of the dominant hegemonic power in the interstate system, the USA. And, as is quite evident, the USA uses force whenever it sees fit, as in Vietnam or in the Gulf. What is important to emphasize, however, is that states, through international agreements, have laid down legally enshrined norms that they claim govern their behaviour in the interstate system. It has therefore become possible in public discourse to challenge the legitimacy of state action, not by referring to 'lofty' philosophical principles, but to the legal commitment made 'voluntarily' by the states themselves. Foreign policy has thus been opened up for a certain kind of principled public control.

For example, as will be remembered, it was the Nuremberg trials of Nazi war criminals in 1945–6 that introduced into international law the idea that citizens have rights in respect of, and duties to obey, a universal moral code, even if this moral code demands actions contrary to the interests of their state as perceived by any given government (Heater 1990: 144–6): obligations to the natural law of humane conduct override national loyalties. But as individuals have duties and liabilities that transcend national obligations, so they have a right of disobedience *vis-à-vis* their own state if its laws and policies violate the universal principles of human morality. The exercise of state power was seen as legitimate only to the extent that it adhered to these universal principles. The trials subordinated 'the actions of nation-states to a presumed higher law of the human community – a law comprising enforceable rights and obligations for all individuals by virtue of their being members of the human community' (Brown 1992: 107). The trials thus assumed that the world was a moral community and that individuals had rights and duties as members of the community of humankind and that the behaviour of states was rightfully judged by assessing their contribution to upholding the universal moral code. Related to this supposition is the idea that individuals, by the fact of being human, have a right to (at least minimal) satisfaction of basic human needs, such as subsistence, security, love and dignity of the person. Derived from this notion of (inalienable) human rights is the perception that servicing these basic human needs is the prime task of states and that their legitimacy is heavily dependent upon their securing these basic 'human rights' (Brown 1992: 101–14, 125–7).

The debate on the moral significance of human rights centres on the question as to what significance ought to be attached to moral principles that hold universally among individuals who, as bearers of human rights, merit just and equal treatment without regard to their membership in particular nations, states or political communities. If we accept the human rights argument, then violation of these human rights by a state may serve as a ground on which an international organization, such as the United Nations, or a coalition of states could intervene in that state to ensure that human rights are upheld or re-established. We would accept that such a policy of intervention could possibly be detrimental to international peace and security; and we would deny that national boundaries have a moral significance, which is typically asserted in the right of self-determination (Gould 1988: chap. 12; Walzer 1980). But even if we denied such a right on the grounds that self-determination of a group presupposes free and autonomous persons empowered to participate in the decision-making process of their group and who are thus endowed with the conditions of agency (that is, human rights), the debate on human rights has strengthened, rather than undermined, the primacy of the state. It is still the state that is seen as that body that is rightfully and legitimately charged with upholding these human rights, both domestically and internationally (Aron 1988).

To repeat, the transnational social movements can be analysed as a manifestation of a kind of 'Kantian' cosmopolitanism and universalism, and thus of a nascent 'global consciousness'. They demonstrate that the reinforcement of particularistic collective identities, though of the utmost significance and importance in recent years, has not been the exclusive response to the challenges posed by inter-societal, inter-continental, inter-civilizational and inter-doctrinal encounters in a global world. Globalization is a contradictory process. Borne by the increase in the global reach of economic and political processes as well as by the global flow of information, communication and technology, globalization is fostering manifestations of a 'global consciousness' which conceives of the world as 'one place'. Despite (or rather, because of) these processes, there are, however, also to be detected strong pressures towards the assertion of 'regional autonomy', localism and 'local' identities. Homogeneity as much as heterogeneity and fragmentation are constitutive of processes of globalization.

The search for identity within a global world may express itself politically in the formation of a global consciousness that perceives the world as 'one place' and sees individuals as part of an all-encompassing humankind. But it may also manifest itself in religious fundamentalism, ethno-national revivalism and/or a 'civilizational' consciousness. In Eastern Europe and elsewhere, this revivalism still focuses on the creation and protection of 'sovereign' nation-states. The 'state' and the 'nation' are still concepts in which community is 'imagined' (Benedict Anderson). Membership in a territorially demarcated, 'sovereign' political unit is still the relevant precondition for citizenship rights; membership in the 'human race' does not yet translate into universal human rights which would incorporate political, economic, social or ecological citizenship rights. 'Democratic' politics is thus still channelled through the political institutions of the nation-state on the basis of a claim by the nation-state to sovereignty and the principle of citizenship. Despite the rise of global consciousness, there still exists the perception and the widespread normative acceptance of an 'elective affinity' between the state and democracy (Connolly 1991: 201). Thus there does arise the tension between, on the one hand, the particularism of citizenship that, based on state sovereignty, defines the individual as a political being with freedom and duties within a territorially demarcated political unit, and, on the other hand, the nascent universalizing understanding of humanity that defines the individual as a cohabitant of a fragile planet and a member of a global community of fate (Walker/Mendlovitz 1990: 5–6; Walker 1993: chaps 7, 8). In the international arena, this tension translates into the complex and often conflictual relationship between the system of states and a nascent global civil society. And insofar as globalization reinforces ethnic and national identities, it contributes to the resilience of the nation-state and the state system. At the same time, while in this tension between globality and locality the nation-state as a political unit and focus of political loyalty and identity is invoked, globalization challenges the (liberal-) democratic organization of this state form.

These processes of globalization compel us to reconceptualize the social world in which we live. Centralization and hierarchization of power within states and through states in the international system are steadily replaced by the pluralization of power among political, economic, cultural and social actors, groups, and communities within states, between states and across states. We move into a 'plurilateral' world of diffused and decentralized power, into a world characterized by a variety of different loci of power and cross-cutting, and intersecting power networks (Cerny 1993). For Nederveen Pieterse (1994: 166), this 'plurilateralism' can be identified 'in the increase in the available modes of organisation: transnational, international, macro-regional, national, micro-regional, municipal, and local'. These organizational levels are criss-crossed 'by functional networks of corporations, international organisations, non-governmental organisations [and social movements] as well as professionals and computer users'. Those individuals, groups and communities partaking in the creation of these networks and affected by them, will become empowered and constrained by them in ways quite different from the past when it was the nation-state that determined, on the whole, their political 'liberty' and 'identity' and mediated the effects of the 'outside' world. In this plurilateral world, the idea of a *summa potestas* that resides in the state as that institutional arrangement empowered to make, and enforce, collectively binding decisions has lost, if not its appeal, then its justification. And so has the notion of the sovereignty of the people as a united, homogeneous body legitimating the sovereign power of 'its' state through a constitution that manifests the principle of *voluntas populi suprema lex*.

In this complex and fragmented world, where is the place of 'democracy'? If there is no longer a *summa potestas*, who, then, can be held accountable by the 'people'? And if we, as individuals and members of groups and communities, are 'embedded' in a plethora of power networks, bringing us into relationships of dominance and dependency with alternating sets of individuals, groups and communities, who or what is the 'constituency' that can legitimately claim the democratic right of control and participation? In a global world, has the concern with the creation and maintenance of citizenship and rights attached to nationality and territory/place become anachronistic? How to speak of democracy in a plurilateral world and how to institutionalize new forms of democracy commensurate with the complexity and fragmented structure of this world? These are some of the questions we will have to confront as we move into the twenty-first century.

5

European integration, the nation-state and liberal democracy

It was one of the key arguments put forward in the previous chapter that globalization will not usher in the demise of the nation-state. Rather, the nation-state will retain its importance as an actor in the interstate system and as a point of reference for the political and democratic aspirations of its people. Yet, at the same time, the formation of a 'plurilateral' world multiplies the number of international actors and thus relativizes the role of the state in the international arena. This complex and segmented 'plurilateral' world also problematizes our notion of 'democracy' since it results in the transformation of hierarchical power structures and the demolition of clearly identifiable centres of ultimate sovereignty. Yet, as I have also pointed out, one major feature of this emerging 'plurilateral' world is the process of global regionalization. The global economy is dominated by the advanced capitalist countries of North America, East Asia and Europe and is structured by the interpenetration of their economies and the intense transactions and transfers between these three economic macro-regions. Arguably, amongst these three regions, Europe has developed a particularly high degree of regional cohesiveness. Not only do we find here a high density of translocal economic, political, cultural and social relations and interdependencies, but these relations and interdependencies have also been institutionalized in structures of organized co-operation. This institutionalization has occurred to such an extent that 'Europe' as organized in the European Community/European Union has achieved the capability of turning itself into an acting political subject (Hettne 1993). In this chapter, I want to discuss the effects of economic and political integration in Europe via a 'European Union' on the structure of democratic rule and our understanding of liberal democracy.

European integration and the European Union

European political and economic integration as the formation of a regional bloc of nation-states and the interpenetration of national economies has always been closely bound up with global economic, political and military processes as well as with changes in the political power structures of the Western European nation-states. These processes have been closely intertwined. We can find these dynamics at work in the revitalization of the project of European integration since the mid-1980s. This resurgence of the 'Project Europe' manifested itself in a programme to establish a single European market, in which goods, people, capital and services can move freely across the member states' frontiers. This single market programme, that was launched in 1985, led to a renewed interest in the creation of an Economic and Monetary Union (EMU). It was also partly due to dynamics released by these policies for economic integration that attention became focused on considerations for a European Political Union (EPU). The relaunch of the European project in the mid-1980s found its supreme manifestation in the 1992 Maastricht Treaty. Incorporating both EMU and EPU, the treaty established the European Union (EU), basing it on three pillars: amendments to the treaties that founded the European Coal and Steel Community (ECSC), the European Economic Community (EEC), and the European Atomic Energy Community (EAEC) in the 1950s; a Common Foreign and Security Policy; and co-operation in the area of justice and home affairs. The provisions for co-operation in the areas of foreign and defence policies as well as of justice and home affairs have potentially moved Europe closer to becoming an active political subject; however, it is still the process of economic integration that is at the centre even of the new European Union.

To understand the policies of European integration since the mid-1980s we may begin by seeing them as a response to the structural changes of the international political and economic system of the post-war world (Ross 1992; Ross 1995; Sandholtz/Zysman 1989/90; Streeck/Schmitter 1991). Relative American decline and Japanese ascent and the concomitant shifts in technological, industrial, and economic or financial capabilities have forced the European political and economic elites to rethink their economic and political goals and interests as well as the means appropriate for achieving them. Undoubtedly, one force behind the relaunch of 'Project Europe' was the business interest of some large European firms. They came to realize in the early 1980s that the role of protected national markets in the era of global competition was decreasing. Sectors such as telecommunications, electronics, or automobiles were no longer economically viable even in the larger European countries. A 'single market' Europe would allow for economies of scale by easing economic transactions and by creating a large, 'harmonized' consumer market. It would allow to develop Europe-wide delivery systems, corporate alliances, production networks and electronic market-places: 'Rather than just shipping goods across borders, [companies] are seeking customized, in-depth interactions with clients, suppliers and partners, through an expanding gamut of networking strategies, many of which have a strong information and advanced communication content' (Bressand 1990: 58).

As Streeck and Schmitter (1991) have argued, there was an acceptance among many European large firms that such a European orientation was inevitable given the increased size of production runs and investments required for world market competitiveness. This European 'turn' went hand in hand with a move away from the corporatist arrangements of the 1970s that had aimed at managing the macro-economy by direct negotiations among capital, labour and the government. Corporatist concertation had frequently taken the form of 'social contracts' as a national response to the social and economic repercussions of the crises of the world economy and had given capital some protection from foreign competition through state subsidies, wage restraint, technical standards serving as non-tariff trade barriers or privileged access to public procurement contracts. Yet these national economic (crises) management and accumulation strategies were not any longer viable in the face of the international trade challenge from the USA, Japan and the newly industrializing countries (NICs). They had not improved the international competitiveness of European capital, nor had they produced sustained and viable economic growth nor low inflation or low levels of unemployment. The traditional models of economic growth and of economic management were perceived by the political and economic elites to have failed. As long as it was thought possible to embark upon a successful programme of national economic management through corporatist concertation, European economic co-ordination and integration was necessarily considered to be of secondary importance. But once national strategies had exhausted themselves, Europe could be perceived as a viable alternative.

While capital was turning away from corporatism and embraced the neo-liberal policy of market deregulation, both at home and in Europe, the political effects of rising unemployment and capital's restructuring efforts had resulted in the weakening of labour and hence of those political forces that could have been mobilizing in favour of national corporatist strategies. This weakening of the union movements and left political parties was compounded by the abandonment by new social movements of the 'social democratic consensus' as it had become institutionalized after the war in the Keynesian welfare state. It was in this context that moves towards greater political, economic and social integration of the European (economic) macro-region were relaunched by national politicians and the European business elite under the instigating and co-ordinating leadership of the European Commission in Brussels under Jacques Delors. Streeck and Schmitter argue that:

[i]nstead of trying to benefit from the economic nationalism that made European integration grind to a halt in the 1970s, business throughout Europe seems to have become willing in the 1980s to join forces with political elites which, under the impact of their economies' poor performances and with worldwide policy co-ordination with the United States and Japan out of reach, found themselves under pressure to seek a *supranational pooling of eroded national sovereignties over economic policy*, to recapture collective autonomy in relation to the United States, and to begin to organize a competitive response to the Japanese challenge. (Streeck/Schmitter 1991: 148–9)

'Deregulation' was the price governments had to pay for the support by business for the political project 'Europe'. 'Pooled' sovereignty was not to be deployed for internal intervention in the European economy, but exclusively for its external reassertion in the global economy.

While these economic and socio-political changes are undoubtedly of great causal importance for the relaunch of the European project, changes in the interstate system have to be taken into account as well. Concern with developing a common foreign and defence policy, or at least, with co-ordinating the respective national policies, gained momentum when the United States hinted in the mid-1980s at a reduction in their military presence in Europe. It became urgent when the United States did indeed withdraw troops with the end of the Cold War and the break-up of the Soviet Union. Anyhow, as the negotiations of the then superpowers at the Washington summit of 1987 had already demonstrated, without some common position on security issues, decisions about Western Europe's security would be taken over the heads of its leaders and peoples. The repercussions of the collapse of state socialism in 1989 initiated a further reconsideration of a common foreign and defence policy. First, the post-socialist states of Eastern and Central Europe were looking to the European Community for political and security agreements. Second, the war in Yugoslavia required some kind of joint geostrategic position. Finally, and perhaps of the greatest importance, the inevitable effects of the unification of Germany on the structure, dynamics and balance of power of the European Community had to be parried. How best to bind the united Germany even more firmly into the European order became a decisive diplomatic concern. The solution was believed to lie in the linkage between German unification and deeper political integration in Europe. It was in the light of all these developments that the Maastricht Treaty included commitments to the objective of both EMU and EPU.

What kind of European political system does the Maastricht Treaty establish or envisage? Does European integration à la Maastricht lead to a European super-state with features in fundamental ways similar to those of the classical European nation-state? According to Ludlow (1992), the Maastricht Treaty does indeed confer on the European Union important responsibilities in relation to many of the major functions of a modern sovereign state. Amongst other items, Ludlow (1992: 121–2) mentions:

> the creation and management of a single currency; the co-ordination, supervision, and where appropriate enforcement of sound economic policies, particularly in budgetary matters; the establishment and safeguarding of a single market based on principles of free and fair competition; [and] the maintenance of equity, and where necessary the redistribution of wealth, between richer and poorer regions.

It will be above all the envisaged independent European Central Bank that will become a strong centralizing force in economic matters in the Union. Furthermore, the new 'pillar' of co-operation in the area of justice and home affairs has strengthened the role of the EU in the preservation of law and order. And the agreement on the procedures for the management of a common external policy covering all areas of foreign and security policy has strengthened the Union's potential coherence as an international actor. Yet, we should note that the EU does not have 'full' sovereignty in external affairs: member states ultimately retain their sovereignty in foreign affairs, and their security policies are either co-ordinated through NATO and/or are formulated autonomously on the basis of 'classical' sovereignty as in the case of France. There is no 'full' internal sovereignty for the EU, either. On the one hand, the European Court of Justice does create European law in the areas of Community competence that becomes legally binding for member states. On the other hand, however, there are no Union-specific law-enforcement agencies, such as a Union police force, and the Union bureaucracy does not possess a general competence to instruct, supervise and control national bureaucracies.

Despite these necessary qualifications, it is important to emphasize the centralizing thrust of the Maastricht Treaty. The supreme decision-making authority of the Council of Ministers has been reaffirmed and reinforced. The Council of Ministers, which is composed of representatives of the member states, takes policy decisions for the EU in confidential deliberations. The Council of Ministers is the Community's real legislature. Its autonomy and efficiency have been enhanced by qualifying the requirements and policy areas for unanimity in decision-making and by limiting the right of veto for individual countries. The extension of majority voting to key areas of Community decision-making has introduced an element of supranationalism into the essentially intergovernmental character of the Council since member states have agreed under certain circumstances to be outvoted in the decision-making process. As Ludlow (1992: 124) points out, 'Council decisions on economic policy, for example, will be on the basis of qualified majorities. So, too, will decisions on visas, transport policy, large areas of social policy, and, if the Council itself so decides, the implementation of common decisions on foreign policy and judicial affairs.' The Council's autonomy has been further enhanced by providing for a considerably enlarged and reorganized Council Secretariat. All the preparatory work required to enable the Council to make decisions will be centralized in the Secretariat as well as in the Committee of Permanent Representatives (COREPER), an already extremely powerful grouping of national ambassadors to the Community.

The legislative power exercised by the Council of Ministers is, of course, an anomaly if we compare this allocation of responsibilities to that in the political system of Western parliamentary democracy. As we have noticed, in liberal democracy it is parliament that is the legitimate legislature. The European Parliament, however, has only limited legislative competence. First, it generally does not have the right to initiate legislation. This right remains for the most part with the Commission, the *de facto* executive body of the EU. Second, its powers to shape EU legislation are rather limited. Policy areas have been divided up, and in each area the involvement of the European Parliament in the legislative process differs. Under the consultation procedure, Parliament is consulted and has the right to submit an opinion before the Council adopts a Commission proposal, but there is no obligation for either of these bodies to incorporate the parliamentary amendments. Under the co-operation procedure, which was introduced by the Single European Act in 1986, Parliament has the right to a second reading of the draft legislation. Yet again, the Council is not obliged to alter its draft legislation in the light of the position taken by Parliament. A determined Council can push through its proposal even against parliamentary opposition, or, alternatively, may decide to take no action and let the proposed legislation lapse. Finally, under the co-decision procedure, which was introduced by the Maastricht Treaty, Parliament was given the right of a third reading of certain draft legislation and the right of veto. This co-decision procedure comes into operation in a number of areas of which policies related to the internal market and the free movement of persons are by far the most important (Art. 110a and 49 EC Treaty).

The European Union and the democratic deficit

For our discussion it is not necessary to present the legislative procedures in greater detail. The point to be made is simple. According to the model of liberal democracy, in a democratic constitutional state parliament represents the sovereignty of the people. This sovereignty is realized in the legislative competence of parliament. This legislative competence includes the budgetary powers of revenue-raising and expenditure. In the European Union, however, Parliament's rights in these areas are seriously curtailed. There exists a clear imbalance in legislative matters between the Council of

Ministers and the European Parliament. Although it gained the new powers of co-decision with regard to some policy areas in the Maastricht Treaty, the European Parliament is not a genuine legislative chamber with effective powers of sanction against the Council and the Commission. Furthermore, the confidentiality of the deliberations of the Council and the attendant lack of public scrutiny of the decision-making process make it difficult to hold the Council accountable to either the European Parliament or the national parliaments of the member states. Both the marginalization of the European Parliament in legislative matters and the decision-making procedures in the Council of Ministers have given rise to concerns about the democratic legitimacy of the European Union. It has been argued that a 'democratic deficit' has arisen because policy-making in the European Union has been delinked from democratic controls and democratic accountability.

More recently, it has also been suggested that this 'democratic deficit' of the EU has been compounded by the way the Commission is organized and operates. It has been criticized for establishing in effect a kind of 'bureaucratic autocracy' organized around a Byzantine administrative structure. Legislative proposals are drawn up in a cartel-like setting by Commission experts, administrative elites of the member states and special interests lobbying in Brussels in negotiations inaccessible to representatives of parliamentary bodies or the media. Yet, the criticism is not confined to the way in which the Commission initiates legislation or draws up and issues directives, regulations and decisions. It is also directed against its almost exclusive right to make proposals, independent of the Council of Ministers and the European Parliament. These criticisms of the Commission have recently resulted in a determined effort to bring transparency and openness to the activities of the Commission. As far as the charges of secrecy against the Commission are concerned, steps have been taken in the last few years to make the bureaucratic procedures, the policy-making processes and policy-implementation more transparent. Amongst the steps taken are the publication of consultative Green and White Papers by the Commission; the timely publication of work programmes and legislative programmes allowing parliamentary bodies and interest groups to make submissions or instigate public discussion; and, more generally, improvements for easier access to policy-relevant information for both special interest groups and the public at large (Lodge 1994; Dehousse 1995; Weiler *et al.* 1995).

Yet, there is a widespread belief that the democratic deficit can not be overcome by introducing *glasnost* but only by a far-ranging policy of *perestroika* that will give the European Parliament powers similar to those exercised by national parliaments. To surmount the democratic deficit in the European Union, the European Parliament must become a truly legislative body; the central arena for the generation of a European public opinion; and the authoritative supervisory body to which the 'government' would be accountable. As one would expect, the European Parliament itself advocates the parliamentarization of the EU. The 'Draft Constitution of the European Union', which was passed by the European Parliament in February 1994, aims to move the political order of the EU towards a parliamentary system. It stipulates that '[t]he laws of the Union shall be made by the European Parliament and by the Council' (Draft Constitution 1994: Art. 32). This law-making capacity extends to budgetary powers (Art. 40). By providing for joint legislation with the Council, the draft constitutions shies away, however, from a full parliamentarization of the Union. While the Commission is to retain its right of legislative initiative, the influence of Parliament over the Commission has been much strengthened by its envisaged right to elect the President of the Commission, pass a vote of confidence in the Commission, and submit a proposal for a law by common accord with the Council, should the Commission fail to act (Art. 32). Overall, the (draft) Constitution emphasizes the Commission's role as the executive of the Union, supervised and controlled by Parliament and charged with implementing Union legislation in co-operation with the bureaucracies of the member states.

In this chapter I will argue that the expansion of the powers of the European Parliament is not the most adequate and important strategy for overcoming the deficit of political accountability in the European Union. To start with, for a parliament to function as a generator of democratic legitimacy of political rule it must be embedded in the political process of the political community; it must be supported by the intermediary institutions of political society. In all the democratic nation-states in Western Europe, we find well-developed systems of interest formation and intermediation, of institutionalized conflict management and institutionalized norms of social justice. Amongst the forces that have had the greatest impact on the formation of these systems, the political, economic and cultural struggles around the formation of centralized, and secularized, state structures and of industrial–capitalist national economies stand out. Of course, the precise cleavage structure has been different in each country, and so have the course and outcome of the struggles caused by it. As a result, each country has developed complexes of interest formation and intermediation that are fairly idiosyncratic. In the process of democratization and the formation of 'mass politics', each country has built up political parties, trade unions, professional associations, voluntary associations, special interest groups and media for the formation and expression of public opinion. Yet, for example, party systems, structures of industrial relations, the incorporation of interest groups into the political system, or the allocation of jurisdiction and resources to subnational, regional and municipal bodies, have developed in historically distinct ways in each case. However, in all cases these intermediary structures have come to be organized along national lines. They have

151

always remained dependent upon the nation-state. They developed into key institutions of the political system and were instrumental in turning parliaments into elected bodies that represent, at least potentially, the diverse interests of society. Only through this representative function could parliament become a container of democratic legitimacy; a legitimacy that was bolstered by the opportunities for political participation and by political control opened up, and made available, by these intermediary structures.

Even after forty years of European integration, we still find that intermediary structures remain 'nationalized'. As yet, there is no European party system that would aggregate and articulate social and political interests on a Europe-wide level. So far, political parties are national actors that, at best, aim to translate interests of their national constituencies into the European political system. And while there has been an increase in lobbying by interest groups in Brussels since the Single European Act, it has been above all large business interests that have achieved a certain degree of Europeanization of their interests and begun to build up common transnational organizations. Yet, on the whole, the degree of 'Europeanization' of other than business interests has been low. This is part of the reason why there has also not yet occurred the formation of a European public opinion. Under these circumstances, in which the intermediary structures necessary for interest and opinion formation as well as for the constitution of a genuine European 'public' are not in place, whom or what could a European Parliament possibly represent? Only if there is a genuine process of European-wide, transnational interest formation does it become necessary for reasons of democratic legitimacy to institute the European Parliament as that mechanism through which diverse interests have to be channelled, reconciled and acted upon. Without the infrastructure of intermediary institutions, the European Parliament cannot be the representative of a European 'public'.

The lack of a European-wide structure of intermediary institutions thus results in the unrepresentativeness of the European Parliament. Such a structure has to be built up before the European Parliament can justifiably claim to speak for a European 'constituency'. Yet in democracies the function of intermediary institutions goes beyond that of 'mediating' between social interests and the parliamentary and political–administrative system. They are also vital in transferring legitimacy onto the political system as a whole. Neunreither has highlighted two aspects of intermediary institutions that are relevant in this context. First, these institutions are instrumental in allowing citizens to identify with the political community:

> In the familiar environment of a nation-state with all its possible linguistic, historical and cultural identifications, including its daily confirmation by national television and major newspapers that give primary importance to events on the national scene, citizens are nevertheless able to develop and maintain an overall network of orientation. This network is largely dependent on intermediate

structures, that transmit the permanent stream of input necessary for self-iden-
tification. (Neunreither 1995: 12)

Hence, the function of intermediary institutions is not confined to providing
means of political participation and the formation and political expression
of interests. Their function is also to reduce the complexity of the social and
political environment of the citizens so that they can cognitively and emotionally respond to it and act upon it. Without such a system of intermediary institutions on the European level, such an identification is unlikely to
be achieved.

Second, intermediary institutions also function as a 'buffer' between the
citizen and the political apparatus. These institutions are mechanisms of
inclusion, binding the citizen to the political system by providing channels
for participation and the expression of political support for, or criticism of,
specific policies. Intermediary institutions thus articulate both agreement
and disagreement with political decisions. Yet, without such mechanisms,
political discontent is directed immediately at the political system itself.
Thus, policy disagreements can easily be turned into a wholesale attack on
the overall political system. As we have seen, neither the Council nor the
Commission can ultimately be held accountable to the European Parliament
– and given the Parliament's lack of embeddedness in a far-flung structure
of intermediary institutions, such parliamentary accountability is not necessarily desirable. Yet, the lack of an intermediary structure makes it also
impossible to influence decision-making indirectly through the mobilization
of a European 'public' or of genuinely European interests. Taken together,
these two features amount to a situation in which both agreement and disagreement with policies cannot be expressed within the system itself. There
are no channels open for the citizen to express discontent with individual
decisions. Opposition becomes, therefore, directed at the political order itself
(Kaase 1991; Wieland 1992).

Finally, the lack of a European-wide structure of intermediary institutions
undermines the European Parliament's claim to its centrality in overcoming the 'democratic deficit' in yet another way. A key feature of parliamentary rule is policy-making on the basis of decisions taken by a parliamentary
majority. Yet the principle of majority rule does not suffice to generate legitimacy of the political system as a whole. The application of majority rule as
a legitimating principle is premised on a socio-political and socio-cultural
context that is conducive to the defeated minority's acceptance of the majority decision. As we saw in a previous chapter with regard to questions of
multicommunalism, the existence of such a congenial context cannot be
taken for granted. We can generalize from this case and argue that democratic legitimacy as an effect of parliamentary majority rule has a number of
preconditions (Scharpf 1992). First, there must be no fundamental ethnic,

linguistic, religious, ideological or economic cleavages in a society. Second, the political community must have developed a collective identity based on shared citizenship and political equality as well as shared normative orientations so that differences in specific policy areas will not be dramatized into fundamental differences over the institutional order of the political community. In national political systems it is the intermediary institutions that play a central part in the generation of a collective identity as well as in processing conflicts among interests and differences in cultural orientation in such a way that they can be integrated into the political system. And it is the dynamics of the intermediary structure that holds open the promise for minorities possibly to turn their current minority position into a majority position at some point in the future. Neither of these two preconditions for the acceptance of parliamentary majority decisions as legitimate is yet in place in Europe with its historical, cultural, linguistic and political–institutional diversity and economic disparities. To expect that decisions by the European Parliament would meet with widespread acceptance under these circumstances would appear to be unwarranted, even foolhardy.

Despite these structural deficiencies that limit the democratic potential of the European Parliament, there is no denying the fact that its direct election has given it a considerable degree of political legitimacy in the European political order. But the question is how best to build on this legitimacy under the condition of a lacking European intermediary structure. If the objective is to make the decision-making process, policy formation and policy implementation democratically more accountable and more transparent, the way forward would appear to be a closer co-operation between the European Parliament and the national parliaments of the member states. After all, the Council is an intergovernmental institution in which the Ministers act as the representatives of their member states empowered and legitimized by the support they enjoy in their national parliaments. From the point of view of democratic legitimacy, this embeddedness of intergovernmentalism in the domestic political process gives national assemblies a central place in the European political order.

In a declaration annexed to the Maastricht Treaty, the European governments invited 'the European Parliament and the national parliaments to meet as necessary as a Conference of the Parliaments (or "assises")'. This conference would have consultative status 'on the main features of the European Union, without prejudice to the powers of the European Parliament and the rights of national parliaments'. As part of this consultative process, the conference would be addressed by the Presidents of the European Council and of the Commission who would report on the state of the Union. This idea of a 'conference of parliaments' can be traced back to discussions in the European Parliament in the late 1980s when the idea of the convocation of a 'European States General', composed of the parliamentarians of the then twelve member states and the European Parliament, was proposed by the European Parliament. As a result of these considerations, a conference was held in Rome in 1990 that brought together 173 delegates from national parliaments and 53 Members of the European Parliament. While no conference has been held since then, and although the 'Conference of Parliaments' has not been institutionalized in the Maastricht Treaty itself, the idea of 'assises' is of considerable significance. This is for the reason that 'national parliaments, together with the European Parliament are now potentially jointly channelled into the treaty reform process' (Westlake 1994: 57).

It will undoubtedly be difficult for such a conference to arrive at a joint position. Yet, perhaps, such an agreed position should not be its overall objective. Rather, one would expect such a conference to provide one institutional setting in which a European 'public opinion' could gradually form. It would also pull national parliaments more into the European arena and would thus contribute to the 'Europeanization' of national will-formation and policy-making. After all, in the past the national parliaments of most member states did not show any sustained interest in European Communities affairs that would have found expression, for example, in standing committees on Europe. It has only been as a result of the Maastricht Treaty and its protracted ratification process that internal procedures in all national assemblies have been revised so as to reinforce parliamentary scrutiny of EC legislation. The national assemblies have now made 'fresh efforts to enhance their general monitoring of EC activities, both through better documentation and research and through closer relations with the executive', although they have not sought to gain a role in the legislative process in the EU itself (Westlake 1995: 68–9).

Such revisions of the internal structures and procedures in the national parliaments are also the precondition for making the co-operation between national parliaments on European matters politically more relevant. Such inter-parliamentary co-operation has been institutionalized in the conference of committees within the national parliaments specializing in Community affairs (Conférence des organes specialisés dans les Affaires communautaires [COSAC]), which was first convened in 1989 and meets twice a year. But this co-operation manifests itself also in *ad hoc*, bilateral and multilateral meetings between specialized standing committees, in the areas, for example, of finance, the internal market, or the field of justice and home affairs (Westlake 1995). The objective of such modes of co-operation cannot be to define political or legislative competencies for these gatherings; rather, the aim must be to create fora of public deliberation in which national domestic issues can be considered in their European context and in which European policy proposals can be assessed in its impact on the national political systems. It is around such fora that a European 'public' may form, given the lack of a European-wide infrastructure of intermediary institutions. As long as European integration was equated with economic integration, and thus understood as a process organized around the increase in efficiency of economic relations through transactions in a European-wide market, the European 'project' could be interpreted as a technical problem that would develop behind the backs of the citizens according to the logic of economic rationality. The dynamics, and 'spill-over' effects, of this process of integration as well as changes in the international environment have, however, politicized European integration. Economic efficiency is no longer accepted as the dominant political concern. European integration has increasingly raised questions about national identity, cultural autonomy, social justice, social solidarity, and political participation and democracy. These are concerns that have exercised citizens, their parliamentary representatives and the media in all member states. The awareness that these concerns are intricately intertwined has grown, and the need for public debate about how best to accommodate these possibly conflicting concerns has been recognized. These changed circumstances will make it more likely that the new fora of public deliberation through the co-operation of parliamentary bodies will meet with increased interest from the public at large.

The argument developed so far amounts to the claim that national parliaments have a central position in the political order of the European Union; that they are indispensable for securing the democratic character of the Union, but also for enabling the formation of a genuinely European 'public'. Of course, we are well aware of the shortcomings and defects of national parliamentary systems. In almost all member states in recent years there have been debates on constitutional issues, ranging from the reform of electoral systems to regional representation and autonomy or political rights for non-citizens. The argument is not that national parliamentary systems cannot, or should not, be reformed in the light of political, economic or cultural changes and developments. Rather, I suggest that national parliaments enjoy a degree of acceptance and legitimacy that the European Parliament cannot possibly match. They are also central to the political order of the European Union because key intermediary institutions in national political systems are organized around national parliaments as the linchpin of political society. As these institutions are 'nationalized', so are the citizens. They experience and live democracy in the context of the nation-state. The nation-state and its institutional structure thus remain important for most citizens.

Any type of political union in Europe will bring together nation-states which for centuries have had their own political, social and cultural histories and institutional order (Lepsius 1992). The multinationality and multiethnicity of Europe are a fact that cannot be wished away. The post-Maastricht debates on the Union have shown that there is no wide-

spread support for a European integration that would discard these histories, pry open these institutional orders and subdue them to transnational
European organizations. The institutions of intergovernmentalism are the
appropriate reflection of this reality. Indeed, the democratic legitimacy of
European integration stems in large part from its intergovernmental decision-making process. After all, democratically elected and democratically
accountable politicians determine European politics through negotiations in
the Council of Ministers. This creates two distinct sets of problems. First,
there are two operative forms of legitimation to be found in the European
Union. The first type is mediated through the democratic structure of
member states and underlies the institution of the Council of Ministers. The
other form of legitimation is mediated through the European Parliament
and its democratic mandate through direct elections by the citizens of the
member states of the European Union. In a sense, the 'democratic deficit'
can be reconceptualized, not as a lack of democracy, but as a concern, and
debate, about how best to mediate these two forms of legitimacy. In constitutional terms, the tension between the two forms of legitimation would present itself as the ascription of specific jurisdictions and competencies to each
respective constitutional body and the design of mechanisms for conciliation
in case of legislative differences between the Parliament and the Council.
Interestingly perhaps, the 1994 (draft) Constitution passed by the European
Parliament remains silent on this issue.

The second problem is inherent in the very logic of legitimacy on the basis
of intergovernmentalism. For governments to be held accountable by their
national parliaments for decisions taken in the Council, intergovernmental
negotiations have either to be based on rules of unanimity or must provide
for a right of veto for governments. Only on that basis can responsibility for
policies be attributed to individual governments and can governments be
held accountable by their parliament:

> Although majority voting in the Council is inherently democratic, it weakens
> the already tenuous ties between governments and national parliaments on
> Community issues. By renouncing the national veto, governments reduce their
> parliaments' already weak leverage over Community legislation. After all, a
> national parliament could try to punish its government for not vetoing con-
> troversial legislation if the government was *able* to impose a veto. But a
> national parliament can hardly hold its government accountable for being out-
> voted. (Dinan 1994: 252)

We are confronted here with a very real dilemma. Majority voting in the
Council weakens the power of national parliaments over their governments;
it also potentially results in policies being imposed on citizens in those countries whose governments are outvoted in the Council. In a situation in
which democratic politics is still 'nationalized', such a state of affairs is

unlikely to be accepted as legitimate. The right of veto is therefore imperative in order to meet the democratic aspiration of the citizens. On the other
hand, however, the exercise of the right of veto may result in one country
blocking policies agreed upon by all the other member states. Is it politically
acceptable to establish a *de facto* disabling capability for minorities through
the institution of the veto? The argument I have been putting forward suggests that the veto should be defended as a means, first, to protect the interests of the constituent national units within the European Union, thus, in
effect, upholding 'minority rights' in a 'multinational' political community;
and, second, to uphold parliamentary scrutiny over governments.

   From the point of view of democratic legitimacy and accountability, then,
the principle of unanimity and the right of veto occupy a central place in
the decision-making structure of the European Union. However, this produces yet another problem. With the creation of a Single Market, national
governments and parliaments have given up much of their regulatory
powers and competencies in economic policy. If one accepts the economic
logic of the Single Market, then Economic and Monetary Union will deprive
national political actors and agencies of most of their fiscal powers as well.
Political regulation of economic processes can only be exercised on the European level. Yet the principle of unanimity and the right of veto have the
potential of limiting the capacity for common political action. According to
Scharpf (1992: 298), these institutional limitations to the capacity of
common action put a premium on the capabilities and willingness of governments in negotiations to seek flexible compromises and identify opportunities for compensating those partners who have experienced failure in one
policy with a solution that favours them in other policy areas. For Scharpf
such a strategy presupposes that national representatives in intergovernmental negotiations must have a high degree of independence to respond
creatively to any openings for compromise in discussions. Representatives
must not be tied down by an imperative mandate from their parliament.

   If we accept the logic of this argument, as I think we should, then two
considerations present themselves. First, although the right of veto binds
national representatives to their domestic political structure, it also necessi-
tates the acceptance by parliamentary bodies of some degree of independence of these representatives in intergovernmental negotiations. Second,
given the heterogeneity of interests and options within the Union and the
procedural constraints on decision-making by the principle of unanimity
and the right of veto, negotiations between these heterogeneous parties are
always difficult and always threatened by failure. Hence, the policy-making
capacities of the European Union are strictly limited. This means, according
to Scharpf (1994: 222), that 'the limited policy-making capacities of the
European Union ought to be used sparingly, and only for issues that need
to be settled on the European level'. That this ought to be the case must

surely also be in the interest of national parliaments that want to exercise supervisory control over their governments and legislative power in line with the expectations of its national constituency. It is in this context that the idea of 'subsidiarity', which gained prominence in the Maastricht Treaty, must be considered in its impact on democratic rule in the European Union.

Article 3b of the Maastricht Treaty contains the most detailed stipulation of the principle of 'subsidiarity':

> The Community shall act within the limits of the powers conferred upon it by this Treaty and the objectives assigned to it therein.
>
> In areas which do not fall within its exclusive competence, the Community shall take action, in accordance with the principle of subsidiarity, only if and in so far as the objectives of the proposed action cannot be sufficiently achieved by the Member States and can therefore, by reason of the scale or effects of the proposed action, be better achieved by the Community.
>
> Any action by the Community shall not go beyond what is necessary to achieve the objectives of this Treaty.

Subsidiarity is thus introduced as a rule of allocating responsibilities. The principle of subsidiarity 'is supposed to constrain the presumed trend towards an expansion, and extensive interpretation, of European competencies' (Scharpf 1994: 223). In this respect, it is closely tied in with the statement in Article A of the Treaty that decisions in the Union are to be taken 'as closely as possible to the citizen'. Yet this declaration of democratic intent does not amount to much.

To begin with, the principle of subsidiarity is not supposed to apply to matters that are under exclusive European jurisdiction. Yet these European competencies are nowhere explicitly defined. Indeed, Article 235 EC Treaty provides for the possibility of the organs of the European Community to appropriate, at their discretion, competencies which they do not yet possess but which are considered essential for achieving the objectives of the treaty. These objectives, however, are so comprehensive that there is hardly a policy area in which the involvement of the Community could not be justified. After all, the Community is beholden to guarantee the free movement of goods, persons, services and capital, and to work towards the creation of an 'ever closer union among the peoples of Europe' (Article A of the Maastricht Treaty). As the revised EC Treaty demonstrates, these objectives can be interpreted as going beyond a 'narrow' concern with the co-ordination of economic and fiscal policies on the European level, and may therefore also include matters of education, vocational training, cultural activities in member states, public health, consumer protection, regional development, industrial policy, research and technological development and so on (for example, Art. 117–130y EC Treaty). Furthermore, the treaty provides for action by the Community even in those areas which do not fall within its exclusive competence. However, 'in view of the extreme differences in the economic development and financial and administrative capacities of member states, it will always be possible to argue – if the matter falls within the purview of European powers at all – that "the objectives of the proposed action cannot be sufficiently achieved by the Member States"' (Scharpf 1994: 223).

We are thus confronted with a major difficulty regarding the principle of subsidiarity: 'No clear list of subjects which would fall within the scope of subsidiarity has been written, the competences which rest with the union or with the member states have not been set out, nor have residual competence been allocated' (Wincott 1994: 579). Such an explicit and constitutionally binding delineation of respective jurisdictions is warranted, however, because, as the principle of subsidiarity is formulated at the moment, '[i]t is the will of the Council which remains the final voice, and where there is the will, subsidiarity shall not be able to defy it' (Green 1994: 298). Scharpf (1994) suggests that the debate on the justiciable allocation of responsibilities to the various levels of government within the Union could take as its starting-point the commitment of the Union to respect the national identity of its member states (Art. F EU Treaty). He argues that there is reason to think that:

> in the relationship between the Union and its members, just as in federal-state relations within the nation state, the core of reserved rights [for the constituent states] would lie in the protection of the cultural and institutional identity of the members. This certainly includes education and cultural policy and the shaping of the country's internal political and administrative institutions and procedures. In addition, one probably would also have to include historically evolved economic and social institutions [such as patterns of industrial relations or the National Health Service]. (Scharpf 1994: 225–6)

Manifestly, specifying the core responsibilities and competencies of both levels of government in the Union with equal emphasis is a political enterprise; it cannot be, for example, the result of a ruling by the European Court of Justice. It presupposes wide-ranging debate in the member states and on the European level, for example, in the institutions of inter-parliamentary co-operation mentioned above as well as in the European Parliament. However, in its 1994 (draft) Constitution the European Parliament has not advanced this debate. Its endorsement of the principle of subsidiarity remains within the spirit of the Maastricht Treaty (Draft Constitution, Art. 10). And it also fails to list the rights and responsibilities for each level of governance in the Union.

This debate about the allocation of governmental responsibilities is bound to be complicated by demands for the institutionalization of competencies for regions. After all, the logic of subsidiarity does not necessarily stop at the level of the nation-state, but may move 'down' to the subnational level of 'regions.' In a federal system such as Germany, or in quasi-federal states such as Spain or Belgium, such an interpretation of the subsidiarity principle is indeed prominent and determines the policy of the *Länder* and the autonomous regions. Yet we must not overlook that in recent decades there has occurred a process of 'Europeanization' of local government across Europe. This 'Europeanization' was partly the result of a conscious policy by the Commission to bring the Community's regions into the European policy-making forum. Goldsmith (1993: 689–91) gives three main reasons for the Commission's interest in dealing directly with subnational governments. First, most EC programmes are spatially located at levels below the national state, and to deal directly with regional or municipal levels of government may therefore improve policy operations. It may also provide the Commission with an opportunity to obtain information about policy objectives or about policy implementation that is not filtered by national governments. Second, the Commission can increase its regulatory control over programmes by working through regional or local agents. This is of importance for the Commission as the relatively small size of its bureaucracy in Brussels makes policing policies difficult. Finally, many of the Commission's programmes are essentially clientelistic: '[T]he EC has many dependents, for whom it can produce many benefits – in return for support for its overall policies, perhaps?' (Goldsmith 1993: 690). Thus, policies may be used to bind regional and local governments to the Commission in an endeavour to bypass possibly recalcitrant central governments and to break down the nationalistic elements in much of EC work. One favoured strategy in this endeavour is devising programmes for subnational regions that encourage cross-national partnerships and transnational networks as a condition of funding.

As a result of such policies a fair number of organizations have been formed that aim to synchronize and co-ordinate the interests and policies of regional and local actors. For example, the main spokesman for local government in relation to the EC is now the Council of European Municipalities and Regions. There are also, for example, the Assembly of European Regions and the Association of European Border Regions that aim to co-ordinate activities outside the controlling influence of national governments. And it is to be expected that policies drawn up by the Commission as well as economic regionalization as a result of changes in global capitalism and national economies will increase the number of Euroregions, of which the best known and most successful is that comprising the Four Motors: Rhône–Alpes; Catalonia; Lombardy; and Baden-Württemberg (Bianchi 1992; Perulli 1992; Murray 1992; Taylor 1995).

The importance of regions in Europe has found a political manifestation in the 189–member Committee of the Regions that was created by the Maastricht Treaty. Its tasks are described as assisting the Council and the Commission by 'acting in an advisory capacity'. It has the powers of issuing opinions 'on its own initiative in cases in which it considers such action appropriate', and of meeting at its own initiative (Art. 198a–c EC Treaty). While such a committee that represents regions in Europe can be welcomed as a further forum for the generation of a European 'public opinion', some questions have to be raised regarding its relationship to the issue of democratic rule in the European Union.

To start with, in its current form its members have been appointed by their national governments. Hence their democratic legitimation is, at least, questionable, and so is their status as genuine representatives of 'their' regions. Should it be demanded by, or for, the Committee of the Regions that it evolve beyond its current advisory and consultative role and acquire powers of legislative co-determination, then it would have to be composed of representatives with a direct democratic mandate. This presupposes that regions build up a democratic structure that allows for the election of representatives either indirectly through regional assemblies or directly through a regional electorate. While such a democratic procedure is quite feasible in subnational regions, it will be much more difficult to develop such a democratic mechanism in transnational regions. As we have seen, a structure of intermediary institutions is a key element in any democratic system, be it supranational, national, subnational or regional. As far as the formation of such a regional intermediary structure is concerned, Streeck and Schmitter have offered the following hypothesis:

> The emergence of regional arenas of interest politics seems to advance, not the organization of labor or for that matter of capital, but rather its *disorganization* ... In addition to the enterprise, the sector, the nation, and perhaps Europe as a whole, struggling factions inside interest associations, including unions, would have yet another option for pursuing sectional interests separately and on their own in coalition with other categories of equally fragmented interests or with ambitious local governments. (Streeck/Schmitter 1991: 156)

The fragmentation of interests and the pluralist proliferation of political opportunities will undermine associational monopolies and interassociational hierarchies. In these circumstances, it will be very difficult for a 'regional' interest to be formulated that could then be represented on the European level.

The development of a viable and long-term system of interest formation and interest intermediation is also likely to be affected by the location of the region within a transregional network. Arguably, economic regions in Europe are not coherent and self-contained economies but nodes in the European economic system, which is itself part of the global economy. If

162

nation-states are insufficiently powerful to set their own economic policies and exert regulatory control over transnational and global economic actors, then regional 'states' are unlikely to succeed where nation-states fail. Against mobile global capital, regions will ultimately have only limited bargaining power. Furthermore, the competition amongst regions to attract scarce capital will result in an increase in regional disparities:

> A few privileged growth regions *may* be able to exact concessions from 'supralocal' actors but the overall effect has been to *reduce* the power of local and regional states – in terms of economic intervention and the maintenance of progressive social welfare systems ... Furthermore, the process of competition between regions for pieces of global capital raises the constant spectre of 'regulatory undercutting', while the speeding up of turnover times ... makes even the strongest growth regions vulnerable to devalorization and crisis. In other words, the more vigorously localities compete with one another, the more pronounced their subordination to supralocal forces becomes. (Peck/Tickell 1994: 304)

In these circumstances, the development capabilities of regional (or local) states are severely limited and the political system will succumb to the economic logic of global capitalism. This economic dependency is unlikely to be lessened by Commission-led Community policies for the 'less-favoured regions'. In order to 'develop structurally weak regions, convert regions in industrial decline, combat long-term unemployment, increase youth employment and secure the development of the rural areas', real expenditure on the structural funds (regional policy, the social fund, and the guidance section of agricultural funds) would have to go well beyond even the projected 3 per cent of the Gross Domestic Product of the Community (Amin/Malmberg 1994: 240). While an increased commitment to the regions may be warranted for reasons of economic integration and social cohesion, the Commission has, on the other hand, also accepted the need to create political and economic conditions congenial for the development of European firms with a global presence in order to survive North American and Japanese competition: 'Indeed, big firms, by design or effect, are the major beneficiaries both of the various programmes which constitute the Commission's technology policy and of the relaxed stance of EC competition policy towards the market behaviour of large firms' (Amin/Malmberg 1994: 241). In a sense, then, the very policy of the Commission with regard to international competitiveness is thus likely to exacerbate the problem of regional disparities.

Yet there is another question we have to address when we contemplate the democratic effect of a 'Europe of the Regions'. What would the relationship be of a newly empowered Committee of the Regions, made up of elected representatives with direct democratic legitimation, with the European Parliament? As Westlake (1994: 49–50) points out, the creation of the Committee has given rise to profound misgivings within the Parliament. The European Parliament can justifiably claim that it 'has its own specialised Committee on Regional Affairs and Regional Policy, which has traditionally played a pre-eminent role in such matters as, for example, the distribution of the Community's structural funds'; and, furthermore, that 'Parliament's membership itself contains regional representatives', for example, in the case of the United Kingdom, MEPs from Wales, Scotland and Northern Ireland (Westlake 1994: 49). The contentious issue, however, is not the possible duplication of activities in the two bodies, but the emergence of the Committee as a rival to the Parliament should it be legitimated through elections and given more than advisory powers. The supranational character of the European Parliament, its dependence on the formation of a European political system for its own democratic legitimacy and its interest in the creation of a more centralized European order to secure its centrality within the European Union pit it against the Committee of Regions which is likely to be concerned with securing a high degree of political autonomy for its constituent regions and might possibly interpret the principle of subsidiarity as a justification for substantial regional devolution. In this context, it is worth noting that the consultative status of the Committee of the Regions is reaffirmed in the Parliament's 1994 (draft) Constitution (Art. 29). The 'federal-style Union' that the European Parliament embraces as an objective in the Preamble of the (draft) Constitution would not appear to be a 'Europe of the Regions'.

European citizenship and European identity

The central thrust of my argument has been the assertion that a major aspect of the 'democratic deficit' in the European Union is the lack of a European-wide structure of intermediary institutions. As Habermas (1992a: 9) rightly observes, 'democratic processes have hitherto only functioned within national borders'. It is around the conflict and cleavage structure within the bounded territory of the nation-state that intermediary institutions such as political parties, interest groups, voluntary associations, trade unions or the mass media have been organized. Citizens still direct their interests, concerns and demands to their national, or subnational, government, not to 'Brussels'. They tend to avail themselves of the national intermediary institutions as the means of their political participation. To put it differently, the role of the citizen has been firmly institutionalized at the level of the nation-state; and it is the democratically constituted nation-state that, on the whole, reliably guarantees the rights of its citizens.

But can this argument not be challenged by pointing to the introduction of a 'Citizenship of the Union' in the revised EC Treaty (Art. 8)? I do not think so. Citizenship of the Union does not replace the citizenship of member states; citizenship status in one of the member states is the prerequisite for Union citizenship. This Union citizenship gives its holder a limited number of rights. The core and the origin of Union citizenship is the right of free movement. This right is no longer restricted to the mobility of economically active persons, but has now been expanded into the mobility for nationals of member states generally (d'Oliveira 1995: 65–6). While it would be quite wrong to underestimate the importance of this right, it it worth noticing that the essence of citizenship rights in nation-states has rested historically and politically in the exercise of popular sovereignty and the control of state power by the people through political participation that was guaranteed by political citizenship rights. Yet, in Union citizenship this political dimension is underdeveloped. Union citizens are given the right to petition the European Parliament on matters which come within the Community's field of activity. They may also take complaints about possible maladministration in the activities of the Community institutions or bodies to an ombudsman who is elected by the European Parliament and acts independently of any Community institution or national governments. The core of the political rights of Union citizenship is, however, the right of citizens of member states to vote and to stand as a candidate at municipal and European elections in the country of residence rather than the country of nationality.

The political rights of Union citizenship, however, do not cover national parliamentary elections, elections to 'regional' assemblies in member states, or referenda and plebiscites. This restriction is in line with an argument the Commission had put forward in a report on local elections submitted to the European Parliament already in 1986. In it, the Commission argued that '"political" elections (parliamentary and presidential elections, referenda)' were different from local elections since they 'play a part in determining national sovereignty. The national aspect of these elections is clearly incompatible with the participation of non-nationals, even nationals of other Community countries, since the Community is not intended to impinge on national sovereignty, or replace States or nations' (quoted in Rosas 1995: 151). It merits pointing out that the European Parliament, too, would not allow non-national EU citizens to vote in national elections in its 1994 (draft) Constitution (Art. 4). However, the exercise of voting rights for national elections would be a much more relevant aspect of Union citizenship, 'given the involvement of (some) national bodies of representation in the framing and implementation of the European legal and political order' and their pivotal role in upholding the principle of democratic accountability for decisions taken in intergovernmental negotiations (d'Oliveira 1995: 73). Thus, while Union citizenship is premised upon citizenship in a member state, it does not give Union citizens residing 'abroad' necessarily or automatically the same rights, duties, privileges or advantages that are inherent in national citizenship in their country of residence. Hence, non-national EU citizens are second-class citizens in their country of residence. Yet, these limited political citzenship rights set EU citizens not only apart from the nationals of their country of residence; it also separates them from third-country nationals who are still denied any political citizenship although they may have lived and worked in the country often for many years. Their daily experience of marginalization and insecurity is compounded by this new manifestation of discrimination.

A genuine European citizenship will only evolve to the extent that European intermediary institutions are built up that allow citizens political participation in a European political system. But the experience of the development of citizenship rights in the Western nation-states also shows that it is premised on the formation of some kind of national identity that provides the cognitive, normative and emotive framework for the exercise of citizenship rights. We have seen above that the democratic legitimacy of parliamentary majority decisions has a number of preconditions, and one of these is a shared normative orientation. Ultimately, shared citizenship rights presuppose the willingness to live together as a community. Such a *vouloir vivre ensemble* must be reconfirmed in a 'daily plebiscite' (Renan); it must be a will expressed by all members of the community, not just by a small elite of 'Eurocrats' or self-interested business people. So far, such a European consciousness and social–psychological identification with 'Europe' (that is, the European Union) have not yet formed (Angelucci 1993; Reif 1993). The very existence of a multiplicity of national and ethnic communities and identities makes it imperative that European citizenship minimalizes the importance of ethno-cultural criteria for determining membership and rights in the political community. The idea of a European citizenship and a European 'demos' in a multinational and multiethnic Europe must be based on a common political culture which embraces the universalist meaning of popular sovereignty and human rights; it cannot be based on particularist ethnic criteria. What is warranted, therefore, is the development of a European political identity, while ethno-cultural identity remains largely at the national level – or even moves down towards micronational 'regional' identities (Wæver *et al.* 1993: chap. 4). But this collective political identity is premised on the creation of a European-wide civil society through whose institutional structures the value- and norm-constituting communicative processes will have to be channelled. The European collective political identity will have to find its expression and form in a 'constitution' that details not only the institutional structure and the power and authority for the various levels of government, but entails also a vision of a distinct form of politicalness for individuals in their new collective capacity.

However, while the marginalization on the European level of ethno-cultural criteria for the granting of a European citizenship is warranted because of the multinationality and multiethnicity of Europe, we are currently witnessing developments that have already led to a recharging of the 'ethnos'-dimension of political life. In the previous chapter I have highlighted the importance of globalization for this process. My argument centred on the effect globalization has on the formulation and defence of a collective identity. One strand of that argument emphasized the gradual loss of state sovereignty as well as of popular sovereignty. Global forces affect the life of citizens by imposing constraints and limits on democratically constituted political agency while not allowing the citizens substantial control over them. What does it mean to be a citizen of a nation-state, if the political 'fate' of the political community cannot be determined by its own citizenry? Citizenship in the European nation-state was based on two distinct, and alternative, ideal-typical models. The (French) republican model defined the nation as a political community, based on a constitution, laws and citizenship. This political republicanism was premised on the political ideal (and, to an extent, the reality) of the strong, sovereign state which could defend the nation against external threats and act upon the democratically expressed wishes and demands of its citizens. Confronted with the curtailment, if not actual demise, of state sovereignty, a stronger emphasis upon ethno-cultural identity and criteria for national citizenship is to be expected. Political republicanism will thus be challenged by the other major ideal–typical model of citizenship, the folk or ethnic model whose main historical representative has been Germany. In this model, belonging to the nation is defined in terms of ethnicity, with a strong emphasis upon common descent, language and culture.

It is in this analytical context that the resurgence of right-wing extremism may be most usefully discussed. However, we may also place the debates in the member states of the European Union about immigration and asylum laws in this context. They address the question of who should be 'allowed in', and who should be 'kept out' of the European Union. These national debates have been taken up in two ways on the European level. First, a joint EU position regarding immigration has been formulated. It was agreed that the refusal by one member state to allow third-country nationals entry would be tantamount to refusal by all others; and that the member state of first entry must assume responsibility for that immigrant or asylum seeker. This policy has two logical consequences:

> First, it is in the interests of individual member states to develop more restrictive immigration policies. Failure to do so could result in the EC member country with the perceived more liberal immigration legislation facing a potential inflow of third-country nationals. Secondly, there now exists a compelling incentive for EC nations to prevent immigrants from entering their countries in order to avoid subsequent responsibility for them. (Baimbridge *et al.* 1994: 429)

167

This policy found, second, an organizational manifestation in the establishment of a number of decision-making bodies and policing structures on the European level. Operating outside the official Community framework, the Trevi group of interior ministers (since 1976), the Working Group on Immigration (1986), and the Schengen Accords (1985 and 1990) focus on immigration in terms of 'law and order' issues – 'alongside, in the case of Trevi and Schengen, terrorism, drugs, public order and the development of international co-operation on policing' (Bunyan 1991: 19; Macey 1992; Allen/Macey 1991). Stanley Hofmann has put these policies and measures in its proper context:

> It is as if, having gradually become used to seeing in the citizens of other EU nations persons who, while different from true nationals, are nevertheless not aliens, the inhabitants of each of the EU countries had decided to treat those from outside the magic circle with extra suspicion and severity ... Blocking immigration except in the rarest of cases (when asylum cannot be refused under international law), persecuting illegal immigrants with venomous vigor, and, in the French case, making the integration of legal ones more difficult, shows how governments have tried to defuse the arguments and to deflate the growth of xenophobic movements by adopting some of their recommendations and thus by legitimizing their existence – as long, of course, as they do not turn murderous. (Hofmann 1994: 20)

It is likely to be difficult to establish criteria of exclusion which are based exclusively on race for migrants from Eastern and Central Europe because historically they share with Western Europe the same cultural and religious traditions. For migrants and asylum seekers from areas south of the Mediterranean, such cultural links can be more easily denied and religious differences more easily dramatized so that in their case ethnic, cultural and racial criteria are more likely to inform the public and political debates (Balibar 1991). Once again, the argument put forward in the previous chapter would support this view. I pointed out that the search for identity in the context of globalization may express itself in ethnic revivalism and nationalism; yet it may also be couched in politico-religious terms. This manifestation of a search for collective identity may then take on the form of the construction of a civilizational identity, for example, on the basis of the (encompassing) ideology of 'world religions'. European/Latin 'Christendom' could then possibly be pitted against 'Islam', or, in a more secular version, Western democracy against 'Oriental' despotism and theocracy.

Such a civilizational identity could be formulated from within the 'official' discourse on the 'idea of Europe' (Swedberg 1994). In this discourse, a European identity has been constructed by drawing on the interactions of a multiplicity of traditions (Wilterdink 1993). It has been argued that European culture and civilization have been formed by the tradition of critical and independent thought that goes back to Greek antiquity and became the dominant ideal of European 'modernity' in the Renaissance and the Enlightenment. Roman antiquity exerted its influence through the spread of 'Roman law' across Europe. As the third cultural pillar of European civilization, Christianity provided for the normative integration of Europe. But the conflicts and tensions between the Papacy and the secular rulers ensured that a system of states formed in Europe that made theocratic rule impossible. It also contributed to the internal fragmentation, or differentiation, of Christianity. The conflicts between Greek orthodoxy, Roman Catholicism and Protestantism, in turn, set free forces of intellectual creativity and innovation. This theological and intellectual diversity became interlaced with the enormous variety of languages, national traditions, regional and local customs that already existed or developed in Europe. Modern science, the industrial revolution, humanist ethics including the idea of human rights as well as democracy can all be interpreted as resulting from the political and cultural diversity within the overarching unity of European civilization.

On the basis of this interpretation, it is easy to claim a special historical significance of Europe for humanity as a whole. In the nineteenth century, this claim manifested itself in a variety of forms. It found expression, for example, in the benign 'academic' form of Max Weber's assertion of the 'uniqueness' of the West or in theories of evolutionism that foresaw lengthy developmental processes for other peoples to reach the hights of European achievements. Yet it also took the form of the older idea of a struggle of European civilization against 'barbarianism' which manifested itself ideologically as racism and politically as imperialism. On the basis of what I have argued in this and the previous two chapters, there is all reason to believe that an ideological mobilization that aims to turn allegedly unique features of European culture into claims for superiority and the right to defend this uniqueness by excluding 'the other' would find support amongst a considerable number of people in the late twentieth century.

I have argued that the formation of a European-wide civil society through the build-up of intermediary institutions is necessary to provide the basis for the development of a European 'demos' and a political collective identity. This political project faces three major challenges. First, given the importance of the nation-state for the exercise of democratic rights and the emotive force of national consciousness and identity, the structure of intermediary political institutions on the European level must be articulated with the intermediary institutional arrangements on the level of the nation state; it must not aim to replace them. Such an articulation, however, will be a protracted process which will be threatened by controversy over the allocation of authority and power to the various institutions. This is, second, likely to lead to constant political mobilization around demands to renationalize competencies given to European agencies as a result of the pooling of sovereignty. Such political mobilization is likely to draw on ideas of national uniqueness and ethno-cultural particularity. It will thus undermine the project of formulating a political identity that all citizens of Europe will share. Finally, the formulation of such a political identity may also become problematic as processes of globalization may privilege the assertion of a civilizational, rather than political, European collective identity.

Bibliography

Ackerman, Bruce (1989), Why dialogue?, *Journal of Philosophy*, 86, 5–22.

Addis, Adeno (1991), Individualism, communitarianism, and the rights of ethnic minorities, *Notre Dame Law Review*, 67:3, 615–76.

Allen, J. W. (1951), *A History of Political Thought in the Sixteenth Century*, London, Methuen.

Allen, S. and Mary Macey (1991), Minorities, racism and citizenship: the impact of the Single European Market, *European Journal of Intercultural Studies*, 2:2, 5–16.

Amin, Ash and Andres Malmberg (1994), Competing structural and institutional influences on the geography of production in Europe, in A. Amin (ed.), *Post-Fordism. A Reader*, Oxford, Blackwell, 227–48.

Anderson, Frank M. (ed.) (1904), *The Constitutions and Other Select Documents illustrative of the History of France, 1789–1901*, Minneapolis, Wilson Company.

Angelucci, Orietta (1993), Die europäische Identität der Europäer: Eine sozialpsychologische Bestandsaufnahme, in A. von Bogdandy (ed.), *Die Europäische Option. Eine interdisziplinäre Analyse über Herkunft, Stand und Perspektiven der europäischen Integration*, Baden-Baden, Nomos, 303–21.

Appadurai, Arjun (1993), Patriotism and its futures, *Public Culture*, 5:3, 411–30.

Arendt, Hannah (1958), *The Human Condition*, Chicago, University of Chicago Press.

Arendt, Hannah (1961), *Between Past and Present: Six Exercises in Political Thought*, London, Faber & Faber.

Arendt, Hannah (1973), *On Revolution*, Harmondsworth, Penguin Books.

Aristotle, *The Politics*, ed. Stephen Everson, Cambridge, Cambridge University Press, 1988.

Aron, Raymond (1988), Sociology and the philosophy of human rights, in R. Aron, *Power, Modernity and Sociology*, Aldershot, Edward Elgar, 194–210.

Ashford, Douglas (1986), *The Emergence of the Welfare State*, Oxford, Blackwell.

Avineri, Shlomo (1972), *Hegel's Theory of the Modern State*, Cambridge, Cambridge University Press.

Axtmann, Roland (1992), 'Police' and the formation of the modern state. Legal and ideological assumption on state capacity in the Austrian Lands of the Habsburg Empire, 1500–1800, *German History*, 10:1, 39–61.

Ayubi, Nazih (1991), *Political Islam. Religion and Politics in the Arab World*, London, Routledge.

Baimbridge, Mark *et al.* (1994), The Maastricht Treaty: exacerbating racism in Europe?, *Ethnic and Racial Studies*, 17:3, 420–41.

Baker, Keith Michael (1990), *Inventing the French Revolution. Essays on French Political Culture in the Eigtheenth Century*, Cambridge, Cambridge University Press.

Balibar, Étienne (1991), 'Es gibt keinen Staat in Europa': racism and politics in Europe today, *New Left Review*, 186, 5–19.

Bauman, Zygmunt (1993), *Postmodern Ethics*, Cambridge, Polity Press.

Baumgold, Deborah (1988), *Hobbes's Political Theory*, Cambridge: Cambridge University Press.

Baumgold, Deborah (1993), Pacifying politics. Resistance, violence, and accountability in seventeenth-century contract theory, *Political Theory*, 21:1, 6–27.

Beck, Ulrich (1993), *Die Erfindung des Politischen*, Frankfurt a.M., Suhrkamp.

Beck, Ulrich (1994), The reinvention of politics: towards a theory of reflexive modernization, in U. Beck *et al.*, *Reflexive Modernization. Politics, Tradition and Aesthetics in the Modern Social Order*, Cambridge, Polity Press, 1–55.

Beer, Samuel H. (1993), *To Make a Nation. The Rediscovery of American Federalism*, Cambridge, MA, Harvard University Press.

Beetham, David (1984), The future of the nation-state, in G. McLennan *et al.* (eds), *The Idea of the Modern State*, Milton Keynes, Open University Press, 208–22.

Beiner, Ronald (1984), Action, natality and citizenship: Hannah Arendt's concept of freedom, in Z. A. Pelczynski and J. Gray (eds), *Conceptions of Liberty in Political Philosophy*, London, Athlone Press, 349–75.

Bellamy, Richard (1993), Citizenship and rights, in R. Bellamy (ed.), *Theories and Concepts of Politics. An Introduction*, Manchester, Manchester University Press, 43–76.

Bellamy, Richard (1994), 'Dethroning politics': liberalism, constitutionalism and democracy in the thought of F. A. Hayek, *British Journal of Political Science*, 24:4, 419–41.

Benhabib, Seyla (1992), *Situating the Self. Gender, Community and Postmodernism in Contemporary Ethics*, Cambridge, Polity Press.

Benhabib, Seyla (1994), Deliberative rationality and models of democratic legitimacy, *Constellations*, 1:1, 26–52.

Benoist, Alain de (1993/94), Three interviews with Alain de Benoist, *Telos*, 98/99, 173–207.

Bernstein, Richard J. (1986), *Philosophical Profiles. Essays in a Pragmatic Mode*, Cambridge, Polity Press.

Berting, Jan (1995), Patterns of exclusion: imaginaries of class, nation, ethnicity and gender in Europe, in J. Nederveen Pieterse and B. Parekh (eds), *The Decolonization of Imagination. Culture, Knowledge, and Power*, London, Zed Books, 149–65.

Beyer, Peter (1994), *Religion and Globalization*, London, Sage.

Bianchi, Patrizio (1992), What economic scenario for Europe?, in C. Crouch and D. Marquand (eds), *Towards a Greater Europe? A Continent without an Iron Curtain*, Oxford, Political Quarterly Publishing, 64–90.

Bobbio, Norberto (1989), *Democracy and Dictatorship: The Nature and Limits of State Power*, Cambridge, Polity Press.

Bock, Gisela *et al.* (eds) (1990), *Machiavelli and Republicanism*, Cambridge, Cambridge University Press.

Bock, Gisela and Susan James (eds) (1992), *Beyond Equality and Difference. Citizenship, Feminist Politics and Female Subjectivity*, London, New York, Routledge.

Bonder, Michael *et al.* (1993), Vereinheitlichung und Fraktionierung in der Weltgesellschaft. Kritik des globalen Institutionalismus, *PROKLA. Zeitschrift für kritische Sozialwissenschaft*, 23:2, 327–41.

Bressand, Albert (1990), Beyond interdependence: 1992 as a global challenge, *International Affairs*, 66:1, 47–65.

Brown, Seyom (1992), *International Relations in a Changing Global System*, Boulder, Westview Press.

Brubaker, W. Rogers (1992), *Citizenship and Nationhood in France and Germany*, Cambridge, MA, Harvard University Press.

Brubaker, W. Rogers (ed.) (1989), *Immigration and the Politics of Citizenship in Europe and North America*, Lanham, University of America Press.

Brunkhorst, Hauke (1994), *Demokratie und Differenz. Egalitärer Individualismus*, Frankfurt a.M., Fischer.

Brunn, Stanley and Thomas R. Leinbach (eds) (1991), *Collapsing Space and Time: Geographic Aspects of Communications and Information*, London, HarperCollins.

Buchanan, Allen (1989), Assessing the communitarian critique of liberalism, *Ethics*, 99:4, 852–82.

Buell, Frederick (1994), *National Culture and the New Global System*, Baltimore, London, Johns Hopkins University Press.

Bunyan, Tony (1991), Towards an authoritarian European state, *Race & Class*, 32:3, 19–27.

Burtt, Shelley (1993), The politics of virtue today: a critique and a proposal, *American Political Science Review*, 87:2, 360–8.

Calhoun, Craig (1995), *Critical Social Theory. Culture, History, and the Challenge of Difference*, Oxford, Blackwell.

Camilleri, Joseph (1990), Rethinking sovereignty in a shrinking, fragmented world, in R. B. J. Walker and S. Mendlovitz (eds), *Contending Sovereignties: Redefining Political Community*, London, Lynne Rienner, 13–44.

Camilleri, Joseph and Jim Falk (1992), *The End of Sovereignty? The Politics of a Shrinking and Fragmenting World*, Aldershot, Edward Elgar.

Canovan, Margaret (1992), *Hannah Arendt. A Reinterpretation of Her Political Thought*, Cambridge, Cambridge University Press.

Cassese, Antonio (1986), *International Law in a Divided World*, Oxford, Clarendon Press.

Cerny, Philip (1993), Plurilateralism: structural differentiation and functional conflict in the post-Cold War world order, *Millennium*, 22:1, 27–51.

Cohen, Jean and Andrew Arato (1992), *Civil Society and Political Theory*, Cambridge, MA, MIT Press.

Collini, Stephen (1979), *Liberalism and Sociology: L. T. Hobhouse and Political Argument in England 1880–1914*, Cambridge, Cambridge University Press.

Connolly, William E. (1991), *Identity\Difference. Democratic Negotiations of Political Paradox*, Ithaca, London, Cornell University Press.

Copjec, Joan (1991), The unvermögende other: hysteria and democracy in America, *New Formations*, 14, 27–41.

Corrigan, Philip and Derek Sayer (1985), *The Great Arch: English State Formation as Cultural Revolution*, Oxford, Blackwell.

Dahl, Robert (1989), *Democracy and Its Critics*, New Haven, Yale University Press.

Dallmayr, Fred R. (1993), *G. W. F. Hegel: Modernity and Politics*, London, Sage.

Dehousse, Renaud (1995), Constitutional reform in the European Community: are there alternatives to the majoritarian avenue?, *West European Politics*, 18:3, 118–36.

Dicken, Peter (1993), *Global Shift. The Internationalization of Economic Activity*, 2nd edn, London, Paul Chapman.

Dinan, Desmond (1994), *Ever Closer Union? An Introduction to the European Community*, London, Macmillan.

Draft Constitution (1994), Draft Constitution [by the European Parliament] of the European Union, *Official Journal of the European Communities* (OJ) C, 28.2.1994, 156–70.

Eden, Lorraine (1991), Bringing the firm back in: multinationals in International Political Economy, *Millennium*, 20:2, 197–224.

Ekins, Paul (1992), *A New World Order. Grassroots Movements for Global*

Change, London, Routledge.

Evers, Tilman (1994), Supranationale Staatlichkeit am Beispiel der Europäischen Union: Civitas civitatum oder Monstrum?, *Leviathan*, 22:1, 115–34.

Falk, Richard (1992), *Explorations at the Edges of Time. The Prospects for World Order*, Philadelphia, Temple University Press.

Falk, Richard (1994), The making of global citizenship, in B. van Steenbergen (ed.), *The Condition of Citizenship*, London, Sage, 127–40.

Federalist Papers = Madison, James, and Alexander Hamilton, and John Jay [1788] (1987), *The Federalist Papers*, ed. Isaac Kramnick, London, Penguin Books.

Ferguson, Marjorie (1992), The mythology about globalization, *European Journal of Communication*, 7:1, 69–93.

Ferguson, Marjorie (1993), Invisible divides: communication and identity in Canada and the U.S., *Journal of Communication*, 43:2, 42–57.

Flora, Peter (1983), *State, Economy and Society in Western Europe, 1815–1975: A Data Handbook*, Chicago, St James Press.

Forsyth, Murray (1987), *Reason and Revolution. The Political Thought of the Abbé Sieyes*, Leicester, Leicester University Press.

Franklin, Julian (1973), *Jean Bodin and the Rise of Absolutist Theory*, Cambridge, Cambridge University Press.

Frazer, Elizabeth and Nicola Lacey (1993), *The Politics of Community. A Feminist Critique of the Liberal–Communitarian Debate*, New York, Harvester Wheatsheaf.

Freeden, Michael (1978), *The New Liberalism. An Ideology of Social Reform*, Oxford, Clarendon Press.

Fukuyama, Francis (1992), *The End of History and the Last Man*, London, Hamish Hamilton.

Funabashi, Yoichi (1993), The asianization of Asia, *Foreign Affairs*, 72:5, 75–85.

Galeotti, Anna Elisabetta (1993), Citizenship and equality. The place for toleration, *Political Theory*, 21:4, 585–605.

Galston, William (1988), Liberal virtues, *American Political Science Review*, 82:4, 1,277–89.

Galston, William (1991), *Liberal Purposes: Goods, Virtues, and Duties in the Liberal State*, Cambridge, Cambridge University Press.

Gamble, Andrew (1993), Shaping the new world order: political capacities and policy challenges, *Government and Opposition*, 28:3, 325–38.

Gellner, Ernest (1983), *Nations and Nationalism*, Oxford, Blackwell.

Gellner, Ernest (1988), *Plough, Sword and Book. The Structure of Human History*, London, Collins Harvill.

Gellner, Ernest (1992), *Postmodernism, Reason and Religion*, London, Routledge.

Giddens, Anthony (1994), Living in a post-traditional society, in U. Beck *et al.*, *Reflexive Modernization. Politics, Tradition and Aesthetics in the Modern Social Order*, Cambridge, Polity Press, 56–109.

Glennerster, Howard (1991), The radical right and the future of the Welfare State, in H. Glennerster and J. Midgley (eds), *The Radical Right and the Welfare State. An International Assessment*, Hemel Hempstead, Harvester Wheatsheaf, 163–74.

Goldsmith, M. M. (1987), Liberty, luxury and the pursuit of happiness, in A. Pagden (ed.), *The Languages of Political Theory in Early-Modern Europe*, Cambridge, Cambridge University Press, 225–51.

Goldsmith, Mike (1993), The europeanisation of local government, *Urban Studies*, 30:4, 683–99.

Gordon, David (1988), The global economy: new edifice or crumbling foundations?, *New Left Review*, 168, 24–64.

Gough, John W. (1936), *The Social Contract. A Critical Study of Its Development*, Oxford, Clarendon Press.

Gould, Carol (1988), *Rethinking Democracy. Freedom and Social Co-operation in Politics, Economy, and Society*, Cambridge, Cambridge University Press.

Grant, Wyn (1992), Economic globalisation, stateless firms and international governance, *Working Paper*, No. 105, Warwick, Department of Politics and International Studies, University of Warwick.

Gray, John (1993), *Beyond the New Right. Markets, Government and the Common Environment*, London, New York, Routledge.

Green, Leslie (1995), Internal minorities and their rights, in W. Kymlicka (ed.), *The Rights of Minority Cultures*, Oxford, Oxford University Press, 257–72.

Green, Paul (1994), Subsidiarity and European Union: beyond the ideological impasse? An analysis of the origins and impact of the principle of subsidiarity within the politics of the European Community, *Policy and Politics*, 22:4, 287–300.

Green, T. H. [1881] (1986), Liberal legislation and freedom of contract, in T. H. Green, *Lectures on the Principles of Political Obligation, and Other Writings*, eds Paul Harris and John Morrow, Cambridge, Cambridge University Press, 194–212.

van Gunsteren, Hermann (1988), Admission to citizenship, *Ethics*, 98, 731–41.

Gutmann, Amy and Dennis Thompson (1990), Moral conflict and political consensus, *Ethics*, 101, 64–88.

Habermas, Jürgen (1977), Hannah Arendt's communications concept of power, *Social Research*, 44:1, 3–24.

Habermas, Jürgen (1987), *The Theory of Communicative Action, vol. 2: Lifeworld and System. A Critique of Functionalist Reason*, Cambridge, Polity Press.

Habermas, Jürgen (1992a), Citizenship and national identity: some reflections on the future of Europe, *Praxis International*, 12:1, 1–19.

Habermas, Jürgen (1992b), *Faktizität und Geltung. Beiträge zur Diskurstheorie des Rechts und des demokratischen Rechtsstaats*, Frankfurt a.M., Suhrkamp.

Habermas, Jürgen (1993), Further reflections on the public sphere, in C. Calhoun (ed.), *Habermas and the Public Sphere*, Cambridge, MA, MIT Press, 421–61.

Habermas, Jürgen (1994), Three normative models of democracy, *Constellations*, 1:1, 1–10.

Hall, Stuart (1991a), Brave new world, *Socialist Review*, 21:1, 57–64.

Hall, Stuart (1991b), The local and the global: globalization and ethnicity, in A. D. King (ed.), *Culture, Globalization and the World-System*, Houndmills, Macmillan, 19–39.

Hall, Stuart (1993), Culture, community, nation, *Cultural Studies*, 7:3, 349–63.

Havel, Vaclav (1978/1991), The power of the powerless, in Vaclav Havel, *Open Letters*, London, Faber & Faber, 125–214.

Hayek, Friedrich A. (1960), *The Constitution of Liberty*, London, Macmillan.

Heater, Derek (1990), *Citizenship. The Civic Ideal in World History, Politics and Education*, London, Longman.

Hegedus, Zsuzsa (1989), Social movements and social change in self-creative society: new civil initiatives in the international arena, *International Sociology*, 4:1, 19–36.

Hegel, G. W. F. [1821] (1942), *Philosophy of Right*, ed. T. M. Knox, Oxford, Oxford University Press.

Held, David (1987), *Models of Democracy*, Cambridge, Polity Press.

Held, David (1989), *Political Theory and the Modern State*, Cambridge, Polity Press.

Held, David (1991), Democracy, the nation-state and the global system, *Economy and Society*, 20:2, 138–72.

Held, David (1992), Democracy: from city-states to a cosmopolitan order?, *Political Studies*, 40 (Special Issue), 10–39.

Hettne, Björn (1993), Neo-mercantilism: the pursuit of regionness, *Co-operation and Conflict*, 28:3, 211–32.

Higham, John (1993), Multiculturalism and universalism: a history and critique, *American Quarterly*, 45:2, 195–219.

Hill, B. W. (ed.) (1975), *Edmund Burke. On Government, Politics and Society*, Hassocks, Harvester.

Hirst, Paul and Grahame Thompson (1995), Globalization and the future of the nation-state, *Economy and Society*, 24:3, 408–42.

Hobbes, Thomas [1642/47] (1983), *De Cive*, Oxford, Clarendon Press.

Hobbes, Thomas [1651] (1991), *Leviathan*, ed. Richard Tuck, Cambridge,

Cambridge University Press.

Hobsbawm, Eric (1990), *Nations and Nationalism Since the 1780s. Programme, Myth, Reality*, Cambridge, Cambridge University Press.

Hofmann, Stanley (1994), Europe's identity crisis revisited, *Daedalus*, 123:2, 1–23.

Honig, B. (1992), Toward an antagonistic feminism: Hannah Arendt and the politics of identity, in J. Butler and J. Scott (eds), *Feminists Theorize the Political*, New York, Routledge, 215–35.

Hont, Istvan (1994), The permanent crisis of a divided mankind: 'Contemporary crisis of the nation state' in historical perspective, *Political Studies*, 42 (special issue), 166–231.

Horsman, Mathew and Andrew Marshall (1994), *After the Nation-State. Citizens, Tribalism and the New World Disorder*, London, HarperCollins.

Horton, John (ed.) (1993), *Liberalism, Multiculturalism and Toleration*, Houndmills, Macmillan.

Howse, Robert and Karen Knop (1993), Federalism, secession, and the limits of ethnic accommodation: a Canadian perspective, *New Europe Law Review*, 1:2, 269–320.

Hulliung, Mark (1983), *Citizen Machiavelli*, Princeton, Princeton University Press.

Huntington, Samuel (1991), *The Third Wave*, Norman: Oklahoma University Press.

Huntington, Samuel (1993), The clash of civilizations?, *Foreign Affairs*, 72:2, 22–49.

Hurrell, Andrew (1995), International political theory and the global environment, in K. Booth and S. Smith (eds), *International Relations Theory Today*, Cambridge, Polity Press, 129–53.

Janelle, Donald (1991), Global interdependence and its consequence, in S. Brunn, and T. R. Leinbach (eds) (1991), *Collapsing Space and Time: Geographic Aspects of Communications and Information*, London, HarperCollins, 49–81.

Jones, Kathleen B. (1990), Citizenship in a woman-friendly polity, *Signs*, 15:4, 781–812.

Jordan, Bill (1989), *The Common Good. Citizenship, Morality and Self-Interest*, Oxford, Blackwell.

Juergensmeyer, Mark (1993), *The New Cold War? Religious Nationalism Confronts the Secular State*, Berkeley, University of California Press.

Kaase, Max (1991), Politische Integration Westeuropas: Probleme der Legitimation, in W. Zapf (ed.), *Die Modernisierung moderner Gesellschaften*, Frankfurt a.M., Campus Verlag, 318–29.

Kamenka, Eugene (1973), Political nationalism – the evolution of the idea, in E. Kamenka (ed.), *Nationalism. The Nature and Evolution of an Idea*, Canberra, Australian National University Press, 2–20.

Kant, Immanuel [1797] (1965), The Metaphysical Elements of Justice (Part I of *The Metaphysics of Morals*), translated, with an introduction by John Ladd, Indianapolis, Bobbs-Merrill Company.

Kates, Gary (1990), Jews into Frenchmen: nationality and representation in Revolutionary France, in F. Fehér (ed.), *The French Revolution and the Birth of Modernity*, Berkeley, University of California Press, 103–16.

Keane, John (1988a), *Democracy and Civil Society*, London, Verso.

Keane, John (1988b), Despotism and democracy, in J. Keane (ed.), *Civil Society and the State. New European Perspectives*, London, Verso, 35–71.

Keane, John (1991), *Media and Democracy*, Cambridge, Polity Press. ⟸

Keane, John (1994), Nation, nationalism and citizens in Europe, *International Social Science Journal*, 46:2, 169–84.

King, Desmond S. (1987), *The New Right. Politics, Markets and Citizenship*, Houndmills, Macmillan.

King, Preston (1974), *The Ideology of Order*, London, Allen & Unwin.

Konrad, George (1984), *Antipolitics*, San Diego, New York, Harcourt Brace Jovanovich.

Kortian, Garbis (1984), Subjectivity and civil society, in Z. A. Pelczynski (ed.), *The State and Civil Society. Studies in Hegel's Political Philosophy*, Cambridge, Cambridge University Press, 197–210.

Kramnick, Isaac (ed.) (1987), *The Federalist Papers*, London, Penguin Books.

Krumar, Krishan (1993), Civil society: an inquiry into the usefulness of an historical term, *British Journal of Sociology*, 44:3, 375–95.

Kukathas, Chandran (1995), Are there any cultural rights?, in W. Kymlicka (ed.), *The Rights of Minority Cultures*, Oxford, Oxford University Press, 228–56.

Kymlicka, Will (1990), *Contemporary Political Philosophy. An Introduction*, Oxford, Clarendon Press.

Kymlicka, Will (1995a), *Multicultural Citizenship. A Liberal Theory of Minority Rights*, Oxford, Clarendon Press.

Kymlicka, Will (1995b), *The Rights of Minority Cultures*, Oxford, Oxford University Press.

Kymlicka, Will and Wayne Norman (1994), Return of the citizen: a survey of recent work on citizenship theory, *Ethics*, 104, 352–81.

Lash, Scott and John Urry (1994), *Economies of Signs and Space*, London, Sage.

Lechner, Frank (1989), Cultural aspects of the modern world system, in W. H. Swatos (ed.), *Religious Politics in Global and Comparative Perspective*, New York, Greenwood Press, 11–27.

Lechner, Frank (1991), Religion, law and global order, in R. Robertson and W. R. Garrett (eds), *Religion and Global Order*, New York, Paragon Press, 263–80.

Lepsius, M. Rainer (1992), Beyond the nation-state: the multinational state as the model for the European Community, *Telos*, 91, 57–76.

Lipschutz, R. D. (1992), Reconstructing world politics: the emergence of global civil society, *Millennium*, 21:3, 389–420.

Locke, John [1689] (1989), *Two Treatises of Government*, edited with an introduction and notes by Peter Laslett, Cambridge, Cambridge University Press.

Locke, John [1690] (1975), *An Essay Concerning Human Understanding*, ed. H. Nidditch, Oxford, Clarendon Press.

Lodge, Juliet (1994), Transparency and democratic legitimacy, *Journal of Common Market Studies*, 32:3, 343–68.

Ludlow, Peter (1992), The Maastricht Treaty and the future of Europe, *Washington Quarterly*, 15:4, 119–37.

Luke, Tim W. (1993), Discourses of disintegration, texts of transformation: re-reading realism in the new world order, *Alternatives*, 18:2, 229–58.

Macey, Mary (1992), Greater Europe: Integration or ethnic exclusion?, in C. Crouch and D. Marquand (eds), *Towards a Greater Europe? A Continent without an Iron Curtain*, Oxford, Political Quarterly Publishing, 139–53.

Macklem, Patrick (1993), Distributing sovereignty: Indian nations and equality of peoples, *Stanford Law Review*, 45:5, 1,311–67.

Madsen, Richard (1993), Global monoculture, multiculture, and polyculture, *Social Research*, 60:3, 493–511.

Mann, Michael (1993), *The Sources of Social Power, vol. 2: The Rise of Classes and Nation-States, 1760–1914*, Cambridge, Cambridge University Press.

Marshall, T. H. (1963), Citizenship and social class, in T. H. Marshall, *Sociology at the Crossroads. And Other Essays*, London, Heinemann, 67–127.

Martin, Ron L. and Robert Rowthorn (eds) (1986), *The Geography of De-Industrialisation*, London, Macmillan.

Maus, Ingeborg (1992), *Zur Aufklärung der Demokratietheorie. Rechts- und demokratietheoretische Überlegungen im Anschluß an Kant*, Frankfurt a.M., Suhrkamp.

McDonald, Michael (1991), Should communities have rights? Reflections on liberal individualism, *Canadian Journal of Law and Jurisprudence*, 4:2, 217–37.

McLaren, Peter (1993), Multiculturalism and the postmodern critique: towards a pedagogy of resistance and transformation, *Cultural Studies*, 7:1, 118–46.

Meyer, D. S. and S. Marullo (1992), Grassroots mobilization and international politics: peace protest and the end of the Cold War, *Research in Social Movements, Conflict and Change*, 14, 99–140.

Michnik, Adam (1985), *Letters from Prison and Other Essays*, Berkeley, Los Angeles, University of California Press.

Midgley, James (1991), The radical right, politics and society, in H. Glennerster and J. Midgley (eds), *The Radical Right and the Welfare State. An*

International Assessment, Hemel Hempstead, Harvester Wheatsheaf, 3–23.

Mill, John Stuart [1861] (1991), *Considerations on Representative Government*, in John Stuart Mill, *On Liberty and Other Essays*, ed. John Gray, Oxford: Oxford Univerity Press, 205–467.

Milligan, David and William Watts Miller (eds) (1992), *Liberalism, Citizenship, and Autonomy*, Aldershot, Avebury.

Mitchell, Kathleen (1993), Multiculturalism, or the united colors of capitalism?, *Antipode*, 25:4, 263–94.

Mlinar, Zdravko (1992), Introduction, in Z. Mlinar (ed.), *Globalization and Territorial Identity*, Aldershot, Avebury, 1–14.

Mommsen, Wolfgang (1990), The varieties of the nation state in modern history: liberal, imperialist, fascist and contemporary notions of nation and nationality, in M. Mann (ed.), *The Rise and Decline of the Nation State*, Oxford, Blackwell, 210–26.

Morison, Samuel Eliot (ed.) (1965), *Sources and Documents illustrating the American Revolution, 1764–1788 and the Formation of the Federal Constitution*, 2nd edn, New York: Oxford University Press.

Mouffe, Chantal (1992a), Democratic citizenship and the political community, in C. Mouffe (ed.), *Dimensions of Radical Democracy*, London, Verso, 225–39.

Mouffe, Chantal (1992b), Feminism, citizenship and radical democratic politics, in J. Butler and J. Scott (eds), *Feminists Theorize the Political*, New York, Routledge, 369–84.

Murray, Robin (1992), Europe and the new regionalism, in M. Dunford and G. Kafkalas (eds), *Cities and Regions in the New Europe: The Global–Local Interplay and Spatial Development Strategies*, London, Belhaven Press, 299–308.

Nauta, Lolle (1992), Changing conceptions of citizenship, *Praxis International*, 12:1, 20–33.

Nederveen Pieterse, Jan (1994), Globalisation as hybridisation, *International Sociology*, 9:2, 161–84.

Neunreither, Karlheinz (1995), Citizens and the exercise of power in the European Union: towards a new social contract, in A. Rosas and E. Anatola (eds), *A Citizen's Europe. In Search of a New Order*, London, Sage, 1–18.

Nicholson, Peter P. (1990), *Studies in the Political Thought of the British Idealists*, Cambridge, Cambridge University Press.

Nugent, Neil (1992), The deepening and widening of the European Community: recent evolution, Maastricht, and beyond, *Journal of Common Market Studies*, 30:3, 311–28.

Oestreich, Gerhard (1982), *Neostoicism and the Early Modern State*, Cambridge, Cambridge University Press.

Offe, Claus (1985), Challenging the boundaries of institutional politics:

social movements since the 1960s, in C. Maier (ed.), *Changing Boundaries of the Political*, Cambridge, Cambridge University Press, 63–105.

Offe, Claus (1987), Democracy against the welfare state? Structural foundations of neoconservative political opportunities, *Political Theory*, 15:4, 501–37.

Ohmae, Kenichi (1993), The rise of the region state, *Foreign Affairs*, 72:2, 78–87.

d'Oliveira, Hans Ulrich Jesserun (1995), Union citizenship: pie in the sky?, in A. Rosas and E. Anatola (eds), *A Citizen's Europe. In Search of a New Order*, London, Sage, 58–84.

Ortega y Gasset, José (1937), *Invertebrate Spain*, New York, Fertig.

Pagden, Anthony (ed.) (1987), *The Languages of Political Theory in Early-Modern Europe*, Cambridge, Cambridge University Press.

Paine, Thomas [1791] (1985), *Rights of Man*, Harmondsworth, Penguin Classics.

Parekh, Bhikhu (1981), *Hannah Arendt and the Search for a New Political Philosophy*, London, Macmillan.

Parekh, Bhikhu (1991), British citizenship and cultural difference, in G. Andrews (ed.), *Citizenship*, London, Lawrence & Wishart, 183–204.

Parekh, Bhikhu (1992), The cultural particularity of liberal democracy, *Political Studies*, 40 (Special Issue), 160–75.

Parekh, Bhikhu (1994a), Cultural diversity and liberal democracy, in D. Beetham (ed.), *Defining and Measuring Democracy*, London, Sage, 199–221.

Parekh, Bhikhu (1994b), Minority rights, majority values, in D. Miliband (ed.), *Reinventing the Left*, Cambridge, Polity Press, 101–9.

Passerin d'Entrèves, Alexander (1967), *The Notion of the State. An Introduction to Political Theory*, Oxford, Clarendon Press.

Passerin d'Entrèves, Maurizio (1992), Hannah Arendt and the idea of citizenship, in C. Mouffe (ed.), *Dimensions of Radical Democracy*, London, Verso, 145–68.

Pateman, Carol (1989), *The Disorder of Women*, Cambridge, Polity Press.

Peck, Jamie and Adam Tickell (1994), Searching for a new institutional fix: the after-fordist crisis and the global-local disorder, in A. Amin (ed.), *Post-Fordism. A Reader*, Oxford, Blackwell, 280–314.

Pelczynski, Z. A. (1984a), Introduction: the significance of Hegel's separation of the state and civil society, in Z. A. Pelczynski (ed.), *The State and Civil Society. Studies in Hegel's Political Philosophy*, Cambridge, Cambridge University Press, 1–13.

Pelcyznski, Z. A. (1984b), Political community and individual freedom in Hegel's philosophy of the state, in Z. A. Pelczynski (ed.), *The State and Civil Society. Studies in Hegel's Political Philosophy*, Cambridge, Cambridge University Press, 55–76.

Pelczynski, Z. A. (ed.) (1984), *The State and Civil Society. Studies in Hegel's Political Philosophy*, Cambridge, Cambridge University Press.

Pellerin, Hélène (1993), Global restructuring in the world economy and migration. The globalization of migration dynamics, *International Journal*, 48:2, 240–54.

Perulli, Paolo (1992), The political economy of a 'mid-European region': the Alpe Adria community, in C. Crouch and D. Marquand (eds), *Towards a Greater Europe? A Continent without an Iron Curtain*, Oxford, Political Quarterly Publishing, 154–69.

Peters, Ronald M. (1978), *The Massachusetts Constitution of 1780. A Social Compact*, Amherst, University of Massachusetts Press.

Phillips, Anne (1987), *Divided Loyalties: Dilemmas of Sex and Class*, London, Virago.

Phillips, Anne (1991), *Engendering Democracy*, Cambridge, Polity Press.

Phillips, Anne (1992a), Democracy and difference: some problems for feminist theory, *Political Quarterly*, 63:1, 79–90.

Phillips, Anne (1992b), Must feminists give up on liberal democracy?, in *Political Studies*, 40 (Special Issue), 68–82.

Phillips, Anne (1992c), Universal pretensions in political thought, in M. Barrett and A. Phillips (eds), *Destabilizing Theory. Contemporary Feminist Debates*, Cambridge, Polity Press, 10–30.

Phillips, Anne (1993), *Democracy and Difference*, Cambridge, Polity Press.

Pierson, Christopher (1991), *Beyond the Welfare State? The New Political Economy of Welfare*, Cambridge, Polity Press.

Pitkin, Hanna Fenichel (1967), *The Concept of Representation*, Berkeley, University of California Press.

Plant, Raymond (1992), Citizenship and rights, in D. Milligan and William Watts Miller (eds) (1992), *Liberalism, Citizenship, and Autonomy*, Aldershot, Avebury, 108–33.

Pocock, J. G. A. (1975), *The Machiavellian Moment: Florentine Political Thought and the Atlantic Republican Tradition*, Princeton, Princeton University Press.

Poggi, Gianfranco (1978), *The Development of the Modern State. A Sociological Introduction*, Stanford, CA, Stanford University Press.

Poggi, Gianfranco (1990), *The State. Its Nature, Development and Prospects*, Cambridge, Polity Press.

Raz, Joseph (1994), Multiculturalism: a liberal perspective, *Dissent*, Winter, 67–79.

Reif, Karlheinz (1993), Cultural convergence and cultural diversity as factors in European identity, in S. García (ed.), *European Identity and the Search for Legitimacy*, London, Pinter, 131–53.

Reiss, Hans (ed.) (1991), *Immanuel Kant: Political Writings*, Cambridge, Cambridge University Press.

Rieff, David (1993), A global culture?, *World Policy Journal*, 10:4, 73–81.

Robertson, Roland (1990a), After nostalgia? Wilful nostalgia and the phases of globalization, in B. S. Turner (ed.), *Theories of Modernity and Post-modernity*, London, Sage, 45–61.

Robertson, Roland (1990b), Mapping the global condition: globalization as the central concept, in M. Featherstone (ed.), *Global Culture. Nationalism, Globalization and Modernity*, London, Sage, 15–30.

Robertson, Roland (1991), Globalization, modernization, and postmodernization: the ambiguous position of religion, in R. Robertson and W. R. Garrett (eds), *Religion and Global Order*, New York, Paragon Press, 281–91.

Robertson, Roland (1992), *Globalization. Social Theory and Global Culture*, London, Sage.

 Robertson, Roland and J. Chirico (1985), Humanity, globalization and worldwide religious resurgence: a theoretical exploration, *Sociological Analysis*, 46:3, 219–42.

Robertson, Roland and Frank Lechner (1985), Modernization, globalization and the problem of culture in world-systems theory, *Theory, Culture and Society*, 2:3, 103–17.

Rodwin, Llyod and Hidihiko Sazanami (eds) (1989), *Deindustrialization and Regional Economic Transformation: The Experience of the United States*, Boston, Unwin Hyman.

Rodwin, Llyod and Hidihiko Sazanami (eds) (1991), *Industrial Change and Regional Economic Transformation: The Experience of Western Europe*, London, HarperCollins.

Roper, Jon (1989), *Democracy and Its Critics. Anglo-American Democratic Thought in the Nineteenth Century*, London, Unwin Hyman.

Rosas, Allan (1995), Union citizenship and national elections, in A. Rosas and E. Anatola (eds), *A Citizen's Europe. In Search of a New Order*, London, Sage, 135–55.

Rosenau, James (1992), Citizenship in a changing world order, in J. Rosenau and E.-O. Czempiel (eds), *Governance without Government*, Cambridge, Cambridge University Press, 272–94.

Rosenblum, Nancy (1987), *Another Liberalism: Romaticism and the Reconstruction of Liberal Thought*, Cambridge, MA, Harvard University Press.

Ross, George (1992), Confronting the new Europe, *New Left Review*, 191, 49–68.

Ross, George (1995), *Jacques Delors and European Integration*, Cambridge, Polity Press.

Roszak, Theodore (1979), *Person/Planet. The Creative Disintegration of Industrial Society*, London, Victor Gollancz.

Rousseau, Jean-Jacques [1762] (1968), *The Social Contract*, ed. Maurice Cranston, London, Penguin Books.

Rutherford, Jonathan (ed.) (1990), *Identity. Community, Culture, Difference*, London, Lawrence & Wishart.

Sachs, Wolfgang (1992), One world, in W. Sachs (ed.), *The Development Dictionary. A Guide to Knowledge as Power*, London, Zed Books, 102–15.

Salkever, Stephen G. (1990), *Finding the Mean. Theory and Practice in Aristotelian Political Philosophy*, Princeton, Princeton University Press.

Sandel, Michael (1992), The procedural republic and the unencumbered self, in S. Avineri and A. De-Shalit (eds), *Communitarianism and Individualism*, Oxford, Oxford University Press, 12–28.

Sandholtz, Wayne and John Zysman (1989/90), 1992: Recasting the European bargain, *World Politics*, 42:1, 95–128.

Scharpf, Fritz W. (1991), Die Handlungsfähigkeit des Staates am Ende des zwanzigsten Jahrhunderts, *Politische Vierteljahresschrift*, 32:4, 621–34.

Scharpf, Fritz W. (1992), Europäisches Demokratiedefizit und deutscher Föderalismus, *Staatswissenschaften und Staatspraxis*, 3:3, 293–306.

Scharpf, Fritz W. (1994), Community and autonomy: multi-level policy-making in the European Union, *Journal of European Public Policy*, 1:2, 219–42.

Schecter, Darrow (1994), *Radical Theories. Paths beyond Marxism and Social Democracy*, Manchester, Manchester University Press.

Schott, Jeffrey (1991), Trading blocs and the world trading system, *World Economy*, 14:1, 1–17.

Schwartz, Joseph M. (1989/90), Arendt's politics: the elusive search for substance, *Praxis International*, 9:1/2, 25–47.

Scott, Andrew *et al.* (1994), Subsidiarity: a 'Europe of the Regions' vs. the British constitution, *Journal of Common Market Studies*, 32:1, 47–67.

Shaw, Martin (1994), Civil society and global politics: beyond a social movements approach, *Millennium*, 23:3, 647–67.

Sieyès, Emmanuel Joseph [1789] (1963), *What Is the Third Estate?*, London, Pall Mall.

Simhony, Avital (1993), Beyond negative and positive freedom: T. H. Green's view of freedom, *Political Theory*, 21:1, 28–54.

Singer, Brian C. J. (1986), *Society, Theory and the French Revolution. Studies in the Revolutionary Imaginary*, Houndmills, Macmillan.

Sivan, Emmanuel (1985), *Radical Islam. Medieval Theology and Modern Politics*, New Haven, Yale University Press.

Skinner, Quentin (1981/1992), Machiavelli, *Great Political Thinkers: Machiavelli, Hobbes, Mill and Marx*, Oxford, Oxford University Press, 1–106.

Skinner, Quentin (1984), The idea of negative liberty: philosophical and historical perspectives, in R. Rorty *et al.* (eds), *Philosophy in History*, Cambridge, Cambridge University Press, 193–221.

Skinner, Quentin (1990a), The republican ideal of political liberty, in G. Bock *et al.* (eds), *Machiavelli and Republicanism*, Cambridge, Cambridge

University Press, 293–309.

Skinner, Quentin (1990b), Thomas Hobbes on the proper signification of liberty, *Transactions of the Royal Historical Society*, 5th series, vol. 40, 121–51.

Skinner, Quentin (1992a), The Italian city-republics, in J. Dunn (ed.), *Democracy. The Unfinished Journey, 508 BC to AD 1993*, Cambridge: Cambridge University Press, 57–69.

Skinner, Quentin (1992b), On justice, the common good and the priority of liberty, in C. Mouffe (ed.), *Dimensions of Radical Democracy*, London, Verso, 211–24.

Sklair, Leslie (1991), *Sociology and the Global System*, Hemel Hempstead, Harvester Wheatsheaf.

Smith, Anthony (1980), *The Geopolitics of Information. How Western Culture Dominates the World*, London, Faber & Faber.

Smith, Anthony D. (1990), Towards a global culture?, in M. Featherstone (ed.), *Global Culture. Nationalism, Globalization and Modernity*, London, Sage, 171–91.

Smith, Anthony D. (1991), *National Identity*, London, Penguin Books.

Smith, Steven B. (1989), *Hegel's Critique of Liberalism. Rights in Context*, Chicago, Chicago University Press.

Sternberger, Dolf (1977), The sunken city: Hannah Arendt's idea of politics, *Social Research*, 44:1, 132–46.

Stoesz, David and James Midgley (1991), The Radical Right and the Welfare State, in H. Glennerster and J. Midgley (eds), *The Radical Right and the Welfare State. An International Assessment*, Hemel Hempstead, Harvester Wheatsheaf, 24–42.

Strange, Susan (1995), Political economy and international relations, in K. Booth and S. Smith (eds), *International Relations Theory Today*, Cambridge, Polity Press, 154–74.

Streeck, Wolfgang and Phillipe Schmitter (1991), From national corporatism to transnational pluralism: organized interests in the Single European Market, *Politics and Society*, 19:2, 133–64.

Swedberg, Richard (1994), The idea of 'Europe' and the origin of the European Union – a sociological approach, *Zeitschrift für Soziologie*, 23:5, 378–87.

Taguieff, Pierre-André (1993/94), From race to culture: the New Right's view of European identity, *Telos*, 98/99, 99–125.

Taylor, Charles (1984), Kant's theory of freedom, in Z. A. Pelczynski and J. Gray (eds), *Conceptions of Liberty in Political Philosophy*, London, Athlone, 100–22.

Taylor, Charles (1989), *Sources of the Self: The Making of the Modern Identity*, Cambridge, MA, Harvard University Press.

Taylor, Charles (1992a), *The Ethics of Authenticity*, Cambridge, MA, Harvard

University Press.

Taylor, Charles (1992b), *Multiculturalism and 'The Politics of Recognition'*, Princeton, Princeton University Press.

Taylor, Keith (1995), European Union: the challenge for local and regional government, *Political Quarterly*, 66:1, 74–83.

Tismaneanu, Vladimir (1992), *Reinventing Politics. Eastern Europe from Stalin to Havel*, New York, Free Press.

Tocqueville, Alexis de [1835/40] (1945), *Democracy in America*, 2 vols, New York, Alfred Knopf.

Tocqueville, Alexis de [1856] (1966), *The Ancien Régime and the French Revolution*, London, Collins/Fontana.

Thränhardt, Dietrich (1992), Globale Probleme, globale Normen, neue globale Akteure, *Politische Vierteljahresschrift*, 33:2, 219–34.

Turner, Bryan S. (1994a), *Orientalism, Postmodernism and Globalism*, London, Routledge.

Turner, Bryan S. (1994b), Postmodern culture/modern citizens, in B. van Steenbergen (ed.), *The Condition of Citizenship*, London, Sage, 153–68.

Vincent, Andrew and Raymond Plant (1984), *Philosophy, Politics, and Citizenship: The Life and Thought of the British Idealists*, Oxford, Blackwell.

Waldron, Jeremy (1992), Minority cultures and the cosmopolitan alternative, *University of Michigan Journal of Law Reform*, 25: 3/4, 751–93.

Walker, R. B. J. (1993), *Inside/Outside. International Relations as Political Theory*, Cambridge, Cambridge University Press.

Walker, R. B. J. and Saul Mendlovitz (1990), Interrogating state sovereignty, in R. B. J. Walker and S. Mendlovitz (eds), *Contending Sovereignties. Redefining Political Community*, London, Lynne Rienner.

Walzer, Michael (1980), The moral standing of states: a response to four critics, *Philosophy and Public Affairs*, 9:3, 209–29.

Walzer, Michael (1989), Citizenship, in T. Ball *et al.* (eds), *Political Innovation and Conceptual Change*, Cambridge, Cambridge University Press.

Warren, Mark (1992), Democratic theory and self-transformation, *American Political Science Review*, 86:1, 8–23.

Wæver, Ole *et al.* (1993), *Identity, Migration and the New Security Agenda in Europe*, London, Pinter.

Weber, Max (1978), *Economy and Society. An Outline in Interpretive Sociology*, Berkeley, University of California Press.

Weiler, J. H. H. *et al.* (1995), European democracy and its critique, *West European Politics*, 18:3, 4–39.

Wei-ming, T. (1991), The search for roots in industrial East Asia: the case of the Confucian revival, in M. Marty and R. Scott Appleby (eds), *Fundamentalism Observed*, vol. 1, Chicago, University of Chicago Press, 740–81.

Westlake, Martin (1994), *A Modern Guide to the European Parliament*, London, Pinter.

Westlake, Martin (1995), The European Parliament, the national parliaments and the 1996 Intergovernmental Conference, *Political Quarterly*, 66:5, 59–73.

Westphal, Merold (1984), Hegel's radical idealism: family and state as ethical communities, in Z. A. Pelczynski (ed.) (1984), *The State and Civil Society. Studies in Hegel's Political Philosophy*, Cambridge, Cambridge University Press, 77–92.

Wieland, Beate (1992), *Ein Markt – Zwölf Regierungen? Zur Organisation der Macht in der europäischen Verfassung*, Baden-Baden, Nomos.

Williams, Geraint (1991), *Political Theory in Retrospect. From Ancient Greeks to the 20th Century*, Aldershot, Edward Elgar.

Willke, Helmut (1992), *Ironie des Staates. Grundlinien einer Staatstheorie polyzentrischer Gesellschaft*, Frankfurt a.M., Suhrkamp.

Wilterdink, Nico (1993), The European ideal. An examination of European and national identity, *Archives Europeénes de Sociologie*, 34:1, 119–36.

Wincott, Daniel (1994), Is the Treaty of Maastricht an adequate constitution for the European Union?, *Public Administration*, 72:4, 573–90.

Wolin, Sheldon (1977), Hannah Arendt and the ordinance of time, *Social Research*, 44:1, 91–105.

Wood, Allen (1993a), Hegel's Ethics, in F. C. Beiser (ed.), *The Cambridge Companion to Hegel*, Cambridge, Cambridge University Press, 211–33.

Wood, Allen (1993b), Hegel and Marxism, in F. C. Beiser (ed.), *The Cambridge Companion to Hegel*, Cambridge, Cambridge University Press, 414–44.

Wood, Ellen Meiksins (1990), The uses and abuses of 'civil society', *Socialist Register*, 1990, 60–84.

Young, Iris Marion (1989), Polity and group difference: a critique of the ideal of universal citizenship, *Ethics*, 99, 250–74.

Young, Iris Marion (1990), *Justice and the Politics of Difference*, Princeton, Princeton University Press.

Young, Iris Marion (1995), Together in difference: transforming the logic of group political conflict, in W. Kymlicka (ed.), *The Rights of Minority Cultures*, Oxford, Oxford University Press, 155–76.

Zürn, Michael (1992), Jenseits der Staatlichkeit. Über die Folgen der ungleichzeitigen Denationalisierung, *Leviathan*, 20:4, 490–513.

Index

G.G: free communication
└ power of pen
  └ informed of how we are
    implicated in modernity
    ° post-modernity.

  − feeds both dev of moral conscious^{ness} (evolution)
  + dialectical modes of pol dev.

  ───────

  − accountability

  − devolution of knowledge,
  − expansion of responsibility
  − charting of the economic, culturally made [i.e. human
    constructed] nature of our world.

  ① lit
  ② Various debates/issues
  ③

let each live to their
conscience, but know
of its burden, shame,
evolutionary change.